LISA'S STORY

The Interrupted Life
Of Petoskey, Michigan's
First Female Police Officer

LISA M. PIEL

Compiled by
ART PIEL

Edited With Commentary By
MITCHELL JON MACKAY

ADAMS PRESS
CHICAGO, ILLINOIS

Manufactured in the United States

Jacket design by MJM Art Studio

Dedicated To:

All those who have been
discriminated against

Lisa's Story

Contents

Introduction
Madam Butterfly
Preface By The Editor

Statement By Art Piel

Epilogue

Introduction

Lisa's Story

As told through her own journals, transcripts, recordings,
interviews, and statements of those who knew her,
the majority of this information having been compiled
and sworn to be true, to the extent of verifiable
certainty, by Art Piel, father of Lisa.

Organized and prepared by
Mitchell Jon MacKay

This is the story of the first FEMALE POLICE OFFICER in
Northern Michigan, town of Petoskey, a lake-side community of
6200, known for its pristine beauty, lack of crime, and congenial
atmosphere for both its permanent residents and its many
summertime visitors.

The anomalies herein will come as some surprise in an area
perceived as such by the world, and indeed the eyes of the world
are upon it as these events add to the awareness of historic small-
town life as it is encompassed by the greater events of the
metropolitan society encroaching.

LISA'S STORY is one which will shock the reader into the
realization of misconduct by powers of authority, cultural fear and
prejudice, cover-up, and seeming victory by those entities that
heretofore have prevailed. This story seeks to reveal much of this
malfeasance by bringing facts, attitudes, and vague assumptions
into the light of acculturation.

Though there are culprits to be found, it will be seen that the
greater culprit is society itself in its acceptance of allowing such
stories to be enacted. This writing hopes to bare some causes of
the sequences leading to the death of one individual whose role
now transcends the individual and bespeaks of a concept that
needs constant addressing by society as a whole.

The facts herein are true and verifiable. Other allegations unsubstantiated by documents may be considered "hear-say" in legal terminology, but are included as true links in the chain of events to follow inasmuch as they round out the story by providing what must be termed "the other side." There is always another side to any story.

There is much suppression of evidence as will be indicated. The best-documented aspects of the story are the police files on Lisa, as may be imagined, by dint of mandatory record-keeping on their parts. Naturally there is scanty hard evidence to tell Lisa's private story, but fortunately we have her own journal notes to fill in many discrepancies and blurry sequences.

The purpose of this book is to tell the true story as near as may be arrived at. Persons' testimonies and comments alluded to are true to the best of verification considering the now three-year lapse since her death. As only one "side" of the story is told through conversational mode we state blankly that these are unverified comments and not to be considered defamatory but merely opinion. The other "side," of course, remains incommunicado but for written records, most of which have finally been released. With this somewhat unequal balance of fact and opinion—and rarely do the extremes meet—the tale is told.

The reader is free to perceive it any way he or she wants to. The intent is to shed light upon a death and the reasons leading to it. No harm is intended to any of the players within. Each will convey his or her own personality through the records, comments, rebuttals, journal entries, etc. as the scenario unfolds in its kaleidoscopic patterns.

It is thought that a clearer picture will emerge for the reader as fact is played against the behind-the-scenes reality leading to the fact. Legalistics speak in their own peculiar nomenclature for their own purposes. The rest of the story, while attested to be true, cannot be viewed in the cool light of bureaucratic oak-panelled rooms but is left to the discretionary perceptions of the reader him-or-herself.

In short, it is not the intent of this writing to slander and it is in no way to be inferred that any one player is being pointed out as being to blame for the many wrongdoings committed. The stage was set far before the actors arrived. We reenact each part as best as it may be remembered.

It is for LISA, family and friends, that this story is told. Perhaps she has more friends than are willing to come forward and speak in her behalf. Maybe this story will provide the impetus for more people to reveal what still remain mysteries in this tale.

**Lisa's Story, by Lisa and friends,
that her life and passing
be not in vain nor
forgotten.**

MADAM BUTTERFLY

A butterfly of red, green and yellow.
A symbol of freedom. Papillon! A need to be free,
with no obligations—one striving for independence.
My tattoo represented all that. A belief that would
be imbedded in me for the remainder of my life.
Condemned by society, but a reminder to me,
for freedom would soon come with time. These
are such deep beliefs and set ways for a
sixteen year old.
Four years later I'm lying on a table in a clinic.
A nurse is covering my entire body with paper,
while the doctor administers zylocane into a
syringe. My emotions start to drain and I am
thoughtless. My arm is placed on my stomach
and the doctor injects the needle several times.
My butterfly swells and is deadened.
He then turns on a sander, which resembles my
father's. As he sands the surface of the tattoo,
blood splatters in my face and in various
directions. A few more minutes of this nightmare
and surgery is completed, my arm is bandaged.
The doctor gives me certain instructions,
I nod and leave feeling empty.
My eyes begin to tear as I run to my car,
I can't utter a sound. I can't believe what I
just let happen. It would now be part of my past.
It was silly of me to once believe I could really be
"free" in such a conforming society.

Lisa M. Piel
English 102
1977

Preface By The Editor

PREFACE BY THE EDITOR

A reporter learns that there is not so much "action" as there is "reaction;" that is, covert masterminded sequences tend not to occur in most situations wherein reporting is wanted. Most stories tend toward the mundane in their precipitation and conclusions, the middle ground being just the facts between here and there which are usually not premeditated but rather spontaneous.

It is only when dealing with large organizations of long-standing that subterfuge tends to be the occasional story. Thence come cover-ups–like Watergate, etc. The mystery and intrigue of most stories disappears when the facts are reported and the tale turns out predictable and not unusual. It seems only in government agencies, big business, and Mafia activities that premeditated intrigue actually happens, and this because the facts are so difficult to get at. John Q. Public tends not to harbor that many twisted and complex tales worthy of Sherlock Holmes interpretations. The intrigue lies with larger cover-up schemes carried out on large enough scale to become so big that they are obscured by their quality of being bigger than life, bigger than the individual by far. In the case of the UNABOMBER the anomaly of one man's intrigue stands out remarkably to the contrary, but the this singular sequence was brought about in considered retaliation to a much larger syndrome as perceived by this protagonist–that of governmental culpability in league with technology and hence business interests.

Society itself creates its intrigues by the accumulation of standards of morality, ethics, acceptances and prejudices. In times of cultural change, such as we have known for as long as most of us have been alive, the acceptance quotient is constantly bombarded with input and need of questioning and realigning values and understanding. In the larger city conurbations acceptance is arrived at more definitively–and usually more violently. The underlying reasons for conflict usually remain the same, however, and tend to flare up again and again to be exposed, publicized, negotiated and thence to be assimilated in perpetuity until the antagonistic force builds in intensity once again.

In the rural areas things work differently. Neighbors farther apart have buffer zones around them that prevent crises from coming to explosive terms. This allows for a silent buildup of powers, surreptitious acceptances of behavior and prejudice that go largely unspoken and certainly unwritten but accepted nonetheless.

When Art Piel approached me about editing this story, he'd already put three years of frustration into its assimilation. His copious notes, files, transcripts, articles, letters and sundry must have numbered six hundred mostly typed pages since the stack was thicker than a standard 500-sheet box of paper. I was immediately interested due to his mention of "female police officer" and her untimely "death." I told him I'd see what I could find out initially without actually getting into it. I called the Traverse City newspaper office to see what they had done with it since Art had been in contact with them. After an introductory warm-up an editor told me that one reporter had conducted some twenty interviews and they had enough copy for a lengthy story but kept it shelved due to some disagreement within their offices. This was explained as "no blacks and whites" to the story which I assumed to mean no verifiably conclusive resolutions could be made. I thanked this editor for his time, saying I doubted that I would take this on either, taking his pose of "no blacks and whites" literally.

But then when I saw the voluminous stack of background on it, and was told that the reporter who did most of the information gathering was somehow related to law enforcement in the same area of Art's daughter, Lisa's, demise, I began to wonder why indeed the Traverse City paper had bothered to do twenty interviews if they felt there was not enough story there. This was the first hint of the "C" word of reportage: cover-up. I was hooked. The more I looked into the story the more discrepancies I found. There came into focus a dickensian scape albeit updated and superimposed upon the bright and well-kept streets of Petoskey, Michigan rather than the foggy, narrow passageways of London, England.

Even containing a couple Pantagruelian-like players, this story expanded itself in the telling as the kaleidoscopic pieces slowly assembled themselves, eventually revealing some very discernible "blacks and whites" too obvious to be negligible. Then as I talked further with Art Piel, and we discussed legal retribution possibly attendant to our delving into matters mostly of police concern, I realized that a story not only existed, it was being suppressed. And, as usual, in that most subtle of ways: fear.

What? . . . here, in Petoskey, Michigan?! The answer came wafting back with a most conclusive, "uh-huh."

Should there be any legal retribution, perhaps the tactical recourse would be to contact "Citizens Against Legal Misconduct," a newly-formed watch-dog group which monitors police actions, whose founder, J.D. Reed, features somewhat largely in this book, he being one of the last persons to see Lisa Piel alive.

Dave Reed, as he goes by, created quite a stir with his implementation of this service—which is an actual non-profit concern—though no mention of Lisa Piel's circumstances have yet issued forth from these offices. The monitoring relates mostly to current affairs, and Reed's point has apparently been made: not everyone is silent anymore. Just as in some documented police methods, a little pressure gains a lot of attention. It is rumored that some TV talk shows have expressed interest in happenings in Northern Michigan due to Dave Reed's efforts. The pen is mightier than the sword; the TV screen and the Internet are as a trillion pens.

This writing ultimately became a labor of compassion. Of empathy. I perceived and became acquainted with people who are sincere in their telling of dealings with authorities—people who are decent, upstanding members of the community—that tell of serious misgivings as to factors of trust in these authorities. Actually, quite to the contrary. The cop on the beat, who historically was given a free lunch in gratitude for his needed presence, sometimes evidently takes his free lunch for granted now, even when not offered or earned.

This story aims to weed out the negative influences inherent behind the convoluted issues of this tale of a lady cop in a former all-male domain. We do not mean to take issue with any segment of the populace who maintain that woman's place is best left to maternity and domestics. Lisa knew what she was doing; it was her battle. It is the perfidy, the hypocrisy, and the legal malfeasance that are at issue, not societal mores and changes. Injustice, under legal auspices.

Every document contained herein was found in Lisa's personal papers. It is on this basis that we print this information as that found in her possession. Authority, as an entity guided by individuals threatened, may take exception at the printing of some of this evidence as being not exactly in the public domain. This ploy is easily countered by expostulation of "the truth, the whole truth, and nothing but truth" as a guide. This story is indeed Lisa's story as everything written here is from her thirteen-year collected experiences. She was a careful chronicler of events. As she is deceased, this telling is just that: Lisa's Story as she lived it and recorded it. It is with gratification that Art Piel and myself have been allowed the telling of it. But it is for Lisa, her voice beyond the grave, that our efforts are bestowed. To give the every man and woman his and her due as an individual with right of free speech and action without fear of recourse by authority is the overtone of intent; Art Piel and family would settle for a clearing of Lisa Piel's name and a possible indictment of a few figures of authority involved in decrying her honor.

As it is presupposed that authority will indeed react with some vindictiveness upon the publication of this book, the evidence within will stand as factual data and theory of jurisprudence in abjuration of any claims made by authority of imprudence as to use of documents or summations of misconduct and malevolence by said authority. What this paralegal jargon means to say is that reprisal is anticipated, and the First Amendment to the Constitution stands ready for battle.

Mitchell Jon MacKay, Editor

1

Lisa's Journal

"**L**isa Piel was young, beautiful, and a very caring person. She loved and was loved by many. She died a lonely, gruesome death."

These are the words of Henry Arthur Piel, Lisa's father.

"10/18/80 1:05 A.M. Writing. Tears flow. I can't believe this is happening. Why? Why? Getting many comments on a commercial I did last winter, for N.C.M.C., also—my weight-loss. My back's bothering me . . . I'm so tense, I can't relax."

These are the words of Lisa Piel, Petoskey, Michigan's first female police officer.

- - - - - - - - - - - - - - - - - - - -

The Petoskey News-Review, the leading (and only) newspaper in Northwestern Lower Peninsula of Michigan, on February 8, 1979 printed this article by Betty Washburne:

"Lisa Piel, 21, is the newest addition to the Petoskey Police Department.

"In addition to being the newest, she is also a first for the city law enforcement agency.

"Miss Piel was hired by the police department last September and now has four months of service under her belt.

" 'I love it!' exclaimed the lady police officer. And the fact that she is currently on the 'graveyard shift' hasn't seemed to dampen her enthusiasm.

"The graveyard shift means Lisa goes to work at 11 p.m. and gets off at 7 a.m. Those are mighty difficult hours in any working gal's book, but Lisa seems to thrive on her vocation.

"Lisa, the daughter of Mr. and Mrs. Art Piel of Harbor Springs, has been in the area the past three years. She grew up in the Detroit area and this is where her first interest in law enforcement began.

" 'My grandfather, Raymond Piel, was a detective with the auto recovery squad of the Detroit Police

2

Department and retired in 1955, and my great-grandfather, Henry Piel, was chief of detectives in Detroit in the late 30's. In the early 40's he was chief of police in Grosse Pointe Park,' explained Miss Piel, 'I still have their badges,' she added fondly.

" 'I like being the first woman police officer in Petoskey,' said Miss Piel proudly. 'It's really an honor and I intend to do a good job.'

"Lisa received an associate degree in criminal justice from North Central Michigan College. She then attended the police academy at Grand Valley State College where she received her certification as a police officer on Aug. 18, 1978.

"The female officer 'mans' her own patrol car and answers all kinds of complaints. When asked if she gets any doubletake from complainants when a woman shows up, she answered, 'Not really, in some instances I think they are kinda glad, depending on the situation or problem.'

"Lisa has issued her share of speeding tickets. She was given a thorough ordination in traffic control at the police academy including various procedures in apprehending speeders.

"In the local department, Lisa does her share just like her male counterparts. She is one of nine officers and they all take turns on a rotating shift basis that includes morning, night and midnight shifts.

"Having a woman on the force is a new experience for the male police officer, but according to Chief Ernest Kraus, officer Piel is fitting in well, and there's been no conflict with other officers accepting her.

"This brings to three the total number of women in police work in Emmet County.

"The Sheriff's Department has two women deputies. Kit Lieberman was the first woman in

3

their department having joined the force Sept. 4, 1977. She is the daughter of Mr. and Mrs. Robert Lieberman of Charlevoix.

"Kit received her bachelor's degree in criminal justice from Northern Michigan University at Marquette and is now the veteran lady law enforcement officer in the county.

"Not too far behind Kit as far as veteran status goes, is Linda Schiller, 24, who joined the sheriff's force as a lady deputy just a couple weeks after Kit.

"Linda, the daughter of Mr. and Mrs. Maynard Wiertalla, hails from the Brutus area.

"She graduated from the police academy in Benton Harbor, 'The toughest one in the state!,' says Linda.

"She has two children, Kendra, a first grader in the Pellston elementary school and David, a preschooler.

"The three lady law officers all have one thing in common. When asked how they like their jobs, which has only recently become popular as a profession for women, they all agreed they love it."

Fourteen years past the above journal excerpt in Lisa's own hand, Lisa Piel was found dead by bullet wound in bed at her home in Petoskey.

Lisa Piel was trained under the auspices of the C.E.T.A. program of the late 1970's. In her own words:

"Equal Employment Opportunity Commission
%Intake Supervisor
600 1st National Building
Suite 600
Detroit, Michigan 48226

4

"To whom it may concern:

"I would like to file a complaint with you concerning possible discrimination against me at my place of employment, this being, Petoskey City Police, Petoskey, Michigan.

"I was hired under C.E.T.A. September 24, 1978, as a patrol officer. C.E.T.A. terminated March of 1980. At this time I was picked up by the City of Petoskey to fill a needed position.

"Note: I am the first and only woman patrol officer hired in the City of Petoskey. —Also, at the time of employment I was the youngest and only single member of the department.

"I.   I was hired because I was the only one who fit C.E.T.A. requirements.

"A.   Emmet County Resident.

B.   Certifiable.

C.   Unemployed over 15 weeks.

"II.   I was told Chief Kraus would not hire a female patrol officer.

"A.   Kraus stated he did not like/want a woman working road patrol.

"1.   Kraus told several Law Enforcement classes he instructed at North Central Michigan College.

"2.   On several occasions, (prior and after employed) Kraus told Detective Burke the same.

"3.   At a dinner party Kraus told my mother, along with other guests, he had reservations about hiring a female (me).

"4.   Prior to August 31st, 80, Kraus told a female.

(Editor's note: omissions and inconsistencies are verbatim transcriptions from Lisa's handwriting. The following reference to locker room convenience remains unaddressed; female officers would be expected to share with secretaries.)

"III.   After employed Sept. 24, 1978, I was not issued the same necessities as all other patrol officers.

"A.   A locker was not issued.

1.   Men have a locker room along with lockers and showers to use.

B.   My uniform and badge indicated I was a "Patrol Man," not a "Patrol Officer," "Patrol Person," or a "Patrol Woman."

"C.   I was not issued a protective vest until two years after employment.

"IV.   Summer of 1980, an attempt to terminate my position was made, ending in suspension November 24, 1980.

"A.   A biased internal investigation conducted by Chief Kraus. Those involved:

"1.   Detective Hartman, Emmet County Sheriff's Dept.

2.   Capt. Shalk, Petoskey Police Dept.

3.   Sgt. Doernenberg, Petoskey Police Dept.

4.   Detective Watts, Harbor Springs Police Dept.

Please Note: this investigation has/was the most extensive investigation the Petoskey Police Department has made, with a goal to terminate a position, based on allegations made by two subjects arrested, (known hearsay).

"1.   Improper investigative techniques, questioning citizens.

A.   Detective Watts advised Anita Walker he was involved in an internal investigation concerning the Petoskey Police Dept., who

6

was attempting to "clean up their backyard," Officer in question Officer Piel.

"B.   Sgt. Doernenberg approached Gladys Ann G __ (sp.?), who said she did not know officer in question but knew who she was. Sgt. asked if she was sure she wouldn't sign a statement (assuring her she was (Ed. note: End of sentence and possible C. listing are missing or never completed)

"D.   9/17/80, working 11-7, Sgt. Doernenberg repeatedly asked me to take a polygraph to prove my innocence, then I would not have to put up with this "shit" anymore . . . Because it would continue.

"E.   On Nov.   , 1980 I picked up Detective Burke for work. He stated he was investigated for rape and selling marijuana, and he could not understand why they were coming down so hard on me, that his investigation was not as involved. At this time he brought up how the Chief did not like, nor want a woman on the force.

"F.   Theresa Lungin (former Juvenile Officer) applied for an open position for Patrol Officer. Kraus told her he did not like women patrol officers.

"V.   Sexual Harassment by fellow Officers.
1.   Making sexual advances
2.   Insinuating my flashlight was a vibrator.
3.   Continued sexual connotation in conversations.
A.   Sexual embarrassment in the presence of others. (not alone) after he knew the women did not know me.

(Ed. note: this lapse is apparently due to emotional aggravation since no other connective pages are to be found)

"2.   Continual Harassment due to non-common practices in an internal investigation by this dept.

"A.   9/5/80, Fri., I was in a cycle accident injuring my right leg. 9th and 10th I called in sick (contract states officer calling in "3" days will have doctor's note) – After the second day I called in, Chief Kraus and Det. Hartman came to my residence to see if the call was of actual nature. (Petoskey Police Dept. does not make house calls).

"B.   9/19/80 12:20 p.m., working 7-3 p., Capt. Schalk informs me of an informal hearing set for 1:30 p.m. I did not have time to obtain proper representation. Meeting turned out to be an interview-interrogation.

"C.   9/25/80 app. 1:00 a., working 11-7 a.m. I was ordered to take a blood test or I would lose my job. In uniform I was taken to the hospital, (weapon taken from me) where a blood test was taken improperly.

"1.   No vital signs taken.

2.   No consent form signed by me.

3.   Alcohol solution used to sterilize skin. Instruction stated not to use alcohol.

"Investigating Officer,

Please be advised I am presently suspended as of Nov. 24, 1980. Allegations based on a bias and discriminant investigation. Please help me. More involved. I've done as much leg work as possible.

Helpless,

Lisa M. Piel

P.S. Enclosed is a resume."

- - - - - - - - - - - - - - - - - - -

To interject here for purpose of perspective on what may seem to the reader a quantum leap from a joyous career beginning to an alleged misconduct on Lisa's part, along with her own assertions of harassment, a brief letter by then Prosecuting Attorney John F. Salan of September 19, 1980 to Chief Ernest Kraus:

> "Chief Ernest Kraus
> Petoskey Police Department
> Petoskey, Michigan
> "Re: Officer Lisa Piel
> Dear Sir:
>
> "Please be advised that I am aware of the investigation that you are conducting pertaining to the above named officer. You are hereby advised by this letter that I have no intention of pursuing criminal charges from items that may be developed during the course of your investigation.
>
> Sincerely,
>
> John F. Salan
> Prosecuting Attorney"

Quantum leap? To be sure. No "hard" evidence of drug use ever surfaced against Lisa, yet, as follows, the "drug use" wedge was continually utilized to discredit her. Why? It is the purpose of this book to delineate all known issues and hopefully arrive at a clearer picture through the confusion.

This letter of Sept. 19, 1980 to Richard Schaefer indicates the influences that were beginning to undermine Lisa's tenure.

> "Richard Schaefer, President
> Petoskey Patrolmans Association
> Re: Lisa Piel interview.

"President Schaefer,

At approximately 12:00 Noon, September 19, 1980, I was requested by Officer Lisa Piel to accompany her to a meeting at 1:30 P.M., 9/19/80, regarding allegations made against her. I agreed after learning that she had been unable to contact yourself or any other officer of the association.

"I later checked with Captain Schalk to determine if this was to be a formal hearing or proceeding. Captain Schalk stated that no formal disciplinary action would be taken at this interview.

Being unfamiliar with procedures and in an attempt to safeguard Officer Piel's rights, I contacted our Association legal advisor, Dean Burns. I explained the circumstances and that the Patrolmans Association was not officially involved as of this time. Mr. Burns advised that Officer Piel had to answer questions as a condition of employment, but that answers could not be used against her in criminal proceedings. The meeting, later learned to be an "interview," started at 1:45 P.M. in Chief Kraus' office. Present were investigating officer Det. Sgt. Jerry Hartman, Darvin Schalk, Captain, Petoskey Police Dept., Officer Lisa Piel, and myself, Officer Norman Shivly, representing Petoskey Patrolmans Association.

"Officer Piel was advised by Captain Schalk that this was an administrative interview regarding certain allegations of frequently places and/or associating with persons using narcotics. Piel was also advised that the interview was being taped and that she was required to answer all questions truthfully as a condition of employment. Officer Piel was also given a statement from the prosecutor's office that the statement/interview would not be used in the event of criminal proceedings (see attached). (?)

"Officer Piel, on the advise of Norman Shively, then read statement of rights (from POAM card), at 1:52 P.M.

At this time Officer Shively inquired if a copy of the taped interview would be available to officer Piel and/or association. Capt. Schalk checked with Chief Kraus and returned stating that copy of tape would not be available. Captain Schalk also advised Officer Shively that he was allowed as an "observer" only and that Officer Shively was not permitted any input to the proceedings or was he to give Officer Piel any advice.

Officer Shively stated at this time he was opposed to the proceedings and that at this time he was formally notifying Capt. Schalk that he was taking the first step (oral notification) in the Grievance Procedure, effective immediately.

"Grievance is for:

1. Insuffient notification of Administrative Interview (approx. 1-1/2 hr.)

2. Refusal to make copy of tape available until disposition.

3. Prohibiting representative of Association to advise Officer Piel or any input to the proceedings.

Detective Hartman proceeded with the interview based on allegations by two (2) un-named persons. Officer Piel answered all of the questions. Officer Shively interrupted proceeding when Det. Hartman repeated a question to Officer Piel, after restating Officer Piel's obligations to answer truthfully, Officer Piel had answered the question, and in the absence of anything mentioned contrary, answered to the best of her ability.

"When Det. Hartman concluded his questions, he asked Capt. Schalk if there was anything he wished

11

to ask. Capt. Schalk replied "No" and then concluded the tape. Officer Piel was not asked or given the opportunity to ask any questions or make any statement regarding the allegations.

"At the informal meeting after Officer Piel had left, Capt. Schalk explained his understanding of the "observer" priveleges and suggested that the grievance be held until consultation with President Schaefer. Officer Shively admitted that he was in total ignorance of his obligations and/or rights as an observer even though he was representing the Patrolmans Association. But until talking with President Schaefer the grievance still stands. If it should be determined that there were no grievable offences the grievance may be withdrawn at a later date. It is Officer Shively's suggestion that a full meeting of the Petoskey Patrolmans Association be held to determine the Association position on this matter. It is further suggested that this meeting be held as soon as possible.

Respectfully submitted,

Norman L. Shively, grievance officer."

While it will of necessity be constantly reiterated that there are no true "black and white" facts to this story but for the most obvious and salient, each piece of the puzzle presented herein, often in its blatant and somewhat ungrammatical format, may be seen to compose the elements of bureaucratic malfeasance, in the sense of bending or accentuating the rules, that attends the entire sequence of Lisa's experience from inception to demise—literal demise.

Bureaucratic rhetoric, for the record, speaks its own allegorical nomenclature, incorporating such oxymorons as "criminal justice" and similar such terms as tend to confound the ordinary citizen in their totalitarian methodology. But piece by piece the story will surface as one in which the between-the-lines images gain credibility through constant pointing to discrepancies in the "official" wording.

Lisa's own journals, of course, and her letters to some extent, bridge the gap between bureaucracy and opinion with believable clarity in her ingenuous striving for balance in this tenuous see-saw battle she was inexorably pulled into, and held there stretched resiliently until the stress finally overwhelmed the taut tension spring.

This next letter to a Ms. Gorden from Lisa, while reiterative, sheds a bit more light on the subject which must have been all-inclusively bearing on her mind in the second year of her career.

"Wednesday, October 01, 1980
Lisa M. Piel
2250-B Harbor-Petoskey Rd.
Petoskey, Michigan 49770

"Ms. Gorden
920 Ford Building, Griswald
Detroit, Michigan 48238

"Ms. Gorden, First I would like to thank you for your concern in handling my case referred to you by Ms. Lutz, September 30, 1980.

"Enclosed is a resume, a newspaper article which appeared in a local paper here in Petoskey, February 08, 1979. Also, personal notes taken by myself pertaining to the matter in question. Along with this is a copy of a letter sent to the Chief of Police and minutes taken from a so-called meeting, September 19, 1980, by Patrol Officer Shively. Please see attached "SPECIAL ATTENTION."

"I hope the following will give you a better understanding as to the matter in question. This is also to confirm an appointment you set for October 10, 1980.

"10/01/80, No formal charges brought forth as of this date.

"09/11/80, On this date I saw Dr. Pollack at Burns Clinic for leg injury (motorcycle accident, 09/05/80). Requested by Chief Kraus before returning to work. Dr. Pollack found no broken bones, but ordered I was not to return to work until the 18th day of September. Also a prescription for Tylenol #3 was issued.

"On this date, in the presence of Officer Schaefer, President of the Petoskey Patrolmans Association, And Captain Schalk I was handed a letter signed by Sgt. Detective Hartman of the Emmet County Sheriff's Department. This letter pertained to an internal investigation himself and Detective Watts, of the Harbor Springs Police Department, were conducting. The letter stated certain allegations such as associating with persons using narcotics; and use of same. A copy of the letter was requested by Officer Piel, and the Chief stated one would not be available at this time. Chief Kraus requested that Officer Piel take a polygraph to clear herself or else an extensive investigation would continue. Piel's reply was no, she did not feel she should have to prove her innocence. Nor, she did not personally feel they were reliable.

"09/19/80 At approximately 12:20 p.m., (Piel working 7am-3pm) Capt. Schalk requested Piel to come into his office. He advised her of an informal "meeting" set at 1:30 p.m., same date. He also informed Piel that Officer Schaefer was out of town and that I should get someone to sit in on the meeting to represent her. At approximately 12:45 a.m. Piel contacted Officer Shively, also on duty, of the meeting that was to take place. At this time she briefly filled him in as to what the meeting might be about. The meeting which took place was in the

14

office of Chief Kraus. Present was Capt. Schalk, Sgt. Det. Hartman, Officer Shively and Piel. See minutes of alleged "meeting" (interview-interrogation), typed by Officer Shively. Also at this time a letter from the Prosecuting Attorney was presented to Piel, stating that no criminal charges would develope; see copy of letter enclosed.

"09/25/80 Piel was on duty from 11 p.m.-7 a.m. At approximately 1:00 a.m. Piel was ordered to return to the police station by Sgt. Doernenberg. Upon arrival Piel was met by Sgt. Doernenberg, Chief Kraus and Officer Schaefer. Chief accused Piel of being on something (?). Piel reply was she had taken nothing. SGt. Doernenberg stated two officers had confronted him in reference to her behavior. This being: Auxiliary Smith and Officer Vargo. Later learned Vargo had said nothing. Sgt. Doernenberg also stated he had noticed a difference in behavior. Piel replied she had taken a Tylenol and took a nap prior to coming to work. She also said she was under a great deal of strain due to the allegations and rumors. In addition, mental pressures of the investigation which she was told very little about. Such as: no formal charges, no names of the persons making allegations, or evidence which was not brought forth. Chief requested Piel to take a polygraph. Piel replied no. As before, she stated she did not think they were reliable, nor did she feel she should have to prove her innocence. Chief then demanded that Piel have a blood test taken. And under conditions of employment she had no choice but to comply. Sgt. Doernenberg and Officer Schaefer were present when demand was made. Officer Schaefer, at the request of Piel, called legal advisor Deam Burns concerning same. Burns stated, yes, under the conditions of employment, Piel must consent or be dismissed. Sgt. Doernenberg then drove Officer Piel in a marked unit to Little Traverse Hospital E.R. At this time her duty weapon was taken from her. Piel was then asked to wait in the waiting room while he talked to the Doctor (Clark) on duty. Piel, in uniform, was then asked to have a seat on a table in room three. Dr. Clark then, under the direction of Sgt. Doernenberg, removed 20 cc of blood, first using an alcohol solution to sterilize the skin of right arm. Piel signed nothing prior to nor after the removal of blood. See attached "SPECIAL ATTENTION." Sgt. Doernenberg then drove Piel back to her personal vehicle where she was sent home with pay for remainder of shift. Time approximately 2:30 a.m.

"09/27/80 Officer Piel on duty 11 p.m.-7 a.m. Auxiliary Paul Rybinski was to ride with above officer. Piel politely asked if he would not mind riding patrol this shift. Piel explained her state of mind and the need to be alone. She also stated it was nothing personal (pertaining to him). Department policy states officers will ride with auxiliary, grounds for dismissal if refused.

"At approximately 11:10 p.m. Sgt. Doernenberg was phoned by Officer Vargo in reference to a misunderstanding between Officer Piel. This was in reference to Vargo's accusations of Piel's condition the night before, 09/26. Conclusion was that Vargo did not confront the Sgt., as understood by both Officers Piel and Schaefer. Piel had then left office to back up another unit on a family disturbance. After clearing, Piel returned to station to see if Vargo wanted or needed a ride home. He stated it would be a couple minutes, for he was tied up on some paper work. Within minutes Sgt. Doernenberg was observed walking towards the police station in uniform by both Officers Piel and Schaefer (working a separate job, Bay View Patrol, at time). Piel and

16

Schaefer talking in front of police station at time of occurance. Sgt. stated he wanted to talk to Piel inside, Schaefer followed. Chief was called by Sgt. prior to coming in. In the presence of Officer Schaefer Sgt. asked Piel if she had refused to ride with auxiliary. Piel's reply was no, but a request because of emotional condition. Statement of this was made out by Auxiliary Rybinski, requested by Sgt. Sgt. had then repeatedly asked Piel why she would not take a polygraph to get this investigation cleared up. (Schaefer still present) Sgt. requested Piel to take one, then she would not have to put up with the "shit" anymore. He (Sgt.) stated it would continue. Still no formal charges made, nor names of people making accusations and allegations were brought forth. Sgt. also stated the investigation would continue after the results came back from Lansing (blood withdrawn 9/26/80). Also, another blood test may be requested/demanded at any time felt necessary. Again, Sgt. advised me to take a polygraph to prove innocence and put an end to this.

"10/02/80 No formal charges made, results of test unknown.

"Officer Piel's feelings as to the allegations made and the internal investigation are as follows:

1. Failure to protect officer's reputation due to not conducting a proper investigation.
2. Slander.
3. Defamation of character.
4. Harassment and coercement into taking polygraph to determine innocence.
5. Possibly civil rights violated.
6. Libeled (letter in writing shown to officer by Chief, written by Sgt. Det. Hartman.
7. Mental anguish.
8. No formal charges brought forth.

9. No names produced in reference to allegations made nor evidence pertaining to same.
EVERYTHING BASED ON POSSIBILITIES AND HEAR-SAY.

*Add. Officer Piel's understanding that a subject named John Kasimer Walenta, D.O.B. 4/24/64, adress, 7833 Indian Garden Rd., Petoskey. Phone: (616) 347-4847, made verbal statements 08/25/80 that he had witnessed Officer Piel using narcotics at a Sheridan St. address. This statement was made in the presence of Officer Vargo and SGt. Doernenberg. Later, same statement made in presence of Sgt. Det. Jerry Hartman (Emmet County Sheriff's Department), investigating officer. While pressured and read rights (Maranda Warning), Walenta made statement/confession that he did not actually see Officer Piel using narcotics, but knew of someone that did. This information was enclosed in letter read by Officer Piel 09/05/80. (See info. dated same). Letter in possession of Chief Kraus, Petoskey Police Department. SLANDER!?

Respectfully submitted,

Lisa M. Piel"

The "SPECIAL ATTENTION" referred to parenthetically throughout this last letter emphasized specifically that "*NO CONSENT FORM SIGNED BY OFFICER PIEL," adding that this is "*HOSPITAL POLICY," and pointing out that on the attendant "Alcohol or Drug Determination" form, when the 20cc of blood was drawn by Dr. Clark at Little Traverse Hospital, 09/26/80, an alcohol or alcoholic solution *was* used to sterilize the skin surface. Instructions on these forms clearly state, "Do not use alcohol or alcoholic solution to sterilize skin surface, needle, or syringe," the inference being that this could taint the blood test.

These following, brief notations are apparently from Lisa's journal though were found typed:

18

"09/29/80 at 6:00 p.m. Phone call at residence. Piel answers:

"Good afternoon." Pause . . . reply, "Queer bitch, why don't you leave town." Hung up.

"6:13 p.m. Phone call. Piel answers: "Good afternoon." Pause . . . no reply . . . Piel hangs up.

"6:14 p.m. Phone call. Piel answers: "Good afternoon." Pause . . . no reply . . . Piel hangs up.

"10/06/80 Piel working 7 a.m.-3 p.m. Request to pick up Deputy Jim Hemstreet at Buck's Body Shop. Hemstreet inquires as to how problem is with chief. Piel's reply is that she has not heard anything. Hemstreet states that he and Sgt. Det. Hartman interviewed subject LARRY JOHN COLE, D.O.B. 8/15/56. Cole states he saw a "police person" sniffing cocaine. Hemstreet said he took for granted it was Cole was talking about you because you do not call men "police persons." Hemstreet then stated he thought Cole had made statement to "get his butt out of a jam."

"10/06/80 10:10 a.m. Piel at Emmet County Sheriff's Dept. Sgt. Deputy Hayes says to Piel: "Gee, I didn't know you were a coke sniffer." Inquires about. Piel inquires to see criminal history on Cole. Piel did not recognize subject. Bad record. Subject from Cross Village area.

"Date unknown. Det. Watts from Harbor Springs Police Dept. contacts Anita Walker (friend-acquaintance of Piel's). Asks if she would come down and talk with him at P.D. Insures her she is not in any trouble. Walker calls back at later date and inquires nature of visit. Watts tells her he was requested to assist a Police Department who was trying to "clean up their back yard." Walker asks which officer he was referring to. Watts' reply was, "I think you know who." Walker answers, "no, I don't." Watts says, "Officer Piel." Walker answers, "no, I

19

don't care to get involved, I want to keep my back yard clean." (Poor investigated technique) (?)

"Above information given to Piel by Walker, by phone. Concerned."

Concluding this earliest of unwarranted onslaughts are excerpts from Lisa's own journals of the time. It's hard to imagine the grief she must surely have felt through her valiant efforts to calmly and painstakingly elucidate each and every nuance of this portion of her ordeal. Lisa was young at this time, just twenty-three years of age. Her journals and photos of this era portray a pretty and "perky" young girl, interested and aware. It is clear even at this stage that some harassment was present in that no verifiable charges had been named, only vague allegations by one or more suspected felons under pressure of being charged themselves.

These concluding journalized statements by her offer the reader the insights she felt, the frustration, and also the obviously earnest propriety she maintained while trying to cope with the persecution she was experiencing.

"10/12/80, return to work 11p-7a–nothing said.

"3:20 p.m., Tuesday, Oct. 14, 80, 3-11p shift. At this time and date I gave Officer Schaefer a ride home. When dropping him off he advised me that the Chief told him, 10/13, that the test results came back. Findings indicated there was another prescription drug besides codine in my blood system (?). Chief also told Schaefer he was getting another doctor's opinion, which was needed.

"7:40 p.m., Tuesday, Oct. 14, 80, 3-11 shift. Auxiliary Taylor riding with me. At this date and time Sgt. D. radioed to my unit asking to talk with Taylor. Taylor went in Sgt's unit. Sgt. D. apparently pumped Taylor for information regarding myself. At 8:05 p Taylor got back into my unit. (Sgt. D. off at

8:00 p.) He was very uncomfortable and said to me, "you know and I know what he (Sgt.) talked with me about." I said, "well, I have a good idea." Taylor then said, "Lisa, talk to me." I replied, "I have nothing to say," but would like to know what was said between the Sgt. and him. Taylor then said the Sgt. wanted to know if he knew anything (about me). Taylor also said to me during the conversation, "Lisa, you know they're after you." He really did not specify what was said when he was with Sgt. Taylor, while riding, asked to drive to the Captain's residence. (Capt. home sick). Taylor did not see him and did not want to stop. He then asked to go by Det. Burke's residence. He then went in with a portable radio for about 5 min. He came out stating we was relieved. Burke had told him Sgt. D. was a dumb x*.!x*! farmer and did not know what he was doing. He also told me no one in the department knew how to conduct an internal investigation.

"5:05 p.m., Wednesday, Oct. 15, 80, 3-11 p shift. At this time and date Det. Burke motioned me to pull in a parking lot by Petoskey Motel (Spring and Charlevoix Ave.). Burke was in his unmarked unit, I was driving unit 448. I walked back to Burke who informed me that Taylor was at his residence the night before. He said Taylor was upset and that Sgt. D. had pumped him. He also told me that the Chief tried to get friendly with him (location - Petoskey Towing). (Burke and Chief not seeing eye-to-eye) Burke went on to say . . . Chief asked him if I was going to him (Burke) with my so-called problem. Burke told me he said, "no" to the Chief, only that I said, "that I was upset because everyone was on my ass." Burke stated he then said to the Chief, "Hasn't that case been closed." Chief Kraus replied, "Oh no - no, you should of seen her that night, you should have seen her." Burke thought he was referring to the

21

time Sgt. Det. Hartman (E.C.S.D.) and Chief came to my residence, 09/10/80. (I called in sick because of leg injury 09/15/80).

"I trust no-one, don't know what or who to believe.

"3:45 p.m., Friday, Oct. 17th, 80, 3-11 p shift. Petoskey Police Dept. Office of Chief of Police. At this time and date I asked Chief Kraus who was in his office, door open, reading, if he had a couple of minutes and if I could talk to him. Kraus answered, "yeah, sure, come on in." I then requested to see my personnel file and then requested a copy of the same. Kraus said he would show me the file but would not give me a copy. I informed him that under law I was entitled to one. Kraus replied he would not give her (me) a copy until he was ready to do so. I said "OK," setting the "Employee's Guide To Personnel File Access In Michigan" next to my clipboard on the Chief's desk. Then I started reading my personnel file, handed to me by Chief Kraus. While I was reading Chief Kraus asked me what part of the file I wanted a copy of. I replied, "All of it." Kraus then picked up the Employee's Guide To Personnel File Access In Michigan" and started reading it. I then found a written complaint against myself, dated June 1979, written by Auxiliary Denny Bargaron. This complaint also stated it was not to remain in my file for a period exceeding 6 months. Sgt. D. then walks in Chief's office. Door still open. I then pointed out the written complaint and the time which stated it should not remain in my file (6 mo.). Now, still in my file 1 year and 3 months. And, asked that it be removed. Kraus reply, "Don't worry about it, I know." I answered, "Well, I am worried about it." Kraus said, "are you through?" (getting hostile). I answered, "I'd like to read the last few pages." Not letting me finish, Kraus advised me to read the act (in the Employee's guide) on the proper way to go

about seeing my file . . . Not to come storming into his office, demanding a copy of my file. Kraus also said he was not going to put up with any "bullshit." He said he could put up with so-much "bullshit" and he wasn't going to put up with this "bullshit." He then ordered me to "get back on the road." I then said, "oh–fine," leaving with my clipboard. Kraus said a few more things as I was leaving. Something about "bullshit." I had to bite my tongue! Wanted to cry. I never cry!

"6:30 p.m., Friday, Oct. 17th, 80, 3-11 shift. I was sitting stationary on Charlevoix Ave. Jim Pierce (friend-acquaintance) pulled up next to me and asked how I was. Then he said that he had heard that I was under investigation, and what it meant. I asked where he had heard this. His reply was, in a bar, Nancy. He then asked if I could possibly lose my job. My reply was, "yes." He then sympathized by saying, you know when someone works hard for something and then gets it–and it's taken away . . . I said, "yes, I know–it hurts." I almost broke down–cops can't–I told myself.

"8:05 p.m., Friday Oct. 17, 80, 3-11 p shift. I was called to Little Traverse Hosp. E.R. to unlock a vehicle. After doing so I went in to E.R. to wash my hands. Upon leaving Dr. Clark ran after me out the E.R. doors. Dr. Clark asked if they (Police Dept.) were still hassling me. My reply was, "yes, they are." He said he was shocked when they brought me in. He also said not to worry, that my blood did not show anything. He also stated he would testify that my eyes, nor anything showed anything. He went on to explain that he talked to a few people and everyone agrees they're doing this because I'm a girl. Again he said, "if you need anything," to call, and to keep my chin up. I said Thank you, Dr. Clark.

"10/13 (?) - 10/17 - My duty pants are getting bigger, I force myself to eat. My headaches each night as I end my tour of duty. I have had trouble sleeping throughout this week. I hate going to work. I cried and sobbed Wednesday. I'm a hermit. I'm paranoid.

"I got my phone # changed Tuesday - Only my parents, one friend, and my office have it. 10/18.

"6:00 p.m., Wednesday, Oct. 15, 80, 3-11 p shift. (Ed. note: this date is correct for this day though appears chronologically confusing. Perhaps Lisa had inadvertently skipped a page in her spiral notebook. At any rate, the conversational tone does not reflect any sense of lacuna). Tim Mahoney riding. Tim Mahoney told me that a certain officer had said something to him (referring to rumors spreading), thinking this (certain) officer might be responsible. He told me something this officer said in reference to the so-called crowd I was hanging around with (using drugs, etc.). Mahoney stated he did not believe this officer and became "upset and mad." He asked me to guess what officer. My reply was Buchner. He (Mahoney) said, "How did you guess?, right." I assured Mahoney that the rumors were not true. He stated he knew that. He went on to say that he was behind me 100% and that he would back me. He also said that there were probably 20 auxiliary that would. And, many thought I was one of the best officers. He said the allegations were getting him very mad—and that he does not get mad. Adding, he's only been mad once. He also said Danny Bargaron (Auxiliary) told him I was one of the better officers. Mahoney added that he thought they were discriminating because a female could do their job.

"3:20 p.m., Friday, Oct. 17, 80, 3-11 shift. At this date and time I was picking up a certified letter at the Post Office when Kim Glascox drove up—stopped

24

to say hello. Glascox is a so-called friend-acquaintance. She inquired as to how I was doing. And, if I was going to stick around. She said that she had heard a couple of rumors. I asked what. She said she just heard that I caught with some drugs and that someone (?) narced on me. She also added that, "you know how rumors are" (meaning they get blown out of [proportion] and that's why she wanted to ask me."

(Chronologically, this point in Lisa's personal journals contained the entry that began this book. This is reprinted for emphasis.)

"10/18/80, 1:05 a.m. Writing. Tears flow. I can't believe this is happening. Why? Why? Getting many comments on a commercial now appearing on TV that I did last winter for N.C.M.C. Also—my weight loss. My back's bothering me . . . I'm so tense, I can't relax.

"6:30 p.m., Wednesday, Oct. 22/80. 12-8p shift. At this date and time I was asked to meet the Det. (Burke) at Dawn Donuts. P.P.D. assisting Marcia Elliott, Dept. of Soc. Ser. In the presence of Marcia Elliott I asked Burke why the Capt. (Shalk) was working 9 to 5 p in plain clothes. (Usual shift is 12-8 p). Burke answered by saying "watch your ass." he also added: "If I was a certain individual and know how to get in the Chief's office, I'd try to get ahold of this month's issue of Chief Of Police, and read the article on "How to hire and fire." Burke also added that the way the book is bent, it's been open to that page. He also overheard Capt. talking to Chief (pertaining to article) and using the pronoun "she." Capt's been playing Det!

"12:00noon, Thursday, Oct. 23/80, 12-8 p shift. For the past three days the Capt. (Shalk) has worked 9-5 in plain clothes. This shift is normally worked only by the Detective and Chief. (Captain's been

playing Detective, working on my internal investigation).

"5:00 p.m., Thursday, Oct. 23/80, 12-8 shift. At this date and time I went to Dean Burns' office. Burns advised he would take Kraus out for a social drink and discuss putting this ordeal to an end. He stated Kraus was like a push-button phone. You just have to know the right buttons to push. He thought he knew the ones. He said he'd wait for the right moment, maybe a week or two. Burns advised he'd let me know (good or bad).

"8:30 a.m., Monday, Oct. 27/80, 7-3 p shift. At this date and time I picked up Det. Burke for work. He told me the Chief "jumped on his ass" about me. He went on to explain, the 24th, Friday, after work, he, along with Jack Hamill (aux.), his wife, Marsha Elliott (D. of S.S.), her husband, and possibly a waitress at Vic's were present when the chief accused him (Burke) of giving me legal advice. Chief also advised Burke, when Piel gets fired she's going to take everyone down with her, including him. He demanded if Burke had or knew something he'd better come up with it. Chief went on to say everyone's got something in the closet. He also told Burke I was taking notes. (Burke has been investigated for an alleged rape and selling pot, a joint, in the past; the Patrolmans Association and many Aux's. feel if I get fired, Burke should be). On the 22nd of Oct. Capt had an interview. I asked Burke who it possibly could of been. Burke thought he saw Mrs. Zaremski. At this time Burke also advised me that whoever I was talking to was running to the Chief. Schaefer was his guess. I kinda thought so too. Chief received my written request for my personnel file on this date, this being Friday the 24th. Burke also informed me of Theresa Lungin (former Juvenile Officer previously

26

*mentioned) wanting to apply for open Patrol Officer's
position that was open. Chief told her on TX (phone)
he did not like woman patrol officers.*

*"10/31/80, Friday, 7-3 shift. At app. 1 p.m. I
picked Burke up for work. He told me Ed Ward
(Probation), P.O. confronted him asking what was so
secret-secret. Asking why the Capt. wanted to talk–
find Marcy Newton (who's on probation for
possession of cocaine). Ward thought Burke wanted
to see her. Burke said he could not understand why
they were going "so down" on me. Burke informed me
of him being investigated for an alleged rape and
selling a joint, and was not investigated to this
extent. Burke also thought the Chief was
discriminating against me and needed to use me to
show the (new) city manager he had a back bone.
He's afraid, Burke said."*

This completes the extant record of Lisa's journals throughout
her initial harassment which began in earnest in 1980 and which
led to her suspension on November 24 of that year. Some
repetition was unavoidable herein due to the plethora of notes to
be sorted through in order to garner a comprehensive overview of
the sequences leading to this suspension. The police-like manner
in which the journal is maintained in itself bespeaks of her
youthful dedication to her new job, though apparently even this
sort of record-keeping came under scrutiny by her superior officers.

As of the Nov. 24, 1980 suspension there existed no charge
against Lisa Piel nor relevant accuser. Everything thus far was
based upon "hear-say" and the malicious prejudice indicated by
Lisa's journals.

2

Good Ol' Boys

While the written information in the foregoing chapter underlines the seemingly sudden attritional harassment on the part of authorities, when considered in context of the latter 1970's it is seen that this was the "coming out" era for women, especially in the work-force. The C.E.T.A. program of this era provided the training vehicles in which both men and women were enabled to be schooled in areas that they were previously excluded from, both by economic and traditional role inhibitions.

Cities and towns across the U.S. were animated with implementing the means to locate, verify, and provide the means for education and training for tens of thousands of persons who were otherwise left to their own devices in finding traditional work. Although it was to be proven that many, perhaps most, of the C.E.T.A. training sessions were never followed up by actual representation in the work-force, much opportunity for vistas of new horizon were opened up for the recipients.

In Lisa Piel's case, with her perseverance, the program allowed everything it was extolled to usher in. The government paid Lisa's salary for eighteen months as its commitment, with no cost to the City but for essentials she only in part received. Women were trained in police work, heavy equipment operation, and many other aspects of labor that were up to then taboo to them. Men and women were allowed the same opportunities vocationally under equal-opportunity law for the first time in American history.

This was the official terminology, at least. Indeed many were taught the methods and tools of the trades and reckoned proficient enough at them to seek work beyond school. There was, in fact, a directive circulated by federal bureaucracy from whence these monies came to city and provincial offices and state-run institutions of a mandatory hiring policy not to exclude minorities based on gender, race, etc. There were quotas—into which Lisa fit quite well.

The traditional work-force, however, did not always prove to be willing to accept this revolution of co-workers, and indeed many felt it to be an intrusion upon their intrinsic domination of a career deemed to be "man's work" in the case of a woman being introduced against the wishes of the male hierarchy into the inner sanctums of labor.

As mentioned in the foregoing, Lisa entered a world where there was no provision for her as a woman. She was not issued a locker–a seemingly simple convenience–due to the fact that the other officers, all male, used the locker room as a changing room. The shower was off-limits to her obviously as well, there not being need for such formerly. There were, to be sure, comments of feigned acquiescence by the male officers to the effect that she could use the shower freely, this with all the attendant sexual nuance one might presume. There was, by Lisa's own telling, a poster on one wall showing a graphic representation of fellatio, supposedly to inform the officers of its illegality. In reality it was a combination of shock treatment directed toward her while at the same time serving as an auto mechanics calendar poster for the boys.

This treatment, of course, was to be expected, and is fairly-well chronicled by C.E.T.A.-trained recipients country-wide, mostly those of the female gender. The bastions of maledom did not open wide to encompass women in their domains. Especially not in their locker rooms.

Most of these situations are now termed "co-ed." Provisions have been made in some cases to allow for the separation of the sexes in the same work place. In 1978, however, no separation existed. Lisa took it in stride for a time, ultimately suggesting that some implementation be considered. None was. The initial bemusement seems to have turned rapidly into hostility. Not all male officers were openly hostile. Some of the Auxiliary considered her one of the better officers. The immediate superiors in her position seem to have vented the most antagonism, as evidenced by the many references to this in her journals and letters. It appears possible that with some cooperation from the influential ranks of the department Lisa might have been made to feel comfortable in a situation that would improve as everyone became used to the adjustments necessary.

Lisa's conduct on the job was exemplary. In becoming accustomed to the wielding of authority she retained a compassion for people, not choosing arrest when a situation could be dealt with with tact. By many accounts she was "always getting thanks for caring about the under-dog," which in so many cases means the ordinary person as this note pertains to:

". . . Recently we had a VCR stolen by a local person and after all our resources failed, we phoned your department. Officer Piel responded and after outstanding detective work, perseverance, and determination she finally acquired our VCR from people who never rented it. If she had not continued the case as diligently as she did we would have never recovered our equipment back. We are very thankful and wanted to share this information with you."

(undated)

And this letter of Sept. 17th, 1984:

"Recently, while on vacation in Petoskey, my husband and I pooled our intellectual resources and managed to lock our keys in the trunk of our car.

"We soon discovered how efficiently General Motors secures the rear-end of their products . . . either that, or we learned what lousy car thieves we were.

"However, luck was on our side, when a member of your police force arrived. Policewoman Lisa Piel managed, with a tremendous effort on her part, to finally get into the trunk, allowing us to continue merrily on our way.

"My encounters with the law have been few and far between, thank heaven, but none has been so pleasant as this latest meeting.

"We would very much like her to know how grateful we are.

"Enclosed is a golf token which my 9-year-old daughter won while playing at the Pirate's Cove in your city. She wants Officer Piel to have it as her personal thank you . . . for rescuing her and her somewhat scattered parents."

And this by Roy C. Hayes, former Prosecuting Attorney for Charlevoix County:

"Last Spring while I served as Prosecuting Attorney for Charlevoix County I taught Criminal Law at North Central Michigan College. Lisa Piel was my student. I found her to be sincerely interested in Criminal Justice and appeared to be pleasant, dependable and intelligent."

Though these kind of letters are scanty in number the truthfulness of them is accentuated by the fact that they were unsolicited, heartfelt reactions to a caring individual in the person of Lisa Piel.

Where then do the problems emanate from?

As noted in the earliest newspaper article about Lisa, Chief Kraus stated there was no problem with Lisa's fitting in with the male officers, yet this viewpoint for the public was negated many times in verbal communications as transcribed by Lisa and others. The public statements do not equate with the clandestine.

By Lisa's own account Chief Ernest Kraus kept a pint of vodka in his desk drawer. There is naturally nothing to substantiate this allegation, and in fact, was never made public by Lisa herself. She apparently would not stoop to the low tactics employed by her detractors but rather maintained her integrity by sticking to the issues of conduct on the job as pertained to herself. She did confide to friends and relatives, however, some startling clues to malfeasance.

This allegation, for instance, was never publicized nor acted upon in any way: Lisa confided to intimates that Ernest Kraus was caught in the bedroom closet of a girlfriend–with pants down!– by the woman's husband, a scene which, while soap-operatic in nature, was never pursued even for its misconduct aspects. If proven true, this alone might have cost the Chief his career. Add to that a vodka bottle in the desk drawer and there emerges a scenario of the "old school" town marshall riding herd on the wild

32

West towns of earlier times, a situation that hardly warrants more than comedic status anymore. But in Petoskey, Michigan, perhaps to this very day, this situation goes unpublicized and perhaps even unabated, by at least several accounts, again, "hear-say" and undocumented, but sworn to be true by the anonymous (for safety's sake) statements gathered.

One "anonymous" statement goes like this: "These are not Clark Kent/Superman types conceived and raised in moral rectitude; these are ordinary people, blue-collar workers, who for whatever reason joined the force, certain and aware that The Force would be with them and they with it. The Fraternal Brotherhood protects its own and rejects its non-complaints. As with all brotherhoods, it's "them" against "us.""

At this juncture of democratic evolution from the 1960's to the 1990's, and in particular the latter 70's to early 80's, the forced aspects of integration of women, blacks, etc., into the work-force were met with hostility, though not so much violently as bureaucratic. Bureaucracy had learned from the 1960's clashes, both on the street and in the courtroom, that publicity was a tool to be kept under constant control, utilized by documentable means.

Lisa's "file" was burgeoning while her superiors suffered no complaints whatsoever.

Ken Burke, an ambivalent figure in Lisa's career, at once a confidant and an informer, was said, by Lisa, to have reported for work many a morning with liquor on his breath. This may have been acceptable in times past–a "bracer" to fortify oneself–but was hardly tolerable in 1980. This same officer was said to have been forced out of duty in the Gaylord precinct for similar misdeeds. It is also alleged that Commander Burke was consistently seen at a Boyne Falls area tavern, cruiser parked outside, for hours at a time, this for many years standing.

While none of the immediately foregoing can be verified by written and signed "proof," the allegations remain unchallenged, the burden of disproof reverting to the accused, there being no means of researching these stories further since recourse to verification lies with the bureaucracies involved. These have not been contacted due to the assumption of lack of cooperation on their parts and the very real possibility and likelihood of retaliation in a "legal" sense.

If these allegations were proven true, and if they are accepted as such, the question immediately comes to mind of hypocrisy. The emphasis on Lisa Piel's "behavior, and any and all miniscule peccadilloes on her part, used against her in her burgeoning file were directed toward her by persons who were indeed breaking the codes of behavior themselves in somewhat more heinous fashion than anything attemptedly "pinned" on Lisa. The illegal retainment of Lisa's file of complaints against her was, in fact, an attempt to build up a discrediting influence, as seems obvious by dint of relatively no files being held against any other officers either directly concerned or otherwise.

It was also alleged that Burke's wife "did drugs" though nothing of this can be substantiated. Ken Burke, himself, was said by many to be "into drugs." Though these statements remain "allegations" they equate with allegations used against Lisa in that they are unproven but taken into account by witnesses and commentators both for and against. If one "side" can allegate, then surely the other may with the same impunity of the former. Imputations formed the greater part of that used against Lisa and that ultimately resulting in her withdrawal from police work. No "hard" evidence was ever found and by this token these allegations herein are printed as both rebuttal and insight into the greater picture of Lisa's tenure in the Petoskey Police Force.

To impact this "good ol' boy" brotherhood are stories such as this about one of Lisa's contemporaries on the force: Officer Matt Breed was said to have hit a utility pole, while drunk, driving a cruiser, and on duty, with NO REPERCUSSIONS. No record exists of this occurrence, no report, but for the barest mention buried in the inner pages of the local newspaper.

To return to black and white, verifiable facts, Lisa's qualifications continued to expand. Since being hired in September of 1978, having brought with her the myriad training necessary for an officer such as "Fingerprints and Criminalistics" 1977, three hundred hours of Police Academy Training 1978, Advanced Firearms Instructions in Michigan Law Enforcement

Officers Training Council approved Combat Revolver Course 1978, with areas of special interest being in Sex Motivated Crimes, Juvenile Matters, Photography, and Investigation, she continued her education while serving as an officer. In 1981 she completed an In-Service Training Course, "Stress and The Police Officer." Also this same year she successfully completed and received accreditation for: "Michigan Traffic Radar Operator's Course" through Kirtland Community College and "Deviant Sexual Behavior" training through the Michigan State Police Training Academy. In 1982 she received the award of "Advanced Police Officer Certificate" from the Department of State Police under the auspices of Frank Kelley, Attorney General. In 1983 Lisa completed a course in Scuba Diving through P.A.D.I. (Professional Association of Diving Instructors). In 1984 she participated in the "Shoplifting Prevention Program and performed a presentation to local third graders, this latter signed by then attorney (not yet prosecutor) Diane Smith.

It seems clear from the above that Officer Piel was not only not shirking any responsibilities but in fact adding to them continually, upgrading her potential. Why then the confrontations? The "good ol' boy" syndrome is not easily changed or ameliorated.

A Performance Evaluation filled out by Ernest Kraus of October 10, 1982 shows some of the ambivalence between Lisa and the Department, not so much in performance as in attitude. Under Knowledge Of Work, from a rating of Poor to Exceptional, she is scored as "Fair knowledge of work," the Basis for Rating being (in Kraus' handwriting) "Has the knowledge to handle routine tasks. Needs some motivation for self-improvement." Under Dependability, she scores in the middle as, "Can be trusted to do a job with routine checks." The Basis for Rating adds, "generally handles assignments thoroughly." The Quantity of Work scores acceptable and average again, though Kraus points out here that, "Self-initiated work is above Dept. average." Quality of Work is rated Average with the comment, "Makes good effort to be thorough." Professional Development analysis states, "Should do some self study in the more technical areas." Appearance:

Personal & Dress scores "Satisfactory," with the comment, "Needs to gain some weight." Under Attitude, the average dips to "sometimes has difficulty getting along with others–often cooperates reluctantly." Kraus adds here, "Needs to realize the importance of team work. Also the fact that police are public servants and act accordingly." Versatility rates "Satisfactory," comment, "Makes good adjustment." Punctuality and Attendance states "Record needs improvement," with this addition, "Record indicates a consistency in sick time use which is above average." Where Chief Kraus is asked by this form what Assets, what strong points are warranted, he writes, "Shows a high degree of interest in police work. Accepts and follows directions from superiors. Practices aggressive patrol methods." He concludes under Areas Of Improvement, "Make a self-improvement effort through study in such areas as procedural law. Try to improve cooperative effort with fellow officers. Improve attitude and demeanor towards other officers. Make every effort to recognize the fact that an officer is not above the law and behave accordingly."

Splendid advice from a man alleged to be drinking on the job and fraternizing with married women.

Lisa was allowed her rebuttal on this evaluation. On November 8, 1982, she wrote this:

> "In the field of Law Enforcement there's a never-ending need for up-dated knowledge in the areas of police procedure and forever-changing laws. Only one other officer and myself in this department have worked towards and received their Advanced Police Officers Training Certificate from the State. Is this not motivation?
>
> "The average sick days figured for this year, to date 11/08/82, for this department (totalling eleven), including Chief and Detective, is 7.9. Excluding the Chief, 7.6. And excluding both Chief and Detective, 7.0. To date this officer has taken seven sick days. Is this not average?

"This officer feels her height and weight are proportioned. The uniform may be deceiving; it's a Men's Small. She was not fitted for a woman's size, therefore it's very ill-fitting.

"This officer has attended several training seminars on her own time, and has used comp-time as well. In April of 1979 this officer attended a 24-hour "Sex Crimes" seminar at the Kalamazoo Regional Training Academy on her own time. In October of 1981 she had a written request, which was granted, to attend a 40-hour "Sexual Deviation" seminar at the Michigan State Police Academy. Are these not technical areas?

"Until now this officer was not aware of any conflict with her fellow workers nor the public for which she works. For the past year and a half or so nothing has been brought to her attention. Shouldn't these so-called conflicts when they arise, be brought to the officer's attention . . . and not six months to a year later?

"As brought to her attention, this officer agrees that there is room for improvement, and will make the effort to better serve her public accordingly."

From the foregoing the deceit is apparent since Lisa's credentials bespeak of everything she claims to be true. By twisting words and use of the implications of superiority and paternalism the Chief suggests a wayward protege in need of old-fashioned guidance. It is this guidance that remains in question.

Some other discrepancies appear in Lisa's journal of April, 1983 as to overall conduct of the hierarchy within the Petoskey Police Dept. "Hazing" is not an unknown premise among military-like organizations, and obviously is continued in the police departments of even small-town America. For un-named reasons Lisa was apparently often given "graveyard" shifts, often being told it was "for the good of the Department," when in fact, it proved to be for the benefit of other individual officers. In one case, an Officer

Vargo received a four-day weekend two weeks early and was relieved of the eleven-to-seven shift for two weeks; this in exchange for Lisa's having to work the "graveyard" shift for an unscheduled two weeks straight.

Other officers were stated to have clocked in earlier than actually arriving at work—this stated by Lisa who evidently was called for a ride to work by these officers. Peccadilloes such as appearing in public without a cap by other officers were said, by Lisa, to have gone unremarked, while any and all remarks against herself were duly reported and recorded.

In her journal appears the entry: *"Shiv. (Officer Shively) called in "sick" April 4th, 1983, 3p-11-shift, when in fact, he was up at V-Lanes bowling 7 p.m."* Nothing was ever said about this and presumably no record appears, when, in fact, Lisa's record from 1978, as late as 1990, was known to have been on file and considered "current." Though she complained, in writing, many times about this "oversight," it is presumed that the complaint record against Lisa Piel is still in existence from its inception in 1978 through her forced dismissal in 1992.

Though Chief Ernest Kraus penned some allusion to Lisa's failure to coexist well with auxiliary officers, there exists no written or verbal record of such. To the contrary, the auxiliaries were said to have been impressed by her conduct and abilities. The nit-picking continued.

This following Letter of Grievance was filed by Officers Piel and Schaefer together on April 17, 1983, and directed to Chief Kraus:

> "This letter of grievance is in regards to the investigation conducted by the Petoskey Police Department and Emmet County Sheriff's Department, concerning "rumors and allegations" of on-duty activities. This investigation lasted three months on a limited scope, as well as additional month of more intense investigation. The investigation conducted involved three command personnel. The Petoskey Police Department

maintains this investigation concerns "possible" violations while on-duty, but somehow strayed to off-duty associations as well as outside employment investigations.

"We are pursuing this matter as a grievance because of the following points which will be dealt with in detail in subsequent paragraphs. The points of issue are as follows:

"(1)   The introductory paragraph on the letter from Sergeant Doernenberg dated April 4, 1983 to Chief Kraus is highly derogatory, slanderous and purposefully vague.

"(2)   The same "memo" to Chief Kraus from Sergeant Doernenberg dated 4/4/83 also suggests that the Sergeant checked the "tapes" at the Emmet County Sheriff's Department on 3/12/83 and determined that dispatch was not notified of the location of these officers. This is incorrect on both counts.

"(3)   The disposition of the incident is inconsistent with present and past disiplinary practices.

"(4)   The actual disposition of the investigation is not only inconsistent with the stated disposition (Chief's letter dated 4/7/83), but also is discriminatory between the two officers involved.

"(5)   No access to basic logs for even rudimentary verification purposes.

"(6)   Harassment in non-charge areas.

"(7)   Discriminatory statements made by the Sergeant Doernenberg on 4/5/83.

"(8)   Deliberate, unreasonable and bizarre attempts to exert tension and pressure on these officers totally inconsistent with the investigation and ultimate charges.

"(9)   Slanderous statements, suggestions and innuendos by Sergeant Earl Doernenberg on 4/5/83 and 4/6/83.

"(10)   Conclusions drawn by Chief Kraus in his letter dated 4/7/83 are not supported by facts due to a faulty investigation. However, his comments on integrity and "the standards of conduct traditionally assigned and expected by the law enforcement practitioner" do open the door to some serious questions concerning the integrity and example of the Petoskey Police Department and some members of management.

"(11)   Redundancy of charges, some of which are not relevant to the investigation.

"More specifically the sections enumerated above raise very serious questions about the manner in which the investigation was conducted, as well as the ulterior purpose of the investigation as pursued by the Petoskey Police Department and a member of the Emmet County Sheriff Department. Did this investigation warrant bringing in an outside agency? The points of issue will now be dealt with in detail.

"Issue #1. The subject of the investigation is purposefully vague, allowing the department to investigate the very [in] specific charge of "rumor and allegation." How the department was able to determine that a mode of communication (least dependable as far as veracity) is a "charge" is beyond me. The subject of the investigation does not even contain enough substance to reliably *guess* what the nature of the "rumored and allegated" violations may be. What we have is a "catch all-grab bag" heading, supposedly guiding an investigation by the Petoskey Police Department. Further, and very importantly, the investigation is concerning on-duty conduct of unknown (but rumored and allegated) violations by these officers. Yet the department did not even stay within its own established guidelines of their investigation.

"Issue #2. The Sergeant states on his Memo dated 4/4/83 that dispatch was not notified when these officers checked out at the House of Flavors on the morning of 3/12/83. This is incorrect. If the Sergeant had taken the time to walk into the Emmet County Sheriff Department when we were there or after we left, and had checked with the deputies on duty (Manville and Prell) this could have been immediately ascertained. The tapes were checked, but six days later, by Detective Hartman (ECSD). Sergeant's investigative report can hardly be described as "truthful and complete."

"With the time delay between the date that these officers were "located" at the House of Flavors, and the date on which the tapes were examined, it becomes obvious that the joint meal was not that uncommon (with other officers as well) but also was not considered serious at the time it occurred. However, by the date 3/21/83 it must have been decided that the "all-inclusive" investigation was going to yield nothing better, and maybe that it needed a catalyst.

"On 3/21/83 Officer Piel was summoned to the Chief's office. Piel was told that the Chief wanted to "clarify a few things." She was told that she probably did not want Lieberman there, but that the Chief did. The Chief then proceeded to question Piel about a coffee/meal break on 3/12/83. When Piel asked what day the 12th was the Chief became antagonistic and abusive, stating, "you don't know what day the 12th is? There must be something wrong with you." After more limited discussion, during which Lieberman rendered virtually no assistance, not even the civil action of clarifying that the 12th was on a Saturday, clearly filling an

41

adversarial role to Piel, Piel was summarily dismissed with the caution, "you'll be hearing from me, I'm going to write you up." At no time before or during the interview was Piel advised by the Chief (or Lieberman) that the incident discussed could result in disciplinary action. This is in direct violation of the current contract between the Petoskey Patrolman's Association and the City of Petoskey, as agreed upon the 21st day of September, 1981, SEction 22, paragraph 4, which reads . . . 'When a disciplinary matter is under investigation and it is necessary to interview a member of the bargaining unit, such member will be advised that disciplinary action is contemplated and the member may request representation prior to questioning."

"What the purpose of the meeting was is unknown even to this day. It was clearly harassment in that it served no constructive purpose. If the Sergeant had observed the violation as he states, it is a simple matter to properly document it, asking the proper questions, and then writing the reprimand and presenting it to these officers in a straight forward manner. That is proper and totally acceptable.

"Issue #3. Even at this point there were problems with the disposition of the disciplinary action, which is inconsistent with the present and past practices of discipline by this department. The following will clearly demonstrate this fact even without having to cover a large period of time.

"On 2/25/83 Burke was involved in a situation where he was driving at a high rate of speed, struck an island curb, disregarded a red light and a stop sign. At the time of initial contact the pursuing officer did not recognize the vehicle or driver. The Captain, on duty at the time, attempted to set up an interception, however, the vehicle was stopped prior to the Captain's arrival. Burke was noted to have been drinking and was intoxicated. When the Captain arrived at the scene he stated that he was going to talk to Burke. When it was asked later of the Captain why no disciplinary action was taken he stated because the officer (Piel) did not want to pursue the charges since she was a junior officer, the Captain [then] telling the sergeant that he can do nothing. Not only was this incident in violation of State law, with misdemeanor and civil infractions involved, [it was] as well conduct unbecoming an officer.

"Department Rule 903, Sections 4, 10 and 11 state that it is the responsibility of the supervisory personnel, not the junior officers, to enforce the violations of department policy. In this case the Captain had intimate knowledge of the incident from the beginning. Ironically, several years ago a deputy was chased also by this department in which case speed was the only issue. The pursuing officer (Lieberman) also did not want to be the person to press charges. In that case the Captain did press the matter, with the deputy nearly losing his job.

"On 3/27/83, the State Police had a high speed chase that looked like it may approach the city of Petoskey. Two city units responded and were told by the Captain specifically not to use the patrol cars for a road block. Both units acknowledged the Captain's order yet within a half minute one of the units set up a roadblock, stopping and detaining vehicles in the street in very close proximity to the intersection from which the chase was expected to come. The roadblock presented a double threat to the citizens . . . the first, a rear-end collsion factor, and the second, the very strong probability of a collision if the pursued vehicle were to attempt a right turn onto Spring St. from Charlevoix Ave. and strike the entire group of vehicles/occupants broadside. The officer was advised to get away from the intersection because of the inherent danger. This was not done. After the incident was concluded with the vehicle being stopped outside the city limits on W. Sheridan, this officer advised the Captain about the roadblock and stated that the officer should be talked to about the danger of his actions. The Captain laughed the matter off with the statement, 'you know how the young officers are, Dick.' Even the roadblock action was clearly in violation of Rule 501 A and C, no action was taken, even the suggested talk.

"In talking with the Sergeant (Burke) on 4/5/83 and 4/6/83, acknowledged many of the infractions similar to those in which these officers [were involved], and also agreed that one officer was frequently 'screwing up' but that the Chief was not going to do anything 'because he gets so many OUILS (drunks).' Even when the investigation on these officers was being conducted, other members of the department were openly taking extended breaks, many over the allowed total hour alloted, which is to be taken in the times of two 15 minute breaks, one 30 minute lunch. The Sergeant also acknowledged that the department was aware of persons checking out at the fire hall as well as at parents and in-laws while on portable without notifying dispatch. Apparently the Rules and Regulations apply only to these members, or as the Sergeant stated, 'from here on in the regulations will be enforced.'

*(Issue 4 was purposefully placed out of order)

"Issue #5. When asked what I had to say for myself as to my activities on the date 3/12/83, the Sergeant was informed that I would have to rely on his word since my activity log (which the department is choosing to call a 'police report') has been missing from its folder ever since I first learned of the

44

investigation, and that I could not say what activities were logged. Other than actual calls or traffic stops the dailies are very basic at best as far as specific activities and, unfortunately, I have the nasty habit of doing my daily near the end of the shift from notes.

"Issue #6. The fact that the department has conducted the investigation at the Best Western where these officers work as outside employment, while the original report of investigation states 'on-duty conduct,' is of concern since it too was an effort to hopefully find something that these officers may have done wrong. The managers at the Best Western Motel were genuinely concerned that they were in trouble, and could not figure what the purpose of the investigation was "getting at." They were also concerned that maybe these officers were not supposed to be working at the motel, or that the department was not aware of the employment. The Captain conducted the interview on 3/17/83 and asked the following questions.

"1. How long had we worked at the Best Western?

2. How many hours did we work? What hours? How often?

3. How did we get paid? How much and whether by cash or check?

4. Were we on a payroll? What duties did we perform?

5. Why did we have to work there?

6. Why couldn't someone else do the job?

"Kelly at the Best Western Motel was assured that the department knew of the employment there and had in fact approved the employment at the same time the department acknowledged that the employment was in conformance to department policy. This officer advised Kelly that the approval was on a department form provided for the purpose of listing a request for outside (department) employment. What was the purpose of this non-related investigation?

"*Issue #4. This issue is placed out of order because it is felt that it should follow the section on harassment.

"Once the department (Chief) decided on a written letter of reprimand, the department immediately went one step beyond and decided to change Officer Piel's schedule causing an additional two weeks of night shifts before getting a four day weekend. Further, there was [no] valid reason to change Piel's shift. Why change Piel's and not Schaefer's? This action is clearly discriminatory towards Piel. Both officers were charged with violating the same regulations, yet a decision is rendered in violation of the stated decision of the letters, and is, further, unequal between the two officers involved.

"Issue #7. On 4/5/83, the Sergeant (Doernenberg) made the following statement, 'I feel kind of bad about this, Dick (Schaefer), you're not the problem, Lisa's the one we want.'

"Issue #8. While cleaning a mess on the Sergeant's desk caused by a spilled pop, the following note was observed written by the Sergeant to Captain . . . 'Dick in terrible mood tonight. I think changing this schedule will be the bomb that explodes him.' Explodes? Was that the purpose of the shift change?

"Issue #9. On both 4/5/83 and 4/6/83 the Sergeant made statements that were suggestive about the asociation between Officers Piel and Schaefer. He was very concerned about what we talked about. Why we had coffee or breaks together (even when one of us was not working)? What was going on between us? Also why I (Schaefer) never meet with the other officers? (Sure could have fooled me!).

"On 4/8/83 the Sergeant advised Piel that her schedule was being changed. When asked why the Sergeant advised her that it was for the good of the department. When asked what that meant the Sergeant stated 'you don't know? I'll tell you after the ten-day grace period (?) is over.' Again, what is the subject of the investigation? The shift change obviously has nothing to do with the break together.

"Issue #10. The conclusion arrived at by the Chief is incorrect due to an incomplete initial investigation as to whether dispatch was aware that we were in one car for the purpose of a short breakfast. They were aware. The Chief is also incorrect when he states 'upon closer scrutiny it becomes obvious that these violations are not the result of unintentional carelessness, but are in fact the result of gross and flagrant disregard . . .' Too many officers, deputies and auxiliaries have laughed at my attempts to reconstruct a daily after several hours or near the end of the shift. About the break, yes. Not the daily or dispatch being notified.

"When he gets to the area of integrity, etc., he steps into a very dangerous realm. While I am guilty of taking the break (although I am not convinced it was the 12th) . [. . .] If there is one person on the supervisory level at the department who should be aware of trying to 'paint a picture' of someone else especially with so little subject matter to work with [. . .]. With so many skeletons in the closet (some very serious ones) I would be more inclined to stick to facts and not be so vindictive as to try to make a minor break into such a lofty concern. Especially when the very same thing is happening on a wide level constantly, as well as

47

more serious violations over which no action is taken. I would not consider the example given by this department 'sterling' by any means.

"Issue #11. As this grievance letter states, two of the charges are unfounded. Also the redundancy of charges–same thing, different words–does not increase the seriousness of the charge.

"In closing, we would like to state that after having our dailies monitored for months, the tapes examined, friends and outside employers questioned, being 'tailed,' and restaurant personnel interviewed, we consider it an honor that the only thing that we have done was to have a break together. This taken in perspective is nearly a letter of commendation. I can guarantee that some of the officers/command would be lucky indeed to last three hours under the same circumstances."

This rather lengthy grievance was signed by both Officers Piel and Dick Schaefer. Schaefer was apparently a fairer-minded man than others in the precinct, perhaps befriending Lisa in one of her many hours of need. Dick Schaefer ultimately quit the force and is employed in insurance work now. No attempt was made to contact him for comment because it is not known what his affiliations with the force might be at this writing.

Not to suggest any cover-up, the details of Lisa's death which will be dealt with at length remain open to skepticism, the unspoken inference is bluntly that few are talking, questioners are under suspicion.

This sensed impression remains true three years after her death.

3

Tina Turner

As may be seen, by superimposing the rough edges of facts via police reports and Lisa's writings, a replicate of injustice is arrived at. A Cause and Effect begins to emerge from the seeming chaos of journals and letters against authoritarian paternalism. The previous episode dealing with Internal Investigation of the Petoskey Police yielded "hard" evidence of one improper coffee break. Cloaked in departmental rhetoric this fact remained hidden. Spreading it out on the table, so to speak via this analysis, it becomes clear that improper conduct was initiated and perpetuated by Lisa's superiors.

Most of this remained hidden in the bureaucratic process by which a young officer is "accustomed" to police work. Lisa's complaints went largely unheeded and unacted upon. Her personal file burgeoned. George Korthauer, City Manager in 1985, appears to have been in accord with all actions of Chief Kraus and his trusted subordinates when he concludes in a reply to Chief Kraus concerning a grievance from Lisa:

> "Therefore, it is my opinion that actions by Chief Kraus were consistent with the intent of the City's-FOP agreement and past practices concerning scheduling and limitations on requirements to work extraordinary shift assignments. Thank You."

That brief piece of boondoggle doubletalk reaffirms and negates a single premise simultaneously. So much for taking it to a higher court.

The above reference is to a situation occurring in 1985 in which Lisa was in court, subpoenaed for a certain case, for more than eight hours just previous to her scheduled tour of duty. Lisa was excused from duty after court, seemingly to avoid the mandatory overtime pay she would have accrued. There exist various precedents for in-court time for officers of the law subpoenaed and while it is not known what precipitated the lengthy legal skirmish, it concluded in bureaucratic consistency with all former complaints filed by Lisa, adding only another black mark in the file against her. The almost continual, attritional pressure between Lisa and the department always revolved around the most inconsequential of matters on a grand scale but nevertheless effected her in a most adverse way on a daily basis. This is, of course, how prejudice works, by hitting the victim where he/she lives, in the work place, in the most petty ways. It was primarily "pettiness which plays so rough," as the poet sings, which accosted her up to this point. This abrasion and grinding had its effect, to be sure, but was in the process of being stepped up to new levels of not-so-petty charges to come.

It is to Lisa Piel's credit that she stalwartly stood up to all onslaughts of chauvinism directed against her. Perhaps her lack of acquiescence actually premeditated more abuse against her. She was said to be "perky," intelligent, hard-working; she was, of course, young and full of stamina, still excited about a new career in a heretofore unavailable vocation. She was a forerunner in a new field. She no doubt had feelings of bravery, forging a new course of action for women, perhaps taking courage through the very actions being enacted against her, her will being the will of womankind committed to equitability in the work force as in the home. This was the legacy of the 1970's, nothing less than the equality factor of the 1960's revolution. It was Woman's time. Lisa had to make good. She was in the spotlight. She was the emissary, the prototype. She had to be good. Yet she was human. Improper breaks were not allowed to her, only her male counterparts. Her only recourse was the formal complaint system, which, as is seen, afforded her no more than additional bias from those petitioned.

Petoskey, Michigan, it should be noted, has of this publication, retained intact its natural, pristine beauty. Petoskey is regularly featured in articles pertaining to "best places to live" country-wide. It is touted as "crime free," pure, and affordable. All of these studies are conducted by groups never having set foot in these towns they survey. The summations are based on statistics available through publications such as AAA, Travel Guides, Real Estate brochures, Government pamphlets, and the like. Visually and pictorially, Petoskey is a dream world. Its downtown, while overcrowded, is a scene from a family-rated movie. The view of

Lake Michigan from almost any vantage point looking north and northwest is of postcard loveliness, inviting and beckoning.

The Petoskey Police headquarters, the courthouse, the Public Safety Department, all overlook the same scene that the many tourists revel at. It is serene and beautiful to see.

Heretofore, in years past, in what is now known as "simpler times," crime was virtually no problem, as in, there was no crime other than speeding, altercations of one sort or another, and the occasional thievery of someone's home or store. There were no drugs. Drinking was not illegal. Public display of rites of passage (college beer-busts, etc.) were not frowned upon. Drunk driving was met normally with a ride home and three shakes of a pointed finger. Even into the 1960's long-haired "revolutionaries" were permitted their excursions through the parks and sidewalks without "hassle." Petoskey for many years took everything in stride. Its tranquility seemed able and willing to encompass any passing fancies for, after all, its income was primarily from tourism. A friendly face was their stock in trade. And it still is.

The implementation of D.U.I. arrests and the subsequent velocity of War On Drug legislation escalated the maneuvers of police departments country-wide as new laws produced by necessity new law officers, judges, clerks, prosecutors, juries, right on down to more news reporters to handle the ever-growing case load of malefactors.

In the small town of Petoskey, Michigan there was virtually no criminal activity prior to 1980. Drugs were known to be "around" but simply as a hand-me-down from the latter 60's in terms of a few joints of marijuana and the occasional tab of LSD. Then came cocaine and its derivatives, which somehow became linked with marijuana in terms of its heinousness and illegality. These "party drugs," for this is what they are no matter what social scale level they are purveyed upon, coincident with alcohol use while driving a motor vehicle, became "crime" for North Michigan. Drug buyers of the harder drugs (cocaine) often have no compunctions about obtaining money to buy more drugs in the most expeditious manner at their disposal, namely, stealing things. This compounded the new "crime wave" in Northern Michigan, although it would not be perceived as such by a sampling of the news locally. All crime in the "Tip Of The Mitt" area is treated basically as anomalous and is to be stamped out before it takes root, this via sentencing programs geared to teach the perpetrator a harsh enough lesson that he or she will disavow any further connection with said substances or actions. This said, and the law enforcement bureaus prepped for this premise, the political-minded judges and prosecutors grooming themselves for any openings that might arise from such proceedings of weeding out the few bad apples that might be tainting the barrel, the pristine setting covered effectively the mostly clandestine activities being foisted upon the public's underbelly. The harshest criminals the police forces had to deal with were younger white people selling small amounts of the above-mentioned drugs, an occasional belligerent drunk, and a fleeing burglar hopelessly trying to make a getaway in an area where everybody already knew his/her face, make of car, etc. There are no King-Pin Drug Lords in Northern Michigan.

If it were possible to scan a great portion of the country for illegal activities in perpetuation, barely a ripple or tweak would be perceived from the whole of Northern Michigan in relation to many parts of the country at large. Where the areas of Detroit or Chicago might appear solid black with illegal activities, Northern Michigan would appear almost solidly white in contrast.

The forces of organized police work, however, the County Sheriff Departments, the Police Departments of each town, the State Police, and the Public Safety Departments, along with what is known locally as the STRAIGHTS AREA NARCOTICS ENFORCEMENT (SANE) Department, have been programmed to "nip in the bud" any and all suggestion of illegality especially when it comes to drunk driving and drugs. Anything else just falls in line as subtitle to these headings since it is usually found somehow to be tied in with drink or drugs. This has been the unwritten code behind law enforcement in Northern Michigan for the past two decades.

Small town politics do not replicate big city politics. Though the hierarchies are laid out approximately the same, the emphasis is much different one to the other. The small town's motto is some version of, "keep it clean;" the big city's motto, "sweep up after." The only real minorities in rural Northern Michigan are the indigenous American Indians. These peoples are well-enough integrated into the cultural activities of the area to be considered a heritage to be accepted, even distantly revered, as the original pioneering race that they are.

Drugs, drunk drivers, and the occasional young black man came to be known as the new hate group, the ostracized, the mongers of illicit activities, the minorities without morals or ethics, those to be sought out and persecuted into obeisance or banishment, even though they might be perpetuated by local boys and girls gone bad under these influences. It was as though a whipping boy/girl were wanted to enable the protective forces of law and order to bolster themselves, toughen up for the fight, take action before things got bad, and generally put up a front of water-tight verisimilitude of self-righteousness to ban the slime of undermining consequences that continually sought access to the beautiful north country.

To probe a bit further back into the history of the police versus the lawbreaker it is necessary only to view the Prohibition Era. In this time it is seen that a definitive lack of respect for law and order was instigated in the average citizen due to the obvious corruption inherent in those travesties of legislating amusement. Everybody drank; everybody knew it; everybody knew the cops were on the take; nobody wanted the law; alcohol consumption went up two hundred percent ("Ain't Nobody's Business What You Do," Peter McWilliams 1994). Still, most people in Northern Michigan have a certain reverent respect for the law; this is certainly one reason why the north is a favorite retirement area for down-staters escaping the crime-ridden conurbations of Detroit and other auto centers.

Spousal abuse is lately in the glaring limelight of publicity. In the not-so-distant past these incidents either didn't happen at the same rate they do now or they went undetected and unpunished. Perhaps both these vectors of legal-sophic evolution are true; not much evidence exists to substantiate more than educated guesswork.

Legal certification for police officers was not required, nor indeed extant, prior to about 1975. Officers Schaefer and Piel came in to employment as certified, that is, schooled in all the essential aspects of police work. Prior to this an officer was hired on whatever merits he was shown to have exhibited which presumably were prior police work or military service since no other background was available at that time.

Richard Schaefer, apparently a well-trained and conscientious officer, was able to bridge that gap successfully enough; it seems this certification may have been held against Lisa Piel. A "college kid" hired on fully-trained for work might have ruffled some feathers amongst the old-school way of experience. Lisa was confident, trying to do it "right," while having a natural empathy for people, especially people caught up in situations that threatened both themselves and others. Her self-possessed demeanor may have caused some animosity on the parts of other officers, and assuredly on the parts of certain superiors.

From the scanty written history of this area as to actual crime there surfaces basically only rare murders and larcenies inherent to the lumber industry and its gold-rush like fervor for fast money. Law enforcement came about and evolved in much the same way it did in the old West, which was, essentially, through groups electing individuals willing to do the job, sans training, equipped with only a sense of fair play and a vague directive from the more organized legal forces down-state. Even through the Prohibition Era no more than a Keystone Kops approach was necessary to keep the peace for crime was never the problem that it is at once made out to be locally while disguised as negligible for the tourist trade.

Into this scenario of natural wonder, previously non-existent crime, 1960's "revolution," 1970's "liberation," and new complexities of "crime and punishment" due to cumulative effects of drug trafficking, came one Lisa Piel, Petoskey's first Policewoman. She was, as stated, fully trained in every aspect of "criminal justice" but for the on-the-street experience that weathers an officer to the realities of jurisprudence. Lisa was, however, not trained in the realities of police department hierarchies.

After the initial onslaughts outlined, storms which were weathered with moral fortitude, Lisa Piel was becoming the experienced officer she sought to be. Unfairly and illegally the file of reprimands and elusive charges held against her was kept in active status. As drugs were the new crime wave, it was the drug suggestion that was constantly the supposed investigative impetus implied. As was seen in the first official probe as to drug-taking by her, the only drug found was a legally-prescribed pain-killer. This hint of drug "abuse" somehow lingered though, and was to be the focus of the final inquisition held against her, as will be seen. Drug-abuse, with all its attendant, heinous, parasitical attributes, was to the public–even the hint of–enough to condemn a person once-suspected to constant watch and monitor.

Conversely, no allegations or charges were ever brought against any but one of the many persons, both public and private, who were and still are alleged to have been involved in drug taking. Because this writing is limited to existent documentation and hear-say no names can be printed, only the intimation that it is common opinion locally that certain lawyers, police, business people, and community leaders had been seen at parties where cocaine was visibly displayed on coffee tables for anyone's convenience.

Documentation is sketchy at best for the period of the mid-80's. It is known through this following letter that Lisa applied for a license to operate a private detective agency.

"City of Petoskey
200 Division Street
Petoskey, MI
Attention: Personnel Division

Dear Sir or Madam:
Ms. Lisa Michele Piel, DOB: 07/24/57, has applied to this department for a license to operate a detective agency. Ms. Piel has listed her

employment with your agency as part of her qualifying experience. Please verify Piel's employment giving the following information:

1. Dates of employment
2. Position held
3. Duties performed
4. Percentage of time applicant is involved in investigative activities?

Enclosed please find a Confidential Information Release Form signed by Ms. Piel. This form authorizes the release of information to the Michigan State Police in conjunction with Ms. Piel's application for a private detective agency license.

If you have any questions concerning this matter, please feel free to contact D/Sgt. Thomas Dyer of this office at the above address, or by telephone at (517) 322-1964.

Sincerely,

James L. Baird, D/F.Lt.
Commanding Officer"

By this document and by a form of 4/29/83, it is apparent that Lisa was continually involved in upgrading and extending her status and experience in law enforcement.

"EMPLOYEE ACCEPTANCE FOR THE

CITY OF PETOSKEY

SAFETY MANUAL

I, the undersigned, have read and do understand the purpose for Safety Manual and understand its contents.

(signed) LISA M. PIEL"

From January, 1984, there exists this following letter of commendation on two cases handled by Lisa:

"January 24, 1984
Officer Lisa Piel
Petoskey Police Dept.

Officer Piel:

I would like to take this opportunity to congratulate you on the fine work you did on two recent cases.

#1 - Larceny of lottery tickets from Bill and Carol's. After receiving the complaint and getting a description of the suspect, you contacted several stores to be on the look out for the suspect trying to cash in the tickets. As a result of your immediate actions, the suspect was apprehended.

#2 - B&E of the Baker residence on W. Lake Street. Even though you were tied up on an accident and were not able to get to the scene while the suspect was in the house, after breaking free from the accident and checking the residence, finding the complaint to be an actual B&E, you used good common sense in calling for a dog, which led to the arrest of a suspect and subsequently a confession from him.

On these two cases, I would like to again say, congratulations on a very fine job.

> Sincerely,
>
> (signed) Earl Doernenburg, Sgt.
> PETOSKEY
> POLICE DEPARTMENT
> (addenda) Piel's file
> Chief Kraus"

And this excerpt which includes mention of one other officer who will be spoken of later at length:

"To: Officer Joseph T. Rautio
Officer Lisa M. Piel
Officer Douglas C. Keiser
Auxiliary Officer Paul G. Rybinski

I would like to commend all of you for your professional and efficient work at the scene of the recent fatal accident that occurred on Charlevoix Avenue in the city of Petoskey . . . . .

. . . Officer Piel was called at her residence by Sergeant Lieberman at 10:15 p.m., forty-five minutes before her regular shift was scheduled to begin, and requested to report directly to the scene to assist. She was at the location within a matter of minutes and was of extreme value in helping to organize personnel, process the accident scene, and interview the surviving victims . . .

(signed) Kirk R. Lieberman, Sgt.
Ernest Kraus, Chief of Police
George Korthauer, City Manager"

So, it is clear that Lisa was neither inactive nor ineffective during the mid-80's, even gaining the seeming respect of superior officers. Or so it seemed. At any rate, Lisa was perhaps keeping a low profile while attempting to do an exemplary job as this further commendation from 1987 shows:

"PROSECUTING ATTORNEY
EMMET COUNTY
JOHN F. SALAN
June 4, 1987

Lisa Piel
Petoskey Police Department
Petoskey, Michigan 49770
Re: People of the State of Michigan vs.
Samuel Lee Martin, Jr.
Dear Officer Piel:

As you are already aware, Samuel Lee Martin, Jr. was convicted of the offense of Criminal Sexual Conduct in the First Degree in the Emmet County Circuit Court of May 21, 1987. Your assistance and cooperation were important in securing this result. Without people such as you working with the criminal justice system it could not function.

I would like to personally thank you for the important role that you played in this case. It was only as a result of your testimony along with all the other witnesses' testimony, taken together, that the jurors were able to come up with the verdict of guilty in this case.

Sincerely yours,

(signed) Robert J. Engel
Chief Assistant Prosecuting
Attorney"

These commendations hardly helped Lisa and might even have caused her to drop her guard a little for the sequence soon to follow. Organized law enforcement, much as military strategy, has developed an awareness of how to strike when least expected and in terms of highest vulnerability.

On September 6, 1987, Lisa called in sick, and was seen attending a Tina Turner concert at Castle Farms.

The truth is that she was ill that day, as the transcript will show. The point is, a music concert can be a restful experience, considering the rigors of eight hours plus of police work. So where's the problem? Again, drugs, or allegations thereof. Obviously, calling in sick while being seen at a musical concert would not have the detrimental effect desired by authority since authority is hardly above this peccadillo itself. The worn grooves in this record caused scratchy and distorted, tiresome petulance as the interview shows. The insinuation of drug use, or even awareness, seemed the only aspect of undermining Lisa's career that would stick, whether proven or not. The mere hint of drugs was enough to condemn since drugs were the newest, most feared and hated, evil afoot. It must be remembered through interviews already covered and to be presented that no allegations on the parts of any other officers ever surfaced though there were certainly stories circulating as to the potential of drug use, sales, and general knowledge of the existence of drugs rampant among some members of the police force, other legal representatives, business persons, and lawyers. Up to the date of the Tina Turner concert and somewhat beyond no other drug allegations were ever made even vaguely known by the authorities. This was reserved for Lisa. This interview took place on October 8, 1987:

(The players, per usual, were Chief Ernest Kraus and Officer Piel)

"Kraus: The first thing I would like to address is the possibility of sick time abuse. I would like to bring your attention to a sick day you called in on September 6th, Labor Day weekend.

Piel: Uh huh.

Kraus: Do you remember putting that sick slip in?

Piel: Yes.

Kraus: Ok. We have some information that there is some possibility that maybe you weren't so sick that you should have missed work. Do you want to tell us about it, what the problem was or what happened? You say here that you pulled a muscle, extreme stiffness when I awoke, you got medication from Dr. Postle. Is that basically the facts?

Piel: Yeah, I got some Motrin. Linda got it from her dad and gave it to me.

Kraus: Do you recall what time you called in?

Piel: No.

Kraus: Was it noon, or in the afternoon?

Piel: I don't know what time it was.

Kraus: Did you stay home?

61

Piel: I don't recall, Chief, what.

Kraus: What would you normally do under circumstances like that?

Piel: Most likely stay home. I know if my neck was stiff I probably, every time you come to a stop sign you got to turn your head and you're looking both ways continuously. I just didn't feel that I could ride around in the car all night.

Kraus: Ok.

Piel: You know, turn around.

Kraus: You don't recall then whether you stayed home or not?

Piel: No.

Kraus: And would you recall if I told you that we have two people saying that you at that particular night your tour of duty was to start at 8:00 o'clock, at 8:00 o'clock you were at the Tina Turner concert in Charlevoix? Would that refresh your memory?

(Ed. note: "Ve have vays of making you talk"–circa 1955, Hollywood)

Piel: That's correct, I was there.

Kraus: So obviously, you were not . . .

Piel: Yeah, being there versus riding around in a patrol car, you know, I didn't feel good, I wasn't up to turning my head every time I came to a stop sign, it just entails a little bit, two different activities.

Kraus: You don't think that's abusing sick leave, you're not sick enough to keep you from going to the concert?

Piel: (No reply).

Kraus: Ok, that's the number one issue, so there is no problem, you were at the concert?

Piel:	Yes, I was.
Kraus:	Ok. This particular matter I'm going to take under advice and see if you wish to reply to this particular issue on the sick day, if you wish to make a reply, writing or whatever, or make any statements justifying your actions, you feel free to do so. I would prefer to have it by the first of next week or soon after because I will evaluate it to see if I will be taking any disciplinary action on this.

The other issue is, again I have a citizen that made contact with me and made some allegations against you, concerning events at the concert that particular night. It is our policy here, I assigned Detective Burke to conduct an investigation and the core of the complaint was that you were at the concert and two other young ladies and you were observed smoking what is believed to be marijuana.

Piel:	That's not true. I don't smoke anything. I certainly wouldn't do it in front of 6000 people.
Kraus:	Detective Burke interviewed the people, the complainants and do you want to tell her what these people said?

(Enter Detective Burke)

Burke:	Ok, there was an adult Lisa, and a minor, ok? I went and spoke to the adult first and in the conversation with her I checked records to see if you hadn't arrested them or one of the family.
Piel:	Uh huh, go on, go on.

63

Burke: She states that she got to the concert with her niece approximately at 7:00 p.m. Returning back to their seats after getting coke and that, close to 8:00 o'clock was when she observed you and Linda Postle and a third girl who she didn't know. She says that her niece then directed her to the fact that she had seen Linda Postle go into some kind of container, take out what she believed to be a joint, light it up and pass it back and forth to you and her. She was upset, she was not so upset . . .

Piel: I would like to find out who she is because I will sue her.

Burke: Well let me finish, ok?

Piel: Ok.

Burke: So then I said, well, will the juvenile talk to me, and she made a telephone call and so next day I made an appointment to talk to the juvenile in front of her mother, ok? So I went through the same things, checking on background, or any contact or anything, and she relates the same story. Tried to verify, saying, how do you know who Lisa Piel is, many girls that are her height, weight, hair, she says, well, she identifies you, verbal description of you, she tells me about seeing you in the patrol car and such and then she identified Linda Postle per se. She states same thing in regards to Linda going into something, taking something out, allegedly lighting up a joint. Then I asked her why do you think it was a joint, she gives me the mannerisms of smoking a joint in comparison to smoking a cigarette and I asked her how do you know what a

64

joint is or how do you know as her aunt had said that she had smelled it and also the girl said she had smelled it, well the young lady says, 'I got some knowledge of controlled substances, narcotics.' So she brought out a paper which she had again verbally given to me, to show where she had got her knowledge from. What she says to me is that she was very upset and confused about it. The adult that was with her said on the way back home started talking about the Tina Turner concert, was talking about Lisa Piel, police smoking dope, and they arrest people for it, and as soon as she arrived at her home, juvenile's home, the first thing she blurted out to her parents was 'I saw,' ok? The adult might have complained about it, talked about it, but I guess there was quite a bit of reaction and concern from the parents to see what she saw. So what I did is I tape recorded my conversation with the adult, I taped my conversation with the juvenile and I think you've worked on enough cases, I tried my best not to feed or make it heavier or lighter, whatever, just tried to get them to regurgitate everything they thought they seen or explained what they seen, instead of saying, yeah, I seen Lisa smoking dope, does that mean you saw her smoking five joints, six joints, ten joints, cigar, what, and then I took notes and wrote out a report on it and I taped a report on it.

Piel: That is not true.

Kraus: Ok, one thing I also neglected to tell you that for the purposes of this interview,

	this is strictly an internal matter, it is not intended for the purpose of being prosecuted or anything like that. So I must inform you, you are required to answer any questions because they will not be used.
Piel:	It's not true.
Kraus:	You're saying then you did not smoke anything . . .
Piel:	No, nothing, nothing. Linda smokes cigarettes a lot, but I don't even, nothing was passed to me, I didn't smoke, you know, I'm in front of, I don't know how many people were there, you know, no way, I learned my lesson last time, it cost me thousands of dollars, you know, there's no way.
Kraus:	You are saying then . . .
Piel:	Nothing was passed to me, I didn't smoke anything.
Kraus:	You did not . . .
Piel:	If Linda lit up anything, it was a cigarette. If she would have lit up a joint or anybody else, I would have left. I don't want to be around that crap.
Kraus:	Ok, that's the next thing, on other words . . .
Piel:	It wasn't there. They know better, I don't want, no answer.
Kraus:	You do not use it . . .
Piel:	I don't want to be around.
Kraus:	So you have no problems of taking any kind of test?
Piel:	If there is going to be a test given to the rest of the guys, if everyone's gonna do it or, you know, I would have to consult an attorney first.

Kraus:	That's why, I'm just asking. If you have nothing to do with any drugs, then you should have no objections to taking any type of tests to indicate, no, your system does not have any drugs. Is that right?
Piel:	That's right.
Kraus:	Would you offer one?
Piel:	Oh, I don't know, Chief. I would probably want to consult an attorney, and as far as my personal privacy and all that crap, you know. We have been through this before.
Kraus:	I know, I know.
Piel:	So . . .
Kraus:	I know.
Piel:	Everything zeros, seems to zero in on me all the time, but . . .
Kraus:	Can you think of any reason why two citizens state . . .
Piel:	I don't know, I don't know who they were, Chief, and you know, like I said, I did not, believe me, I did go to the concert, guilty, I didn't smoke anything, I took a Motrin that night, I told Kirk on the phone, I said if you want me to come in I will, if you can get somebody to work, that would be better. I just couldn't imagine riding around in the car, you know, took Motrin, 'I don't want to take anything and come to work, for God's sakes. I don't, take an aspirin, bad cramps not too long ago, and Earl said, well, you should get something like my wife has, whatever that was, you know, I told him I took some aspirin, you think I want to take some other kind of pill and come to work, you're crazy, you know, I never should have come in to begin with so I put in my five hours,

	whatever, and went home, wasn't gonna take Motrin and come to work, you know.
Kraus:	Well, I'm not quite sure what direction to go on this.
Piel:	Why didn't you jump me the next day on that?
Kraus:	On what?
Piel:	On this.
Kraus:	This information did not come through until later.
Piel:	That was over a month ago.
Kraus:	That's right. It only came to me a couple, three, four days ago. It's not a question of jumping you on it, it's a question of . . .
Piel:	Whatever you want to call it.
Kraus:	I don't enjoy this anymore than you do (Ed. note: uh huh) As a matter of fact, I hope I never have to go through this again.
Piel:	Well, that makes two of us.
Kraus:	I certainly . . .
Piel:	I would like to know, these people's names to be available to me, because I will sue for false allegations.
Kraus:	Do you want to respond in writing or any way to this outside of the statements you made already?
Piel:	What do you want now?
Kraus:	Is there any more response that you want to make to these allegations? Other than what we already, you admit you were at the concert, right?
Piel:	Yes.
Kraus:	Ok, and you emphatically deny that you smoked any dope.
Piel:	I didn't smoke anything.

Kraus:	Ok. Is there anything else you want to add at this particular time?
Piel:	No.
Kraus:	Ok.

(Ed note: enter Joseph Rautio)

Rautio:	I don't have anything we need to add. A copy of the tape, is that report available for our copy?
Kraus:	It will be. All of these things will be available to you if anything comes out.
Rautio:	Can she have the names of the people that are making the allegations?
Kraus:	If there is anything comes out of it, yeah.
Rautio:	At this time no?
Kraus:	At this time no. I think what we'll do at this particular time is some further investigation.
Piel:	Ok, that is not true.
Kraus:	To see if we can get to the truth. I can't dismiss anything like this, especially while we're on the subject, obviously to the best of our knowledge.
Piel:	I don't even recall anyone smoking anything in the vicinity. I don't remember, you know, but the people I'm with, they know better, I don't want to be around that, I can't be, I make that perfectly clear.
Kraus:	Ok, I will try to . . .
Piel:	I don't go to any parties, can't go to parties.
Kraus:	Give you some decision within a week, ok? Thanks.
Burke:	Present in this meeting was Patrolman Joe Rautio who is Vice-President of the Association for the Patrolmen, Officer

Lisa Piel, Chief Kraus and Detective
Burke. Meeting ended on this date of
October 8th, 1987, at approximately 2:25
p.m., meeting began at approximately
2:05 p.m."

This is the nomenclatural vernacular of police work as it was recorded by tape machine. More information is forthcoming on Officer Joe Rautio (pronounce Rodeo) as well as Chief Kraus and Detective Burke, in which it will be seen that these slates are far from clean.

Though ostensibly a picayune matter with preposterous insinuations of drug taking by an officer in a crowd of thousands, this investigation seems rather to be one initiated at an earlier time as records indicate. The next chapter deals with the background of this case with attendant statements by several concerned persons, and available data pertaining to the apparent assumption that a case was being attempted against Lisa Piel prior to this incident relating to a Tina Turner concert.

4

Of Friends And Family
And Fraternal Orders

I t should have become clear by now that Lisa Piel was not an acquiescent chore-girl on the job but rather a motivated and self-governed team player up to the point of unequal bending of the rules. At this point she rebelled, speaking her mind freely while staying within the constraints of propriety as to retaining her job. It must be remembered that within any official hierarchy—police, military, court, etc.—one must refrain from comment until one is asked to speak and only then may an individual's truth be told, and this only within certain guidelines as prescribed by the authorities. Not exactly an equilateral equation; as seen, the cards were and are normally stacked on the side of authority. This is where the Defense Attorney comes in, though as will be seen, defense is often not even allowed, and when allowed may turn out to be incompetent if not extremely costly.

In the ranks of police departments everywhere is found a curious montage of colloquialisms and legal rhetoric. "For the record" and "off the record" are very pertinent distinctions, to be sure, although "for the record" sometimes, when examined, belies the rhetorical intent and allows some light to filter through. Since Lisa was continually caught up in the battles for self-preservation, and being a junior officer, she naturally could not arm herself effectively nor utilize the whole picture fully enough, being constantly answerable to a tightly-knit handful of superiors obviously at variance with her every move, both in uniform and out. Being an officer of the law, and being overly scrutinized by both the precinct and the public, she had but few friends she could confide in. It became increasingly difficult for her to bare her soul to anyone but her immediate family, less and less frequently her friends. Perhaps the callous nature of police talk in general— "regurgitate," for instance, by Detective Burke in reference to a witness testimony—added to her hardening and closing in upon herself. Her strong-willed defiance at being singled out combined with her ethical attempts to become a fair-minded officer of the law, with each new allegation wore upon her consciousness in ways she may not have been fully aware of. Being the forerunner in her chosen trade she kept up her front of strength and moral stamina, but underneath she was still a woman, though no man saw a single tear.

About 1984 Lisa had, with the help of her father, a building contractor, bought a house, a nice but modest house, overlooking the Little Traverse Bay of Petoskey and Harbor Springs, again, one of Northern Michigan's most aesthetic geographical features. There appears to have been some jealously on the parts of some other officers, who were all male, of course, at a young officer owning such a desirable property.

A girl named Linda Ann Postle, daughter of a Petoskey physician, had been Lisa's roommate for about three years as of 1987. Linda Postle had attended the Tina Turner concert with Lisa and another girl by name of Susie Wilson. Lisa had friends, of course, but since she was a police officer she naturally assumed a stance of some reticence toward close associations that had any hint of illegal activity–which is nigh unto every person everywhere since everyone breaks some law at one time or another. She did juggle friendships and work, though work seems to have taken the majority of her attention. In the precarious position that she remained in as an officer of the law she dared not deviate far from the upright stance she presented. Still, one needs diversion and entertainment. It seems every diversion was scrutinized and used against her.

There exists a Supplemental Incident Report by the Petoskey Police Department which dates from December 1, 1986, in which the Nature Of Incident is headed in bold letters: CONTROLLED SUBSTANCE. Since the department kept records on Lisa far longer than the normal six months required this journal of events is listed as such:

"Journal:

12-3-86	D/Lt. Hardy	Tape recording and transcript of McNiel's statement attached.
12-3-86	Insp. Holly	Initial Review.
3-1-87	D/Lt. Hardy	Reviewed.

73

5-29-87	D/Lt. Hardy	*Rechecked with Chief Kraus. Nothing new. McNeil has recanted his testimony. SANE Drug Team aware of this information. Will remain open.*
6-1-87	Insp. Byam	*Reviewed.*
10-23-87	D/Lt. Hardy	*Recontacted by Chief Kraus. He requests assistance with an investigation into new allegations regarding this officer smoking marijuana during a rock concert. Officer Piel has stated she may be willing to take a polygraph."*

Who McNeil was and is remains somewhat of a mystery. Since he "recanted" his testimony it is assumed that he was intimidated by the police due to charges against himself, charges which were subsequently dropped and hence his recantation of charges against Lisa. More depth of detail is not available at this time and perhaps never will be.

Three interviews, which summations appear as follows, with Linda Postle, Susan Wilson, and Lisa Piel, plus one follow-up contact were conducted to which end a disposition concluded, STATUS: Closed. Yet this file remained more or less active and was cumulatively aggregated in contradiction of all Lisa's efforts to the equitability of moral conduct. With the exception of the missing file of the stated tape recording of McNeil's transcript, the remainder of this police document follows:

"INTERVIEW LINDA POSTLE:

Linda Ann Postle, w/f, 11-12-59, of 218 Arlington Street, Petoskey was (Ed. note: this is the house Lisa bought) interviewed this date at the Perry Hotel where she is employed. She has been the roommate of Lisa Piel for the past three years. Lisa Piel has discussed with her the allegations of Brenda Turk and Melinda Ellen Berger (Ed. note: these were the two aforementioned protagonists). Postle indicated that Piel, Susie Wilson, and she had attended the Tina Turner concert at Castle Farms of September 6, 1987. They had been seated in the center section and in the fifth row. Postle was seated with Wilson on her left and Piel on her right. Postle was smoking Marlboro Reds and Wilson smoked Virginia Slim light menthol cigarettes. Postle indicated that Piel does not smoke. Postle and Wilson did not share or pass cigarettes among themselves. Postle could recall no behavior which could have been construed as smoking marijuana. Postle indicated that Wilson, Piel, and herself had not consumed marijuana or any other drug at the Tina Turner concert. Postle has never known Piel to smoke marijuana or use any illegal narcotic drugs. The tickets purchased for the Tina Turner concert were purchased by Postle from Record World in Petoskey. The tickets were purchased one month in advance of the concert. The pavillion at Castle Farms was full but the concert grounds were not sold out. Postle indicated that 60.00 people attended the concert. During this concert she had detected the odor of marijuana but did not see anyone actually smoking marijuana. Postle drank two or three cups of beer during the concert and [said] that Piel and Wilson had consumed no more than two or three cups of beer each. Piel had spoken to a female seated behind her and Wilson had seen people that she knew seated two rows in front of them. Postle had seen no one she knew at the concert. The three women had arrived at the concert just minutes prior to the performance of Tina Turner. Her performance lasted 1-1/2 to 2 hours. Postle was aware that Piel had reported sick to the Petoskey P.D. that afternoon and that she went to the concert instead . . . Postle indicated that she knew Wilson better than Piel knew Wilson. Postle indicated that she had not consumed marijuana or any illegal or legal drug since the September 6th concert. She was reluctant to submit to a urine or blood test to check for drugs without legal advice. Postle pledged to reach a decision and to notify the undersigned of her decision."

"INTERVIEW SUSAN WILSON:

Susan Jane Wilson, w/f, 11-25-61, of 08998 Susan Shore Drive, Charlevoix, tx. 547-2748, was interviewed this date. (Oct. 28, 1987) Wilson works at Sally Ann Hair Design (tx. 547-6848) and The Beach Tanning Salon in Charlevoix. Wilson is aware of the allegations made to the Petoskey Police concerning Lisa Piel. Wilson has never known Piel to use any illegal narcotic drugs and she has never known Piel to smoke marijuana. Wilson is better acquainted with Linda Postle, but has known Piel since Wilson had been employed at the Holiday Inn in Petoskey.

"The three women had been planning to attend the Tina Turner concert for a month or longer prior to the event. The evening of the concert they met at the Weathervane Tavern in Charlevoix prior to the concert. Wilson's boyfriend drove them to the concert and picked them up from the concert. While at the concert, they each consumed three glasses of beer, but no marijuana. They each went to the restroom together. The only time when they were not together is when one of the three left their seats to go purchase beer. Wilson talked to Theresa Staley, who works at the Weathervane, at the concert. Staley was seated in front of the three women. Wilson also saw other men from Petoskey at the concert that she knew. Wilson smoked Virginia Slim cigarettes and Postle smoked Marlboro cigarettes at the concert. They did not share or pass their cigarettes from one to another. Piel does not and did not smoke at the concert.

Wilson agreed to submit to blood or urine analysis if necessary. She is not a narcotic user and never smokes marijuana. She has not been exposed to marijuana smoke in recent weeks. She did not recall smelling marijuana or seeing such being smoked at the concert."

"INTERVIEW LISA PIEL:

Lisa Piel was interviewed at 1:15 p.m. this date (Oct. 28, 1987) at the Petoskey Post. She had been aware of the allegations of Brenda Turk and Melinda Ellenberger. She brought a tape recorder to this interview and taped same. At the conclusion of this interview she was asked to provide the undersigned with a copy of the tape. She turned off the recorder and declined to agree to provide such a copy. Piel indicated that she had been fired and reinstated 30 days later in 1980 as a result of similar allegations. Piel agreed that there were some hard feelings between her and the police department administrators. She also indicated that different standards were applied to her than the male officers on the Petoskey Police Department.

"Piel could not recall any professional or personal encounters with Brenda Turk or Melinda

77

Ellenberger that may have caused such allegations to be falsely made. Piel could not think of any person or persons that may have encouraged these false allegations. Piel is aware of no motives to make such allegations.

"Piel attended the Tina Turner concert with Wilson and Postle. She had called in sick at work on that afternoon due to stiff neck as a result of her work the previous day. She indicated that she was docked 8 hours pay for making a false claim of illness. She indicated that other officers had made false illness claims and were caught at such but that no reprimands were issued.

"At the concert she sat in the fifth row, which had been occupied by many people from Petoskey. She was seated next to Postle. Postle was smoking Marlboro and Wilson was smoking a white filtered cigarette. Piel does not smoke and nothing that the three females did could have been construed as smoking marijuana. Piel may have held Postle's cigarette while she removed her coat, but no cigarettes were passed back and forth. They had consumed no drugs at the concert. Piel drank one beer and was entirely sober during this concert. No persons were observed smoking marijuana at the concert. Piel may have once detected the odor of marijuana, but she did not know the source of the smell. She was at the concert a total of one hour.

"Piel has used no prescription or illegal drugs in recent weeks. The only drug she has consumed is Motrin for menstrual pain. She has not been exposed to any marijuana smoke and has consumed no marijuana. Piel had sought legal advice from her attorney and the Police Officers Association attorney prior to this interview. She was advised not to submit to urine or blood analysis and not to submit to polygraph examination. She was asked to consult again with her attorney and let the undersigned know if she will submit to urine or blood analysis. She agreed to do such. Terminate interview at 2:25 p.m."

"FURTHER INVESTIGATION:

RAE JEAN VIOLET SWADLING, w/f, 10-4-59, of 1035 Emmet St., Petoskey, tx. 347-4759, was thought to have been a close friend of Piel. She was contacted this date, however, it was learned that she had no recent close association with Piel."

"COMPLAINT DISPOSITION:

This information has been forwarded to the Petoskey Police Department. Nothing further.

STATUS:

Closed."

Such are the tiresome wheels of "justice" turned. Repetition and almost always one-sided interrogation seem the norm though it must be noted that this particular officer, Detective Sergeant John C. Conn, displays a fair-minded approach to his reportage.

"This "case" was closed, as indicated, yet remained and may yet remain on Lisa's permanent record. What promulgated the charges in the first place is not known. As there was mention of the odor of marijuana in the air at this concert it seems probable that there may have been some use of it. This would not be uncommon at a rock concert, no more than imbibing beer. Whether one of Lisa's friends, or a stranger to her, actually did smoke a joint is open only to conjecture. Yet this remained another black mark against Lisa, the mere hint.

From Lisa's personal work journals much of this interview and testimony is reiterated. Brenda Turk was approximately thirty-six years old at the time and Mindy Ellenberger was a fifteen-year-old high school girl. Nothing was ever concluded from these "allegations," but the interminable attrition continued throughout

1987 in terms of more interviews though brief, and comments, minor complaints from other officers (failure to "gas up" a car for another officer), and general implications of misdoings on her part.

Her journal entry of Thursday, January 7, 1988 states:

> *"2-10 p.m. No pay for call in sick 12/21 on paycheck. Chief called me into his office upon coming on duty. Stated he was not going to write me up because in two years "contract" it would be taken out anyway. Would not let me see Conn's investigative report. Stated there would be a "counseling memo" put in my file. Stated the problem was with my personal life - not professional. Personal life effects job. P.P.D. Words exchanged (?)"*

An interesting extract from the journal of Jan. 26, 1988 says:

> *"Picked Lieb up, told me Jim Young from I.R.S. was going to have me audited. I arrested him and his son for OUIL. Stated he'd teach me a thing or two."*

This last reference, of course, only adds to the long, long list of both personal complaints against Lisa and the intimidation by the I.R.S. against any who crossed their paths. The latter, of course, were severely chastised in 1997 by the President on down since one of their numbers turned against these practices and publicly decried this entrenched travesty. The police department locally has yet to purge itself—as has been the case in several big-city departments in the news lately.

As to the Chief's (Chief Ernest Kraus) reference to "two years contract" deletion, this letter was written by Lisa to Chief Kraus on October 12, 1987:

> "Dear Mr. Kraus:
>
> "This is a request for a copy of my personal file made under Section 4 of the Billard-Plawecki Employee Right-To-Know Act (Public Act No. 397 of 1978). I am a present employee of the City of

Petoskey, working as a Police Officer, from September 25, 1978 through present. My social Security number is 373-60-9418.

"I would also like a copy of the Petoskey City Charter and the taped interview which was held in your office, October 8, 1987, at approximately 2:10 p.m. Present were: Det. Ken Burke, Officer Joe Rautio (Vice-President of the Petoskey Patrolman's Assn.), Chief Kraus, and myself. Also copies of any other information I'm entitled to that would be of help in clearing up this matter.

Thank You,

(signed Lisa M. Piel)"

Such documents came into Lisa's hands ultimately but were not forth-coming upon request immediately, rather much belatedly. No request on her part was ever met with compliance but on appeal and much time lapse. Clearly, she was singled out for abuses that other officers (males) did not experience.

The Equal Rights Act by Congress subsequent to the uprisings of the 1960's states that discrimination due to race, gender, disability, etc. is disallowed. Chief Kraus' comment about Lisa's personal life as opposed to her professional life, when scrutinized makes no sense. Unless the vague insinuation of homosexuality is considered, of which only insinuation exists. She, being a woman, had only this in the all-male world she worked within that could be considered the blatant cause of on-the-job petulance by the male members. No charges held against her were ever proved–but for calling in sick and an improper snack break–until the final agglutination of allegations ultimately tipped the scale by sheer weight and viciousness of attack. This will be dealt with at length below, in time sequence chronology.

Meanwhile, through all this, Lisa constantly sought upgrading in her profession. Despite Chief Kraus' unwillingness to expedite her requests for further courses of study, she successfully completed a 23 hour training program in PRECISION DRIVING FOR POLICE OFFICERS at DELTA COLLEGE in September of

1988, then STREET SURVIVAL '89, the Tactical Edge Seminar in Lansing, Michigan dated June 11-12, 1989.

On March 20, 1989 this letter was received at the Petoskey Police Department addressed to Thomas Postelnick:

"Dear Mr. Postelnick:

"I'm writing in regards to the performance of your police officers on 3-17-98 in the Emergency Room.

"The officers on duty, especially Lisa Piel, were very helpful and professional. A client of the Assertive Community Treatment (ACT) had some difficulty and your officers handled the situation very appropriately.

"I do not know the name of the officer who was on duty with Ms. Piel that night, but please thank both officers for being so helpful in this matter.

Sincerely,

(signed) Karla Matchinski BSW
Mental Health Advocate

NORTHERN MICHIGAN COMMUNITY MENTAL
HEALTH SERVICES BOARD
310 Howard St., Petoskey, Michigan"

Always, in the public's eye, Lisa Piel was the paragon of good conduct as an officer of the law. Ever, in the eyes of the Department, she was the black sheep, the unwanted, the recipient of subterfuge. Still she persisted.

The inference of homosexuality seems largely unfounded. This presumably was initiated by male officers who simply were not attractive to Lisa, hence foiling their attempts to "get next to her." This on-the-job attraction has recently led to much of the publicized "harassment" instances in which co-workers, usually superiors, exert illegal pressures upon subordinates in lieu of, or for gain of, sexual considerations. Lisa apparently was having none of that. She had male friends; she had female friends.

The era of freer attitude toward sexual orientation is still upon us, leaving much disagreement in its wake. No proof of any sexual aberrance exists on Lisa's part, yet this alleged "aberrance" was carried as far as an ultimate Grand Jury in the form of insinuation—not of illegal activities, but merely a swaying suggestion made by the prosecutorial team to discredit Lisa in jurors' eyes.

The issue should never have arisen. Whether Lisa harbored thoughts of deviant sexual behavior has nothing to do with anything else concerned but seems to hang on like barnacles to her legacy. It remains one of the "allegations" used against her, another "stake" in the heart, as it were, to castigate and calumniate. But until such time as the gears of justice are realigned to encompass sexual orientation under Equal Opportunity law, this suggestion remains a condemning influence against anyone singled out as a perpetrator of such "irreligious" proclivities.

Discrimination is the issue Lisa dealt with on a daily basis—plain old-fashioned gender-based discrimination. Every shroud available was instigated and perpetuated to hide this fact but as this biography clearly shows, the facts belie the allegations, the allegations become the "facts." This intimation of "lesbian" was apparently what was meant by "personal lifestyle."

As seen, most of the charges brought against Lisa Piel were in fact common practice amongst police officers at that time. Lisa was buying a house; she normally had a female roommate to help with expenses; she had occasional male friends but no live-ins; thus she was open to insinuations of homosexuality. And drug use, though how this came about will be examined further in subsequent chapters.

Corruption in police departments is not a new phenomenon. Certainly the Prohibition Era substantiates this. Forty years after the 18th Amendment to the Constitution, Frank Serpico was set up by his fellow officers for a bullet from drug dealers. He said, "There was no 10-13"—an urgent "assist officer" radio call—"on the night I got hit. I think that tells the whole story." If allegations and hints and unfounded insinuations can be used by the forces of "law and order" then it is assumed that comparisons of any parallels may also be used to offset the one-sided approach allowed the legal/sophic forces up to this point in time concerning Lisa's evolution and demise.

Serpico now says, "I would have these nightmares about being pursued, and I call the cops and who do you think comes? My old buddies." In other words, the threat lies more with the police force than with the actual criminal. This inversion of tenets of "To Serve And Protect" is diagonally opposed to the premise of police work, of course, and this very antithesis of what is supposed is the basis of this writing. As Serpico said in a recent Albany, New York interview (9-21-97), "good guys don't get ahead in the police department, the way it's set up." He added that the recently publicized attack on Abner Louima, a Haitian immigrant, by the New York police, was further proof of his conviction that his department and today's are the same. The cop culture he believes, is infected with brutality, corruption and racism, and immune to quick-fix solutions.

To give the "living legend," Frank Serpico, his full fifteen minutes herein, this conclusion to the same article goes:

' "To make another point, Serpico referred to the night of Feb. 3, 1971, when two back-up cops ignored his pleas for help when he found himself trapped in the doorway of a suspected drug den, looking down the barrel of a gun and feeling the heat of the shot.

"A message that I wanna tell cops is: You know who called in 'Shots fired, man down? A Puerto Rican resident," he said.'

"That's who's going to call. Some black, Oriental, Haitian, law-abiding person. When you're down, that's who's going to call. And that's who you have to gain their confidence and respect. That's your job." '

Well spoken and well taken. Does anyone care about Lisa Piel's personal life as it pertains to her former job? Not hardly. Is anyone now willing to stand up and tell their own truths about the saga of Lisa Piel on the Petoskey Police Force? Not hardly. Yet there are a few, as will be shown, who tenuously step forward. The problem inherent in legalities stems from the fact that charges are easily instigated by officers of the law, much more difficultly by the average citizen. One gets paid for such activities, the other must pay for them—whether it lies in bringing them or defending them. The prosecutor has the upper hand in the police station and the courtroom, the defence attorney must pick up the pieces belatedly and side with the one burdened with defense and labelled "defendant." It is not an equal battle to begin with. It follows logically that the officer of the law will be credited with more persuasive ability than anyone berating his (or her) testimony.

Since the Serpico saga, obdurate forces of "law and order" have come under scrutiny in many instances. Rodney King and Malice Green of L.A. and Detroit respectively, bring up curious points of peace-keeping: who are the criminals and to what degree? And then Mark Fuhrman, formerly of the L.A.P.D., who was brazen enough to give the world an actual taped message of inherent racism, who committed perjury on the witness without recompense, was actually instrumental in getting O.J. Simpson off a murder charge due to "probable cause" being such a muddled issue in a blatantly racist situation.

The impropriety award, however, goes to the New Orleans Police Department of which as of 1996 has two cops on Death Row and many more indicted for various crimes. Conversely, the majority of charges in new Orleans are against black police officers, to which the city responded by hiring Richard Pennington, a black man with impeccable credentials in police work, to clean up an incredible array of corruption suggestive of Al Capones' Chicago in its lawlessness—lawlessness by the cops themselves.

Then in Detroit, four black officers were accused in May of 1996 of running cocaine in a Texas-Michigan operation, while as many as seventeen white officers from Indianapolis, Indiana, while being rewarded for outstanding work, proceeded to consume 6-1/2 cases of beer at a minor-league baseball game, then made racist and sexist comments to passers-by, fighting, pointing loaded guns at people, battered one innocent man, ended with a hung jury for four of them, the defense attorney for these four claiming that the innocent, battered man should be on trial for fighting with the officers.

85

Such "criminal justice" logic defies rationale, but then, lawyers are well paid to come up with such "logic," as prosecutors and judges are well paid to prosecute and to judge.

Also in 1996, a good year for police misconduct, three former prosecutors and four Sheriff's investigators were indicted in Wheaton, Illinois for fabricating or concealing evidence that sent two men to Death Row but who were later acquitted. This case stemmed from 1985, the former prosecutors now holding positions such as judges and U.S. Attorneys; the Sheriff's Deputies are still employed there.

In 1995 dozens of New York City police officers visiting Washington D.C. for a service honoring fallen comrades went on a drunken rampage, said to have been "worse than Animal House," for three days at several hotels around the Capitol area. "Apparently the visiting officers were discharging their weapons out the windows into the sky," said a Mr. Delaney of the Bellevue Hotel, who added that Washington police were called but, "they came, insisted they didn't hear anything and went on their way." So much for policing the police.

There exist hundreds of such reports available cumulatively every day in your local newspaper. In October of 1977 Judge Joseph Troisi actually "stepped down from the bench, removed his robe and as a half-dozen witnesses looked on in the courtroom, bit a chunk off the end of [the defendant's] nose." So much for "criminal justice."

In the halls of Congress itself, former Representative Dan Rostenkowski, the once-powerful House Committee Chairman, pleaded guilty to mail fraud and was sentenced to 17 months in prison and fined $100,000. And then, of course, there is Newt Gingrich. Rostenkowski, despite his conviction, will keep his annual pension, estimated by the National Taxpayers Union at $96,462., as will Gingrich assuredly keep his as well.

All of this puts a different light on the concept of "Equal Opportunity."

The Equal Opportunity law states that discrimination on the ground of race, color, religion, sex, national origin, age, disability, or political affiliation or belief is against the law. Lisa Piel was discriminated against as a woman. The judicial system, taken as a whole, encompasses the protectorship of the rights of all the aforesaid discriminatory potentials yet this flaunting of the law is rampant. The same law protectors then break the very laws they are trusted with keeping, merely juggling the emphasis one to the other as suits their needs and wants. Plea bargaining is an example of this, which subverts the garnered and considered laws extant to diluted form which may be perverted in many perspectives to usurp and supersede the law itself.

In Petoskey, Michigan a sense of self-righteousness prevails in the visible areas of commerce and residence. Overtones of the realities of legalistics are heard but rarely recorded either legally or in the press. What is constantly heard, though in whispered format, is the ubiquitous, "I have to live here," which effectively precludes much dissent or complaint of any wrongdoing on the parts of legal or political parties locally. Recently (1997) issues such as "misconduct" have arisen and have been grudgingly portrayed in the press somewhat, though not in any entirety. This effect will be dealt with at length subsequently since it relates to the premise of Lisa's tenure with the authorities of Northern Michigan.

In 1989 a girl named Alice Jane Waybrant, who chose to represent herself as [   ] met Lisa. She had come from the Upper Peninsula in 1988 to attend college at North Central Michigan College of Petoskey. A talented but troubled girl, she "developed a friendship unlike any I have ever known and one that to most may be incomprehensible. Lisa was older than myself and taught me of self worth and about living within your means to the absolute best of your ability."

She continues, "I grew up in a small town in the Upper Peninsula of Michigan where culture and prestige were quite foreign to me. Lisa took time to help me grow and brought me to a state of awareness that perhaps I may have never known had I not shared a portion of my life with her."

Lisa's brother, at this time, was found to be dying of an incurable disease. This was her only brother whom she is said to have loved deeply. She continued police work diligently, befriended and helped her new-found acquaintance, and concealed the pain of loss as well as she could within the context of her precarious position with the police department.

Her friend was a musician and played in a band in the Petoskey area. The world of music and musicians was here, as perhaps most places, replete with the overlapping world of drugs. She soon became "a full blown coke addict." This fact is relevant to later happenings as will be seen in reference to drug implications against Lisa. She later became a roommate of Lisa's. In her own words,"

"I found myself moving further and further from my family and friends. At 82 pounds it was getting hard to hide the fact that I was in big trouble. I became everything I hate, a liar, a thief, a manipulating user and worse of all, someone who would sell or trade anything and everything to support this horrifying addiction—right down to sexual favors with men I could not even stomach. I lied about damn near everything to avoid admitting what was taking place. I was killing myself. I was suicidal and I hated my entire being, yet was getting so far gone I had no clue as to how to find myself again. I lived with Lisa and she was simply a person. I don't feel a need to enter into the possibility of her committing human error, (humans do that). What I do feel a need for is to let every ignorant, judgmental, clueless member of society know is that Lisa Piel looked at me, gave me a huge dose of Tough Love, all of the support someone in desperate need could ever hope for and basically saved my life. She gave me an ultimatum—get help or get out! I left her home. I stayed in a hotel funded by my drug supplier, John Rautio. (Ed. note: this is the brother of Officer Joseph Rautio previously mentioned. More on these brothers to come). I stayed drunk and high for days until Lisa could no longer dissociate herself and telephoned my parents. Between Lisa and my parents and my siblings I was placed in a rehabilitation unit. Willingly, I might add. Someone showed me a way back to myself and I wanted to get there. Lisa was sick herself, she had just had one of her kidneys removed but that did not stop the letters, cards and phone calls of support from one form or another arriving EVERY SINGLE DAY! Not one day passed where I did not hear her saying you'll be okay, you can do this. I am so proud of you. Not one!"

Slightly after this reference to a kidney operation Lisa had follow-up back surgery performed at Little Traverse Hospital. To accent the preposterous amount of harassment on the parts of other officers, part of her therapy thereafter contained the suggestion of exercise. Sick days were needed for recovery, but when she was sighted riding a bicycle on one of these days a complaint was made about seeing her on a mountain bike after having called in sick. This after almost twelve years of service.

The pressure was building. Lisa's brother had recently died. Her humanitarian attempts of compassion would yield only more fuel for the undermining fires conspiring against her. Her silent and lonely battle for not only propriety of judicial responsibility but equalitarian coexistence on the job was losing ground. Illnesses were encroaching. The skies were darkening.

5

The Apex Of The
Storm Impending

On June 8th, 1989, Lisa's brother passed away. In her own words:

"My brother died at home after a long illness and battle against AIDS, one year ago. We were very close and I continue living with the memories of his and my family's pain and suffering, as we took care of him at home till the day he died. To this day we have not buried his remains (ashes). Yes, June 8th was a bad day for me. I awoke at 7:30 and jumped into the shower having every intention of going to work at 9 a.m. While in the shower I broke down again and couldn't contain myself. I knew I couldn't go to work in my present emotional and mental state. I was a mess. I called the office at approximately 8:40. I spent most of the morning and early afternoon trying to come to grips with my loss.

"At 1 p.m. or so I decided to go to physical therapy, as I called earlier stating I could not make an earlier appointment. I rode my bike as part of my therapy program. On my way to therapy I ran into Officer Breed and asked him if we were busy and who was working 10-6 p, they weren't real busy. I continued on my way to physical therapy and had a hard work out, and returned home.

"On Monday, June 11, I called the office at 8 a.m. and asked for Burke. Deb stated he was at the court house. I advised her I had to see the therapist, had a doctor's appointment, and anticipated outpatient surgery from complications of my kidney removal 3/13. I asked her to relay this to Burke or leave a note. I further told her depending on how I felt on Tuesday I'd check in.

"I went to the Doc's (Hall) at Burns Clinic as stated and indeed had surgery which resulted in having my right side cut open and a plastic (fishline type) suture removed from my muscle. Because of its

91

position this left me quite sore and bruised, as the Doc had a little problem finding it.

"On Tuesday upon awaking from an uncomfortable night at approximately noon I called the office and talked with Chief Postelnick. He asked how I was doing, I assumed he was talking about my minor surgery the day before. I advised him I had just taken off the bandages and my back appeared quite bruised and sore and the doc said another week of physical therapy. He asked if I was going to be coming in the next day. I told him I had every intention of doing so. He told me to see Burke, and added he had some case for me to work on.

"Wednesday morning I got dressed for work and called in for a ride as I normally do. I reported to Burke who told me to sit as he closed the door to his office. Burke stated he had some complaints from my peers."

"Light Duty" was the normal course of actions for an officer recovering from illness, wounds, etc. The implications above are obvious. Lisa was spotted riding a bike when she was known to be recovering from surgery. The doctor's recommendation for physical therapy and light duty seemed to preclude bicycle riding in the minds of fellow officers. Lisa filed the following grievance on June 20 of 1990:

"Name of Aggrieved Employee   Lisa M. Piel Badge No. 10

Classification   Patrol Officer

Assignment _____

Date of Appointment   9-25-78

Employer   Petoskey Police Dept.

Contract Violations: Article and Section No.(s) Sec. 13.2   (B)   & Past Practice Statement of

Grievance   (Giving time, dates, who, where, when, what, and why):

"On March 13, 1990, the grievant underwent surgery which resulted in the removal of a kidney.

"On April 11, 1990, after a meeting with the Chief of Police, the Grievant returned to work performing Light Duties. The performance of these duties and assignments to same have continued with the Grievant working forty (40) hours per week on selected duties.

"On Friday, June 8, 1990, the Grievant was unable to report for work and notified the department of such, requesting a vacation day.

"On Monday, June 11, 1990, the Grievant was again unable to report for work due to physical therapy and doctor's appointments which resulted in out-patient surgery being performed.

"On Tuesday, June 12, 1990, the Grievant was again unable to report for work due to complications arising out of the out-patient surgery of the previous day. Grievant notified the department of this and requested a vacation day, as all of her accumulated sick leave was expended.

"On Wednesday, June 13, 1990, the Grievant was picked up at her residence by a department vehicle for transportation into work as normal. Upon her arrival at the department she was instructed to report to a Commander Burke who is in charge of the Department during the absence of the Chief of Police. Upon meeting with Commander Burke, the Grievant was advised that the assignment to "Light Duty" was being terminated, and that the Grievant would be placed on a Medical Leave of Absence without pay.

"It was stated to the Grievant that due to failure to report for duty on Friday, June, 8, and due to the fact that she was under doctor's orders to limit her to

93

"Light Duty" for another month, that the assignment could no longer be given.

"It is the opinion of the Grievant and the Union that Commander Burke, the designated representative of the Chief of Police, violated Section 13.1 (B) of the current Labor Agreement, in that the section provides for the assignment of personnel to other duties, which had in fact been done, and that in past practice officers have been allowed to perform "Light Duties" until such a time as they were completely physically fit to resume the normal duties, and that the removal of the grievant from the "Light Duty" assignment was initiated in an arbitrary and capricious manner."

"**Describe in detail desired settlement of Grievance:**

"That the Grievant be returned to the "Light Duty" status for the remainder of her recuperative period and that she receive all pay for the time lost while being denied the "Light Duty" assignment.

(signed)   __Lisa M. Piel__   "
Aggrieved Employee

Then followed the inevitable bureaucracy inherent and necessary to procedural inter-office communications. The Labor Council of the Michigan Order of Police stationery records the receipt of Lisa's Grievance as filed 6-20-90 in a letter by Thomas E. Kreis, Field Representative to George Korthauer, City Manager of Petoskey, as notification of intent to arbitrate, etc. Another letter followed this, dated July 23, 1990 suggesting possible arbitrators for the case.

Lisa personally filed a letter dated August 14, 1990 requesting Commander Burke to delete "any and all disciplinary action which remains in my file, dating back to September, 1978, as agreed to by the City of Petoskey and the Michigan Fraternal Order of Police Council, Sec. 14.1."

But the more she fought back the more she was retaliated against. Tom Kreis wrote Lisa on October 8, 1990 of his decision not to proceed with her grievance due to the opinion of a Mr. Lyons of Birmingham, Michigan, a lawyer for the Grievance Committee. In legal parlance John Lyons states:

"As you know, section 13.1 (b) under medical examination states in part, 'the employer shall attempt, but shall not be bound to place the employee in another position with the city, . . .'. The language is a clear escape, if you will, from the employer's obligation to place an employee on light duty status.

"Possibly a past practice argument could be made, but not using this incident. Moreover, I understand that the employer has some adverse evidence such as the grievant riding her bike, and witnesses placing her in a bar, all of which apparently led to the employer's decision to remove her from light duty status. This evidence would weigh against us in addition to the contract language. Therefore, it is my opinion that we would not be successful in grievance arbitration of this case."

Then Thomas E. Kreis, Field Representative of the Labor Council, Michigan Fraternal Order of Police, wrote to George Korthauer, City Manager of Petoskey, Michigan, that, "In reference to the above captioned matter, after further consideration, it is the position of the Union that the matter will not be pursued any further. It is therefore the intention of this communication to inform you that the matter is considered closed by the Union."

Case closed.

For legal purposes this sort of sequence must be enacted, though when perused all at once it is seen that this foregone conclusion was inevitable. A conspiracy, as usual, deprived Lisa of even her "legal" rights through the arbitrary body of the Union. All she did was ride her bike for therapy purposes and maybe (maybe) have a drink in a bar.

At about this time Ken Burke was seen, by Lisa, at a local Petoskey bar drinking beer on several occasions, his police cruiser parked in back, license number 681 YPX, should verification ever become necessary. On one such occasion Burke was noted to have been drinking beer in this bar just prior to active duty one evening. This incident goes unnoted but for Lisa's journals and conversations to friends and families. She, being not vindictive by nature, never chose to file complaints against Ken Burke for any transgressions observed by her on his part. Mr. Burke was apparently, if not an alcoholic, at least a problem drinker. He was seen at Carley's Bar in Petoskey on March 31, 1991, cruiser plates 681 YPX again, for several hours, and again on April 1st and 5th of that year at the same tavern, always with his police vehicle parked outside. He apparently saw no reason to hide the fact that he as a police officer was drinking in a bar while on duty. Neither did any fellow officers see fit to report this fact nor ever speak disparagingly of it to any lasting effect. Burke was evidently immune to chastisement for his transgressions. One presumes that neither the public nor the precinct dared cross him for fear of his vested powers being used against them.

Ken Burke had been fired from a Detroit area Police Department, it is said, possibly along with another officer. These details are not available at this time of publication, but it is also related that Burke worked for the Gaylord Police Department for a time and left under similar circumstances. Why he was hired by the Petoskey Post remains a mystery. Perhaps the gun-slinging, beer-slugging, tough-minded cop image was thought to have been needed at the time to instill fear into the minds of scofflaws. Burke was also reportedly loose with his police revolver, having been seen twirling it while sitting on his front porch, and having been warned by proprietors at the Junction Inn of Walloon Lake not to brandish his gun in their barroom. It is also said that Mr. Burke "set Lisa up" for her ultimate forced resignation, but this cannot be substantiated. Suffice to say that cumulative efforts on his, and many others', part arrived at their desired result: getting rid of Lisa. Mr. Burke is said to be "one of the dirtiest cops" by local sources unnameable herein due to (still) fear of reprisal.

Ken Burke was obviously friendly with Chief Ernest Kraus and this would certainly explain why no formal complaints were ever brought against him. There was alleged to have been an altercation at a local pancake house (since removed) in which Ken Burke was involved in actually assaulting a customer and ramming his car with a police cruiser. Again and per usual, no record of this exists but for local folklore. It is rumored locally that Burke "beat up a kid" in Gaylord, Michigan, which led to his leaving that town, apparently straight for Petoskey and the waiting tenure under Chief Kraus which plays so heavily in Lisa's experience.

There is a man, a mason by trade, living in Petoskey whose name is Ralph Stowe. Ralph has been described variously as, "no angel," as having made "threats about police department," having "brought a lot of problems upon himself," and as someone who likes his drink and doesn't mind a fight after a few drinks. Sort of an Old West character, out of place and time. He naturally had many run-ins with the police.

Ralph Stowe is, at the time of this compilation of sequences, serving one year in the local County jail for what are perceived by some to be "trumped up" charges. In this instance, he simply resisted arrest but the arresting officers had no grounds to be there in the first place, there being no crime committed.

At some point in the misty and murky chronology of Petoskey's legal and semi-legal affairs, Mr. Ken Burke was overheard saying, "I have one good fight left in me and I am saving that one for Ralph Stowe." This was supposed to have been uttered in about 1990-91. A local resident commiserated to this effect:

> "One day Ralph gets a bum rap in court and goes and gets drunk. He had not drank for over five years but he cannot tolerate lies by the police in the court room. His family gets concerned for the police because Ralph is very intoxicated. They call the

police and tell them for their own safety stay away
from Ralph today . . ."

This strategy proved to be antithesis of the feelings that
promoted it as Ken Burke is said to have seen his opening for an
easy arrest, and proceeded accordingly. Burke evidently knew he
could get a warrant for "mental evaluation" which would give him
legal access to Stowe's home. At this time Ralph Stowe was passed
out on his couch inebriated. A judge Mulhauser signed the
requested warrant. However, both Mulhauser and Burke knew
that a mental evaluation could not be performed while someone is
drunk, but the judge was not informed of this complication.

Ken Burke, Lisa Piel, Doug Keiser, and slightly after, Joe
Rautio, descended upon Ralph's domain, supposedly with
ambulances ordered to stand by contiguously. Burke was
apparently ready for a shoot-out. Stowe was a fighter, and a big
fellow.

Stowe, however, was passed out on his couch and attended by a
friend whom he worked for occasionally. As the police converged
on the back door of the house, Ralph's friend, it seems, stepped
outside to explain that Ralph was incapacitated and no threat to
anyone. But, "Burke then rips open the door and charges in after
Stowe," as related by the aforementioned local resident.

Seemingly, what transpired in the ensuing struggle was that
Stowe heard the commotion, rallied himself for a fight, and
attacked Burke. Lisa later said that Burke had said to her upon
approaching the house something to the effect of, "want to have
some fun?". Officer Keiser tackled Stowe at this point of fisticuffs.
Lisa stood back and merely observed, there being no need for any
more action. Stowe, being drunk, was no real threat, with two
large male officers controlling him. Lisa then watched as Burke
proceeded to pummel Stowe with his fists while his victim lay
confined in handcuffs and held by the other officer.

Moments later, all were said to exit the back door, Ralph in
tow, Lisa "Looking disgusted," Officer Rautio then completing the
scenario, and transported Ralph Stowe to a waiting ambulance
which took him to nearby Lockwood Hospital.

Lisa later told friends that she had said at the time of Burke's beating Stowe, "stop it, this is wrong." This was never reported officially, presumably because Lisa was still the junior officer on the scene and subservient to Detective Ken Burke. Her further words to Burke however, of "you can't do this," may have concluded the beating. Stowe was quickly diagnosed as being drunk and not evaluatable for mental status. Mr. Burke then became confused since his warrant was obtained under the mental instability premise and took Ralph to the County jail. At some point the drunken Stowe bolted for a door, causing him to be tackled again, out of which Detective Burke said that he sustained some injuries to his neck and back.

Ralph Stowe was held for about forty-five days in the County jail awaiting trial, a procedure which netted him eighteen months in prison–"for nothing," as his friend later related. This friend added, "there was no physical reason to come to his house."

Ken Burke subsequently retired on a disability pension due to his "injuries" from this escapade. It is known, however, that Burke's neck injuries were previous to this affair, his claim being spurious although effective since this was never challenged. Lisa herself said in private, "Burke did not hurt himself." Burke was seen "out dancing" not long after this.

Burke had had his "fun" and his last "good fight," backed by the Petoskey Police Department and the following judicial rulings. Justice?

- - - - - - - - - - - - - - - - - - - -

On August 30 of 1991 Lisa Michele Piel was arrested by State Police on a five-count indictment: four counts of possession of less than 25 grams of cocaine, and one court of willful neglect of duty. She was immediately suspended without pay.

This was subsequent to a Grand Jury investigation from January through August of 1991, ostensibly researching drug trafficking throughout January of 1992, but actually focused on Lisa Piel during the majority of the aforementioned time span.

As has been reiterated, the "blacks and whites" of Lisa's story are difficult to pin down. The Traverse City Record-Eagle newspaper had become aware of Lisa Piel's struggles but as yet have declined to report on any of their findings, though they have lengthy interviews and copy on hand. Lisa had sublet living space in her home at 218 Arlington Street in Petoskey to other females since purchasing it in 1984. Though little factual matter exists, it was apparently this proximity of other persons–and their problems–which added to Lisa's dilemma. As stated, Lisa tried to help people who were dooming themselves to drug and drink maladies. Adding to the misconduct of Chief Ernest Kraus and Detective Ken Burke were the complications of Joseph Rautio, a Petoskey Police Officer, and his brother John Rautio, a reputed drug dealer, the latter who is said to have dealt drugs within his mother's home–and this while brother Joe was frequenting the house for lunches and family visits, etc. And then, the girl who was said to be receiving drugs from John Rautio was involved in some way with Lisa due either to living situations or having been friends or acquaintances thereof. It would seem incomprehensible that Officer Joe Rautio didn't know about his brother's drug use.

Barely, the only "hard copy" available on Lisa Piel's arrest and subsequent dismissal are newspaper columns and depositions, and the ensuing commentaries thereafter. The multi-county grand jury indicted twenty-two people for drug trafficking during 1991, shutting down January 8, 1992. The Straights Area Narcotics Enforcement (SANE)–an Orwellian doublethink entity– investigated Lisa's activities at least as early as March 1988 through the spring of 1990. The Petoskey News-Review's John Charles Robbins, their primary crime reporter, published the results of the Grand Jury and ultimate resignation in the succinct manner that is their wont, and which want of in-depth background is the impetus for this book. Digging for facts within these "factual" accounts is ambiguous and confusing, the various accounts being slanted toward the official side with little or no reckoning with the personalities involved. Small town newspapers are intimidated by small town politics. This Grand Jury episode seems to have been an attempted springboard for political aspirations as well. Then-Prosecutor Diane Smith used the sensationalism tactic of "busting" a police officer to promote her ambitions toward acquiring a local judgeship–a ploy which ultimately failed.

As reported by the Petoskey paper, the charges against Lisa were initially dismissed "without prejudice" after her attorneys said they hadn't received all requested information and documents from the prosecution–an inference which seems familiar by now to the reader.

The Assistant Prosecutor at that time said he anticipated an indictment would be re-issued against Lisa Piel. Not surprisingly the multi-county citizens Grand Jury did just that six days later on December 19, 1991. "Without Prejudice," another Orwellian term, means legally that the very same charges may be re-issued against the accused. In logical parlance this seems a contradiction of terms until it is realized that the bureaucracy makes all the rules and tenders the linguistic terms to its own advantage.

The Grand Jury transcripts to follow are accompanied by rebuttals written by Art Piel, Lisa's father, garnered from his lengthy collection of Lisa's personal papers, of which contained the successive transcripts, without which this inquiry would not be possible, further information being scanty and witnesses being inhibited.

As reported in the Petoskey News-Review in early 1992, the four counts of indictment were as follows:

> "Count I alleged Piel 'did knowingly of intentionally' possess cocaine from late March 1988 through early April 1988.

> "Count II alleged Piel possessed cocaine from the fall of 1989 through the spring of 1990.

> "Count III alleged Piel 'did, while a public officer or employee charged with enforcement of the criminal laws of the State of Michigan, commit the crime of Misconduct in Office . . .' from the fall of 1989 through spring 1990, according to the court file.

> "Count IV is the misdemeanor charge Piel pleaded guilty to: willful neglect of duty."

The above quote of "according to the court file" is ambiguous in that it states no evidence of controlled substances having been found. There remains only allegations—insidious allegations—unfounded which, as seen, appear as incriminating evidence but which unproven by evidence are only slanderous and not "evidence." This was nothing new to Lisa, of course, as her "file" was burgeoning with reports almost since her beginning as a police officer.

As this inquiry wends its way through the morass of vindictive subterfuge, the content, taken all at once reveals what was previously hidden in the rhetoric of bureaucracy and the one-sided reportage in newsprint ink. The simplicity of report by the authorities and chronicling by journalists belies the true and complete story behind the sensationalist headlines and bias of "copy" by both the court and the press. But this is, of course, nothing to these entities either since these are accepted standards of fulfilling the premise of law and lexicon.

As it is the purport of law and journalism to conclude, the true story is usurped by the most salient facts available, in many cases these "facts" being the ones most advantageous to the condemning body. The very linguistic ploy of using the term, "defendant" assures that the public will view this person or persons as a wrongdoer with prejudice aforethought. The Petoskey newspaper utilizes this precept continually, John Charles Robbins being the chosen emissary of this task.

This circumstance is, of course, not what legalities and journalism were incepted for but what has evolved due to those persons seeking personal gratification through misuse of public duties and responsibilities. Personal gain, self-aggrandizement, slack interpretations of propriety, all these perversions of "right and proper" living standards may be found inherent in smaller town policies of government in the form of, "we do things differently up here." The rural beauty of small-town life has an accompanying down-side which is not much scrutinized by the harbingers of equality whose crusades are largely emanated from the urban acculturation process.

102

When Harvey Varnum, District Court Judge for Emmet County, dismissed the four-count indictment against Lisa, he took the matter under advisement for six months placing Lisa on probation for this term. Presumably it was the Prosecutor's Office—Diane Smith—which reopened the case six days later.

The Grand Jury testimonies, verbatim, follow, with, in all instances but one, an accompanying commentary by Art Piel, Lisa Piel, or other persons unknown.

The foregoing reference to Judge Varnum and Prosecutor Smith is protracted from the actual minute-to-minute sequence of events, the local newspaper reports being a trifle difficult to translate in terms of the devolution of what can only be described, seemingly, as "détente" toward the culmination of Lisa's career, but which is seen in retrospect as a form of entrapment.

In point of fact, the continual "defendant" status applied to Lisa was a misnomer as she had never been arrested for any charge whatsoever. yet the Grand Jury transcripts and attendant data consistently refer to her as the "defendant." Lisa's lawyer, Mr. Abood, was said by Lisa to be, "Not a criminal attorney," and she was quoted as having voiced the doubt as to, "could he handle this?" This, naturally, raises questions about the legality of this Grand Jury—they who were directed to listen to such incriminations as "defendant," "lesbian" insinuations, the fact of no attorney allowed in direct counsel for Lisa, the local, village setting of said jury proceedings, the rural, farm-oriented nature of the jurors themselves, and the very, stated *secrecy* supposedly surrounding this witch-hunt which was held over the course of months within the paper-thin shell of a Topinabee public building in which everyone knew everyone else and everyone heard every word spoken.

In other words, as will be seen, the prosecution was bent toward "getting" Lisa by the relentless stacking of allegations, the set-up circumstances of the Grand Jury, and, most saliently, the forced testimonies of the witnesses against her. Bear witness now to these *testimonies* of local individuals, themselves threatened by court action, and deprived of legal counsel.

103

LISA'S STORY

"It was silly of me to once believe

I could really be free in such a

conforming society"

- Lisa Michele Piel

6

The Grand Jury
And Alice Waybrant
- 1

1   STATE OF MICHIGAN

2   IN THE DISTRICT COURT FOR THE COUNTY OF EMMET

3
       PEOPLE OF THE STATE OF MICHIGAN,
4   Plaintiff,

5   vs.

6   LISA PIEL,
                 Defendant.
7   _____/

8

9

10

11   TESTIMONY OF ALICE WAYBRANDT

12   At a session of the Multi-County Grand Jury

13   for the Counties of Cheboygan, Emmet, Luce,

14   Mackinaw, Otsego, Presque Isle, Charlevoix, and

15   Chippewa, on the 29th day of January, 1991.

16

17   PRESENT: DIANE M. SMITH, ESQ. (P32402)
                         Emmet County Prosecuting Attorney
18
       ALSO PRESENT: JACK FELDMAN, ESQ.
19   Attorney for Witness

20

21

22

23

24   SANDRA K. DAVIDS
       Certified Shorthand Reporter
25   CSR-1033

106

1   MS. SMITH: Okay. We are ready to call

2   our next witness. Is everyone ready? We are

3   calling Alice Waybrandt. Would you come forward,

4   please, and take a seat here.

5   (Whereupon, a brief recess was taken.)

6   MS. SMITH: Thank you all for your

7   patience. We did have a few problems and it took

8   awhile to work those out. I think we are now

9   ready to proceed with Alice Waybrandt. For the

10   record, this is Miss Waybrandt's attorney, Jack

11   Feldman. I'm going to issue the oath.

12   (Whereupon, the oath of secrecy was

13   administered to Attorney Jack Feldman by Ms.

14   Smith)

15   (Whereupon, the oath of secrecy and

16   affirmation was administered to the witness by

17   Ms. Smith)

18   MS. SMITH: You may be seated.

19

20   ALICE WAYBRANDT

21   having been first duly sworn, testified as

22   follows:

23

24   EXAMINATION

25 BY MS. SMITH:

107

1	Q	Would you state your full name, please, and spell
2		your last name for the record?
3	A	Alice Jan Waybrandt, W-A-Y-B-R-A-N-D-T.
4	Q	Have you reached an agreement with the Emmet
5		County Prosecuting office with regard to your
6		testimony today?
7	A	Yes, I have.
8	Q	And, is it a correct statement of that agreement
9		that you will plead guilty to the charge of
10		possession of cocaine under twenty-five grams,
11		when you are charged in Circuit Court in Emmet
12		County?
13	A	Yes.
14	Q	Is it further your understanding that the
15		Prosecuting Office is not bringing a charge of
16		delivery of cocaine for any drug traveling
17		between August of 1989 and February of 1990, that
18		you were involved in?
19	A	Yes.
20	Q	And, is it further your understanding that you
21		will testify truthfully and fully to anything you
22		know regarding drug trafficking before this Grand
23		Jury, and any and all subsequent proceedings that
24		are related to any indictment that may be brought
25		through this Grand Jury?

```
 1   A    Yeah.

 2   Q    And, it is also your understanding that we're not

 3        seeking a Grand Jury indictment against you here?

 4   A    Yes.

 5   Q    Have you been involved in the --

 6             MR. KWIATKOWSKI:  May I interrupt?  That

 7        would be your agreement in the Cheboygan County

 8        Prosecuting Office as well?  Is that right?

 9             MS. SMITH:  Only the Emmet County

10        Prosecutor's Office could bring the charges, but

11        the Cheboygan County Prosecutor was involved in

12        the negotiations.

13             MR. KWIATKOWSKI:  May I make a statement

14        that Judge Porter, in general terms of this sort

15        of agreement, indicates that it's enforceful.

16        Would you agree with that?

17             MS. SMITH:  I have no problem with that.

18             MR. KWIATKOWSKI:  And, you mentioned

19        delivery, but it would be delivery or any lesser

20        or included offense with respect to trafficking?

21

22             MS. SMITH:  Correct.

23             MR. KWIATKOWSKI:  Fair enough.  Go

24        ahead.

25   Q    (Ms. Smith continuing)  Did you at some point
```

1   become involved with using cocaine?

2 A   Yes, I did.

3 Q   When did that first occur?

4 A   I'm trying to think of the month we decided on.

5   I think it was August or September of 1989.

6 Q   Okay, and when and where did it happen?

7 A   At the Riverside Bar in Alanson, in a friend's

8   car.

9 Q   Who was the friend?

10 A   Andrew Sanford.

11 Q   Who provided the cocaine to you at that time?

12 A   Andy Sanford.

13 Q   How much cocaine was involved in that particular

14   occasion?

15 A   Just a line.

16 Q   Was that the first time that you ever tried it?

17 A   I had tried it once a long time ago and I didn't

18   care for it. This is the first time in trying it

19   prior to getting involved.

20 Q   What was the next time then that you used

21   cocaine?

22 A   I was playing in a band with them and we would

23   use it out in the car, on breaks, and whatnot,

24   and do some lines.

25 Q   Excuse me if I interrupt. You say with them.

1		Who are you referring to?
2	A	The band members: Greg Martella (phonetic), Andy
3		Sanford, and I don't remember the names of anyone
4		else. At one point a base player, setting in,
5		got in the car. The next significant time I
6		remember was in the parking lot of Rouch -- I
7		don't remember the name of the nursing home, in a
8		vehicle with a friend.
9	Q	Are you referring to the Rouch Nursing Home?
10	A	Yes.
11	Q	This is a nursing home parking lot?
12	A	Parking lot, in a vehicle.
13	Q	Who did the vehicle belong to?
14	A	Linda Postel.
15	Q	I believe that is P-O-S-T-E-L?
16	A	Yes.
17	Q	Who is Linda Postel?
18	A	A friend of mine, that I met through another
19		friend of mine. She ended up getting me a job at
20		the Perry Hotel.
21	Q	It was just two of you in this car?
22	A	Yes.
23	Q	No one else was there?
24	A	No.
25	Q	Who provided the cocaine on that occasion?

1	A	She did.
2	Q	How much cocaine was involved?
3	A	Just a line, and maybe when we got back in the
4		car another line, or something, just a couple of
5		lines.
6	Q	You, personally, used it?
7	A	Yes, I did.
8	Q	Did Linda, personally, use it?
9	A	Yes, she did.
10	Q	How much is a line?
11	A	Maybe an inch or two long, I guess.
12	Q	Did she have any other cocaine with her at that
13		time?
14	A	Just a little snow seal in it.
15	Q	Do you have any idea how much was in it?
16	A	A quarter of a gram or half a gram.
17	Q	Do you remember about when that was?
18	A	Well, it would have been -- I don't remember, no.
19		* * *
20	Q	Do you know Lisa Piehl?
21	A	Yes, I do.
22	Q	Who is she?
23	A	She is a friend of mine, in the City of Petoskey.
24	Q	Police Officer?
25	A	Uh-huh.

```
1    Q    What is your relationship with her?

2    A    I have been staying at her house.

3    Q    Did you ever do cocaine with her?

4    A    No.  I never have.

5    Q    Did you ever see her do cocaine?

6    A    Never seen her.

7    Q    Did you give her any cocaine?

8    A    No.

9    Q    Did you ever see anyone give her cocaine?

10   A    No.

11   Q    None, whatsoever?

12   A    No.

13   Q    You are under oath now.

14   A    I never seen her do cocaine.

15                        *  *  *

16

17                        -0-
```

```
 1  STATE OF MICHIGAN    )
                         )  ss.
 2  COUNTY OF EMMET      )

 3           I, Sandra K. Davids, Certified Shorthand

 4  Reporter, State of Michigan, do hereby certify that the

 5  foregoing pages 1 through 9, inclusive, comprise a

 6  full, true and correct transcript of the proceedings

 7  and testimony taken in the Multi-County Citizen's Grand

 8  Jury on January 29, 1991, of Alice Waybrandt, as edited

 9  by the Honorable Richard M. Pajtas, Emmet County

10  Circuit Court Judge.

11

12  _____Sandra K David_____10/30/91

13  SANDRA K. DAVIDS, CSR-1033

14

15

16

17

18

19

20

21

22

23

24

25
```

Editor's note: This commentary was written in the 1990's, signed or unsigned as indicated. Where unsigned it is presumed that Lisa had some part in either writing or relating same to other parties. Each of these accompanying discourses are in rebuttal to the Grand Jury proceedings they follow, attempting to shed more light on issues only partly covered by the questionings. Grand Jury inquisitions are held with indictment potential as outcome and do not of necessity include comprehensive analysis of the panorama of person's lives, only those portions which apply directly to the indictments being sought.

This statement is repeated after each testimony and before each commentary for purposes of index clarification and reiteration of reason for inclusion, with the exception of Julie Woodruff's testimony for which no commentary was found.

- -

"ALICE JANE WAYBRANT:

Waybrant pled guilty to one count of cocaine under 25 grams, plea-bargain through prosecutor's office. After testifying in front of the grand jury January 29, 1991, she was advised by SANE Officer Breed that the grand jury wanted to clarify a few things and would be issuing another subpoena. Piel was present, but out of sight when Breed advised Waybrant of this at her residence. Breed further advised Waybrant when this would take place and asked if she preferred mornings or afternoons. Waybrant told him afternoons and requested he call her and she would come down to the MSP Post to pick the subpoena up. Breed advised her he promised they would not come to her place of employment. Waybrant advised Piel that Detective Croton and another SANE officer came to her place of employment at the Winery Goose Deli located on the Harbor-Petosky Rd. They handed her the subpoena and advised her they were giving her one more chance. Waybrant told Piel they stuck around waiting for others to leave the store and started in on her again. She said Croton leaned over the counter and stuck his finger in her face, called her a liar, and told her she was going to bite the bullet for Lisa Piel. Other verbal assaults were exchanged and they left. Waybrant said she was so upset by their visit she cried and had to leave work."

(unsigned, undated)

"Waybrant, Alice Jane:

After meeting up with John Rautio–mid Dec. 1989–she was taking large doses of Valium, Xanax, and Halicon, given to her in sample packs by John Rautio.

Also told Piel he gave her liquid Demeral while at his residence (mother's house on Atkins St.) and white powder which gave her the runs and frequent bowel movements and made her feel like she drank a lot of coffee. She stayed up two-three days at a time without sleep, and admitted to Piel she hallucinated and heard things.

Waybrant told Piel she was sexually assaulted by her uncle Chuck several times when she was around twelve years old. At sixteen she attempted suicide by taking an overdose of Tylenol. She was put into Lockwood Hospital Psychiatric Ward following that attempt. Waybrant told Piel she was there for two months and was transferred to a half-way home per her doctor's orders down by Pontiac, Michigan. There her shoe laces, belts, etc. were taken upon arrival. Her stay there lasted an hour and she left against doctor's orders. She was supposed to take a mood stabilizer but hasn't for years. This information in part has also been told to Piel by her family members.

Waybrant told Piel just before she was to be sentenced that John Rautio made her perform oral sex on him when she could not afford the drugs he had gotten her addicted to . . . She was very ashamed.

Piel asked Waybrant to find another place to live on three or four occasions, unable to help with rent, irresponsible actions, not working full-time, etc. On two separate occasions Waybrant put minor slits on her wrist, then on her neck (photo of same) (?). She got very emotional and carried on, stating she'd change, (These and other mood swings were witnessed by Postle, Woodruff and

116

others on several occasions), if I would let her stay, as she was not happy living in the u.p. and wanted to progress in her musical recordings."

(unsigned, undated)

7

The Grand Jury
And Lora Hinkley

1   (Whereupon, the oath of secrecy and

2   affirmation was administered to the witness by

3   Mr. Kwiatkowski)

4   (Whereupon, the oath of secrecy was

5   administered to Attorney David Fershee by Mr.

6   Kwiatkowski)

7

8

9   LORA HINKLEY

10   having been first duly sworn, testified as

11   follows:

12

13

14   EXAMINATION

15 BY MR. KWIATKOWSKI:

16 Q   Could you state your full name for the record,

17   please?

18 A   Yes. Lora Lynn Hinkley.

19 Q   How do you spell your last name?

20 A   H-I-N-K-L-E-Y.

21 Q   How do you spell your first name?

22 A   Lora, L-O-R-A.

23 Q   How old are you, Lora?

24 A   39.

25 Q   And, where do you presently reside or live?

```
 1   A    At my mom's at 4450 Blackbird Road, one word,

 2        Petoskey, Michigan.

 3   Q    How long have you been a resident of Emmet County

 4        or the Petoskey area?

 5   A    Say ten or eleven years, but my parents are both

 6        from here and I used to visit here in the

 7        summers, but I moved here permanently, I would

 8        say, approximately twelve years ago, with my

 9        grandparents.

10   Q    Okay.  You've been subpoenaed to testify before

11        the Multi-County Citizens Grand Jury today and

12        you are here represented by Attorney David

13        Fershee; is that your understanding?

14   A    Yes.

15   Q    Prior to you coming to the room here today and

16        taking this oath, you met with the Prosecutor

17        from Emmet County, Diane Smith, together with

18        myself and your attorney; is that correct?

19   A    Yes.

20   Q    And, we have reached a plea agreement that we

21        have all signed, or been signed between you and

22        Diane Smith and your attorney, with regard to

23        your testimony here today; is that right?

24   A    Yes, sir.

25   Q    I'd like to go into that plea agreement and see
```

```
 1        if you understand and if that is your

 2        understanding of the agreement, in exchange for

 3        your truthful testimony.  First, that you would

 4        be pleading guilty to one count of delivery of

 5        cocaine less than fifty grams; is that correct?

 6   A    Yes.

 7   Q    And, that the Prosecuting Attorney's Office, for

 8        the County of Emmet, would, in exchange for that,

 9        not prosecute any other drug related charges to

10        this date, and that being January 29, 1991?

11   A    Yes.

12   Q    And, that the Prosecutors for Emmet and Cheboygan

13        County, that myself and Prosecutor Smith, will

14        meet with the judge and defense counsel in

15        chambers and recommend that the judge depart

16        below the mandatory minimum due to substantial

17        and compelling reasons, and this recommendation

18        is not binding on the judge; is that right?

19   A    Yes.

20   Q    And, that you agree to testify truthfully and

21        totally regarding drug trafficking at -- in the

22        Grand Jury proceeding, at any and all subsequent

23        related proceedings; correct?

24   A    Yes, sir.

25   Q    Alright.  Now, Lora, when did you first,
```

```
 1            yourself, become involved in the use or
 2            distribution of the controlled substance cocaine?
 3    A       Approximately three or four years ago it was.  I
 4            lost my grandfather, who I was living with, and
 5            my grandmother and I was having problems dealing
 6            with this and I was married.  Now, before that I
 7            was not married.  And, then the following year I
 8            lost my grandmother and then I was then married
 9            and had a child, and I was having problems and
10            John Rautio happened to be there when -- and I
11            started getting involved with John.
12    Q       Okay.  You say you had been living with your
13            grandparents?
14    A       Yes.  I lived and took care of my grandparents
15            since I moved there.
16    Q       You had the misfortune of losing them in a short
17            period of time?
18    A       One to cancer, and I took care of my grandmother
19            when she lost her leg.
20                              *  *  *
21    Q       Did you ever have any contact with this Lisa
22            Piehl?
23    A       Lisa?
24    Q       Yes, what was your contact with her?
25    A       She would invite Linda's grandmother, Granny
```

```
 1        Postel and my grandmother, because she was in the

 2        wheelchair, and I'd go over and Lisa would let

 3        her use the balcony.  She lives, overlooking

 4        another bay, and they would go and sit and watch

 5        the fireworks.

 6   Q    Any other social activity with Miss Piehl?

 7   A    Up to the Victories Lanes.  One evening she was

 8        up there.  We had coctails.  Right now, I can't

 9        think of any time when we were out.

10   Q    Did you ever observe her in possession or use of

11        cocaine or any narcotics?  Remember, now, you are

12        under oath.

13   A    I knew it, yes.

14   Q    You have?  When was that?

15   A    When Linda picked it up at my house.  Lisa and

16        her did a little bit of it.

17   Q    Linda Postel?

18   A    I'm not sure if Lisa did it.  Linda went in the

19        bathroom, but I was sure Linda was aware of it.

20   Q    What was Lisa's presence there?  Why she was

21        she --

22   A    Her and Linda were friends.

23   Q    Help brought Linda over?

24   A    No.  Linda drove.  I'm not quite sure.

25   Q    Lisa came with her?
```

1   A   Yeah.

2   Q   That's when Linda picked up an 8-ball that you

3   delivered, primarily an 8-ball?

4   A   Yeah, and I gave it to her in the other room, but

5   in front of Lisa, but Lisa was with her.

6   Q   To answer my earlier question, you said that you

7   had knowledge that Lisa had possessed or used

8   cocaine?

9   A   Yes.

10   Q   What did you base that on?

11   A   Well, because she came over that day.

12   Q   After you made the transaction to Linda Postel,

13   did you see her and Lisa go someplace with the

14   cocaine in your house?

15   A   No. I saw Linda, but not -- Lisa didn't go with

16   Linda.

17   Q   Did they leave together?

18   A   Yes, they did.

19   Q   Do you know whose car they used to get there?

20   A   I'm not sure on that day, sir. I didn't look out

21   the patio doors. I can't remember.

22   Q   Did you have any discussion about the transaction

23   with Linda, in the presence of Lisa?

24   A   No.

25   Q   No?

1	A	I have seen Lisa snort cocaine before.
2	Q	Lisa Piehl?
3	A	Yes.
4	Q	When have you seen her snort cocaine?
5	A	At her home.
6	Q	Where was that at, in Emmet County?
7	A	On Arlington, at her home.
8	Q	Who else was present?
9	A	Just her and I and Linda, and it was the day
10		after my grandmother died and I buried her.
11	Q	What date would that have been?
12	A	Well, my grandmother died on Palm Sunday and I
13		buried her, and it was --
14	Q	What year?
15	A	I don't remember, three or four years ago.
16	Q	Where did the cocaine come from that you snorted?
17	A	I got it from John Rautio, and I went on a binge,
18		so called.
19	Q	You met up with Lisa?
20	A	I went over and called for Linda and she said
21		come over, because I was upset, and Linda and I
22		was doing it with Lisa. I offered her some.
23	Q	Lisa partook?
24	A	She saw it there.
25	Q	You saw her snort it?

```
1   A    I was so high, sir, but, yes.

2   Q    She used a straw or how?

3   A    I think it was with a straw.  I know, sir.

4        That's what I used and I passed it.

5   Q    Have you ever talked -- is that line the time

6        that you recall Lisa Piehl using cocaine or

7        possessing?

8   A    Yes, sir.

9                           *  *  *

10                 JUROR #15:  Did Lisa Piehl and Linda

11       Postel come together to your home, two times?

12                 WITNESS:  No, ma'am.  Just the once --

13       one time, that I recall.

14                 JUROR #15:  And, do you recall if they

15       came in Linda's car or --

16                 WITNESS:  I'm not sure whose car they

17       came in that day.

18                 MR. KWIATKOWSKI:  If I understand it,

19       the first time they came over, you don't know

20       whose car they got in, but Linda picked up the

21       8-ball?

22                 WITNESS:  They were only there once.

23                 MR. KWIATKOWSKI:  Okay.  The second time

24       you went to Lisa's house?

25                 WITNESS:  Yes.  It was a separate
```

1   incident, sir.

2   MR. KWIATKOWSKI: Okay. I'm straight

3   now. Sorry.

4   * * *

5   MR. KWIATKOWSKI: Could you give an

6   estimation of what year your grandmother died in?

7   WITNESS: Okay. I lost my grandfather

8   and Fred lost his grandfather three days apart

9   and that was November '88, '87 or '88. I don't

10   remember. I can look it up at home. I lost my

11   grandmother the following year.

12   MR. KWIATKOWSKI: And, it was shortly

13   after that?

14   WITNESS: I think it was only about

15   three years, if I'm not mistaken.

16   MR. KWIATKOWSKI: Alright. This

17   incident, where you snorted cocaine with Linda

18   and Lisa, was shortly after your grandmother

19   died?

20   WITNESS: It was. I remember because

21   the pressure was off me and I loved my grandma.

22   They were like my parents, but I took care of her

23   and it was hard and I was married and I had a

24   baby that was two, then. Fredrick Arthur was two

25   then and it was just difficult.

1   MR. KWIATKOWSKI: Do you remember your

2   grandmother's name?

3   WITNESS: Anna Marie Thomas.

4   MR. KWIATKOWSKI: Any further questions?

5   WITNESS: I have her death certificate

6   at home, if they want to call me tommorrow and I

7   can give them all the information they need.

8   * * *

9   MR. KWIATKOWSKI: Okay. Well, I would

10   excuse you at this time. Remember your oath of

11   secrecy. You may be recalled. Thank you.

12

13   -0-

14

15

16

17

18

19

20

21

22

23

24

25

1 STATE OF MICHIGAN   )
) ss.
2 COUNTY OF CHEBOYGAN)

3   I, Sandra K. Davids, Certified Shorthand

4 Reporter, State of Michigan, do hereby certify that the

5 foregoing pages 1 through 12, comprise a full, true and

6 correct transcript of the proceedings and testimony

7 taken in the Multi-County Citizen's Grand Jury on

8 January 29, 1991, of Lora Hinkley, as edited by the

9 Honorable Richard M. Pajtas, Emmet County Circuit Court

10 Judge.

11

12 _____ Sandra K Davids 10/30/91

13 SANDRA K. DAVIDS, CSR-1033

14

15

16

17

18

19

20

21

22

23

24

25

Editor's note: This commentary was written in the 1990's, signed or unsigned as indicated. Where unsigned it is presumed that Lisa had some part in either writing or relating same to other parties. Each of these accompanying discourses are in rebuttal to the Grand Jury proceedings they follow, attempting to shed more light on issues only partly covered by the questionings. Grand Jury inquisitions are held with indictment potential as outcome and do not of necessity include comprehensive analysis of the panorama of person's lives, only those portions which apply directly to the indictments being sought.

This statement is repeated after each testimony and before each commentary for purposes of index clarification and reiteration of reason for inclusion, with the exception of Julie Woodruff's testimony for which no commentary was found.

- -

"LORA HINKLEY: aka: STOWE

Married with two pre-school boys. Husband Fredrick; self-employed: farming. Pled guilty to one count of delivery of cocaine; plea-bargain with prosecutor's office. Sentenced to lifetime probation with community service. Hinkley told Piel that her $30. a month oversight fees for probation were dropped by the judge.

"Prior to testifying on January 29, 1991, Gerri Zaremski told Piel that Hinkley stopped while she was shoveling the snow at a friend's on US 131 South and Intertown Road. Hinkley told Zaremski she was enroute to testify in front of the grand jury and she was very nervous. She told Zaremski she took a couple of valiums and asked if she wanted one. Zaremski stated she said no, and Hinkley left driving a pick-up. Zaremski told Piel the pills were blue (10 mils).

"Hinkley came over to Piel's residence the day she buried her grandmother. She was dressed up and had her son Fredrick Arthur (F.A.) with her. Postle, Zaremski and Piel were present when she came over to see Postle. Hinkley appeared to be under the influence of something and appeared quite intoxicated. Zaremski asked Hinkley if she could give her a ride somewhere,

131

stating she shouldn't drive. Hinkley declined. Piel and Zaremski left, leaving Postle and Hinkley to visit.

"Hinkley testified Postle picked up an eight ball (3-1/2 grams) at her residence on Blackbird Road, and Piel was present. Piel recalls on one occasion going over to Hinkley's with her, Postle drove. Hinkley had a plastic baggie she retrieved from the freezer. She told Postle they were morel mushrooms her neighbor had picked. Postle loves to cook and cooks gourmet frequently.

"Piel has been involved having to assist in arresting Hinkley's brother, Ralph Stowe. Stowe has had several brushes with the Petoskey Police Department, and has filed formal complaints against them.

"Hinkley told Piel that Jill Simon who cleaned for John Rautio at his mother's residence on Atkins Road, supplied them with Xanax, valium, halicon and other pain meds. These came in sample packet form Simon took while cleaning Dr. Haas' office.

"Please note: Rautio supplied Waybrant with these drugs and others, including liquid demerol, which Waybrant told Piel they took orally.

"Hinkley at some time told Piel Jill Simon was related to her husband in some way and Simon has worked for them on the farm."

(unsigned, undated)

132

8

The Grand Jury
And Linda Postle

1   STATE OF MICHIGAN

2   IN THE DISTRICT COURT FOR THE COUNTY OF EMMET

3

PEOPLE OF THE STATE OF MICHIGAN,
4   Plaintiff,

5   vs.

6   LISA PIEL,
              Defendant.
7   _____/

8

9

10

11   TESTIMONY OF LINDA POSTLE

12   At a session of the Multi-County Grand Jury

13   for the Counties of Cheboygan, Emmet, Luce,

14   Mackinaw, Otsego, Presque Isle, Charlevoix, and

15   Chippewa, on the 10th day of April, 1991.

16

17

18   PRESENT: DIANE M. SMITH, ESQ. (P32402)
                   Emmet County Prosecuting Attorney
19
                   GREGORY JUSTIS, ESQ. (P27148)
20   Attorney for Witness

21

22

23

24   SANDRA K. DAVIDS
     Certified Shorthand Reporter
25   CSR-1033

134

1   MS. SMITH: Before you are seated, I

2   need to administer an oath to both of you. First

3   of all Miss Postle.

4   (Whereupon, the oath of secrecy and

5   affirmation was administered to the witness by

6   Ms. Smith)

7   (Whereupon, the oath of secrecy was

8   administered to Attorney Gregory Justis by Ms.

9   Smith)

10

11

12   LINDA POSTLE

13   having been first duly sworn, testified as

14   follows:

15

16   EXAMINATION

17 BY MS. SMITH:

18 Q   Miss Postle, you please state your full name for

19   the record, please, and spell your last name?

20 A   Linda Ann Postle, P-O-S-T-L-E.

21 Q   Where are you now living?

22 A   In Austin, Texas.

23 Q   Did you at one time live in the Petoskey area?

24 A   I did.

25 Q   Did you have an agreement with the Emmet County

1   Prosecutor's office with regard to your testimony

2   here today?

3   MR. JUSTIS: Yes.

4 Q   Is it your understanding that you will be charged

5   and you will plead guilty to one count of use of

6   cocaine?

7 A   That is correct.

8 Q   Is it further your understanding we will bring no

9   further drug related charges against you for any

10   drug activity up to today's date?

11 A   That is correct.

12 Q   Is it further your understanding that you will

13   testify totally and truthfully regarding drug

14   trafficking before the Grand Jury and any

15   subsequent proceeding, if necessary?

16 A   That is correct.

17 Q   Have you -- you are represented by an attorney

18   here today. Have you discussed this matter with

19   your attorney?

20 A   I have.

21   MR. JUSTIS: There are some additions I

22   would like.

23   MS. SMITH: I'm looking at our

24   correspondence here.

25 BY MS. SMITH:

```
1   Q    Is it also your understanding that the

2        Prosecution will make no recommendation with the

3        Court with regard to the sentencing?

4   A    Yes, it is.

5   Q    Is it also your understanding that you will not

6        be charged in any of the counties covered by this

7        Grand Jury, this eight-county Grand Jury, and

8        none of the counties will seek an indictment

9        against you?

10  A    Correct.

11  Q    Is it further your understanding any information

12       we obtain here today would not be provided to the

13       federal government or any other agency?

14  A    Yes.

15            MS. SMITH:  Have I covered everything,

16       Mr. Justis?

17            MR. JUSTIS:  I think you have.  I would

18       also confirm, on Miss Postle's behalf, that is my

19       understanding of the agreement and that it has

20       been incorporated in a written document, which we

21       all signed.

22            MS. SMITH:  Thank you.

23  BY MS. SMITH:

24  Q    Did at some point in your life become involved in

25       the use of cocaine?
```

```
1   A   I did.

2   Q   When did that first occur?

3   A   In 1982.

4   Q   Did you become a regular user?

5   A   It was an occasional user until -- between July

6       of '89 until March of '90.

7   Q   What happened then?

8   A   At that point, I was using more cocaine.

9   Q   How frequently were you using it, yourself,

10      during that time?

11  A   Approximately two or three times a month. (LIES)

12  Q   A month?

13  A   Yes.

14  Q   Was there ever anything significant that happened

15      during that time that caused you to use more

16      cocaine?

17  A   I would say its accessibility, and just

18      frustration in my life at that point.

19  Q   Where were you living during that time period, of

20      July of 1989?

21  A   North Conway Road.

22  Q   Were you living with anyone else?

23  A   No. (She was living w/ Woodruff)

24  Q   Pardon?

25  A   No.
```

```
1   Q    Is that in Emmet County?

2   A    Yes.

3   Q.   And, where were you living just prior

4   A    218 Arlington, in Petoskey.

5   Q    Is that in Emmet County?

6   A    Yes.

7   Q    Were you living with anyone at that

8   A    Lisa Piel.

9   Q    What was the time period that you li·
10       with Lisa Piel?

11  A    From July of '85 until February of '

12  Q    When you were living with Lisa Piel,
13       use cocaine yourself?

14  A    I did.

15  Q    How frequently?

16  A    Maybe once every two or three months

17  Q    Did you ever use cocaine with Lisa P

18  A    I did.

19  Q    Where did you do that?

20  A    Typically, at her house.

21  Q    Is this the house that you referred
22       on Arlington?

23  A    That is correct.

24  Q    Do you recall the first time that th
25       used it together?
```

139

```
 1   A   Not specifically the time, but it would have been

 2       in 1984.

 3   Q   Who provided it?

 4   A   I did.  I'm sorry, that would have been 1985.

 5   Q   1985?

 6   A   Yup.

 7   Q   Was anyone else there?

 8   A   No.

 9   Q   Did you, personally, use some of this cocaine

10       yourself?

11   A   I did.

12   Q   What effect, if any, did you get from it?

13   A   Kind of an up, maybe, speedy-type feeling.

14   Q   What did it look like?

15   A   It was in a white powder form.

16   Q   How did you use it?  What did you do?

17   A   Snorted it.

18   Q   Did Lisa Piel do the same thing?

19   A   Yes, she did.

20   Q   Had you gotten that same effect when you used

21       cocaine prior to that incident?

22   A   Yes.

23   Q   Was the cocaine that you used out of the same

24       container as what she used?

25   A   Yes.
```

1	Q	Did you ever use it with her again, then?
2	A	Yes.
3	Q	What is the next time you remember?
4	A	We probably used it together fifteen to twenty
5		times throughout the period of time that I lived
6		with her.
7	Q	Were -- all the time at the apartment that the
8		two of you shared?
9	A	Normally that would have been the case. There
10		was one case when we went to the Venetian
11		Festival, in Charlevoix, that we would have used
12		it in the vehicle, prior to participating in the
13		festivities.
14	Q	Do you recall which one the Venetian Festivals
15		that you used cocaine at?
16	A	It would have been 1987.
17	Q	Did the two of you go there together?
18	A	No.
19	Q	Did anyone else go with you?
20	A	No.
21	Q	How did you get there?
22	A	I believe in Lisa's vehicle.
23	Q	Who provided the cocaine?
24	A	I did.
25	Q	How much did you have with you?

1	A	A gram.
2	Q	And, the two of you shared that?
3	A	That is correct.
4	Q	Did you consume it altogether on that one time?
5	A	I believe so.
6	Q	Where, exactly, were you when you used the
7		cocaine?
8	A	That particular time?
9	Q	Yes.
10	A	I believe we parked in the vicinity of the
11		Weather Vane Restaurant.
12	Q	Were you in the car when you used it?
13	A	Yes.
14	Q	How did you use it? What did you do?
15	A	Put a couple lines out on some kind of a surface
16		and snorted it.
17	Q	On some sort of a what?
18	A	Surface.
19	Q	And, did you get the same effect from it that you
20		had in the past from cocaine?
21	A	Yes.
22	Q	What did it look like?
23	A	It was white powder form.
24	Q	Were there any other occasions, other than the
25		times that you used cocaine at the apartment,

1   that you can recall?

2 A   There was one time at my apartment on North

3   Conway. That would have been in the middle of

4   March, of 1990. *(I WAS IN THE Hosp. gETTING My KidNey REMoved)*

5 Q   Who else was there, if any?

6 A   Just the two of us. *(the whole thing is lies)*

7 Q   You said on Conway?

8 A   That is correct.

9 Q   And, how did it come about that you used it

10   there?

11 A   I provided it. Lisa came to see me, and we

12   shared it.

13 Q   How -- what amount?

14 A   A gram.

15 Q   How was it packaged?

16 A   In a small square piece of paper.

17 Q   How did you use it?

18 A   In lines, and snorted it.

19 Q   Who would actually put out the lines?

20 A   I would do that.

21 Q   And, did you get the same effect that you

22   normally did from using cocaine?

23 A   Yes.

24 Q   Do you remember any other times, at your

25   apartment?

143

```
 1   A   No.

 2   Q   No one else was there?

 3   A   No.

 4   Q   Were there any other occasions?

 5   A   There was a birthday party for me.  That would

 6       have been in November.  Again, I believe of '87,

 7       in which prior to people coming over to celebrate

 8       my birthday, Lisa and I shared cocaine.

 9   Q   This would have been back at her --

10   A   At her house, on Arlington.

11   Q   On Arlington?

12   A   Uh-huh.

13   Q   Was anyone else present at the time the two of

14       you used cocaine together?

15   A   No.

16   Q   Who provided it?

17   A   I did.

18   Q   What did it look like?

19   A   It was white powder substance.

20   Q   You used some yourself?

21   A   That is correct.

22   Q   Did you get the same effect from it?

23   A   Yes.

24   Q   Back to the other times, at Lisa's house that you

25       said -- how many times, total, that you used
```

1		cocaine together at her house?
2	A	I would say approximately twenty.
3	Q	Of all those times, was anyone else there?
4	A	No.
5	Q	What was the last time that you used cocaine with
6		her?
7	A	It would have been on Conway, in March of '90.
8	Q	The incident that you just testified to?
9	A	That is correct.
10		MR. JUSTIS: Excuse me a second. My
11		client has additional answers to give to your
12		question about any other people.
13		MS. SMITH: Okay.
14		WITNESS: Rather than stating that I'm
15		definitely sure no one else was present, I would
16		like to make it, that, to the best of my
17		knowledge, I don't recall other people being
18		present when Lisa Piel and I were doing it.
19	BY MS. SMITH:	
20	Q	It is possible that someone else may have been
21		present?
22	A	It's a possibility, yes.
23	Q	Did you use cocaine with other people yourself?
24	A	Yes, I did.
25	Q	Did you use cocaine with other people at the

145

1		Arlington house, Lisa's house?
2	A	Not that I recall.
3	Q	Did you use cocaine with other people at your
4		apartment?
5	A	Yes.
6	Q	Other places also?
7	A	Yes.
8	Q	Has your own use of cocaine affected your memory
9		at all?
10	A	I would not be able to say it's specifically due
11		to the cocaine, but I have trouble remembering
12		specific dates and places where --
13	Q	Have you stopped using cocaine, yourself?
14	A	Completely.
15	Q	When did you stop?
16	A	April 1st of 1990.
17	Q	What caused you to stop?
18	A	I left Petoskey and had no longer contact or
19		desire to use cocaine.
20	Q	Do you recall using cocaine with Lisa Piel in '85
21		and '86?
22	A	I think that's very possible, yes.
23	Q	Where would that have been?
24	A	At her house.
25	Q	Would be just the two of you again?

146

1	A	Right.
2	Q	Did she ever provide any of the cocaine?
3	A	Never.
4		* * *
5	Q	Were you pretty good friends with Alice
6		Waybrandt?
7	A	During that time period she worked with me at the
8		Perry Hotel.
9	Q	Was she also friends with Lisa Piel?
10	A	She was.
11		* * *
12	Q	Do you still have contact with Lisa Piel?
13	A	I do.
14	Q	How does that take place?
15	A	She has visited me once since I have been in
16		Texas, and I talked to her on the phone once
17		every two or three weeks.
18	Q	Have you discussed your testimony here today with
19		her?
20	A	I have not.
21		* * *
22	Q	Was there ever a New Year's Eve party, where some
23		cocaine was used?
24	A	It was not a party. One New Year's Eve, Lisa
25		Piel and I used cocaine together.

1	Q	Where did that take place?
2	A	At her house on Arlington.
3	Q	Do you recall what year it was?
4	A	If I'm not held to it, I would say 1987.
5	Q	The old year '87 or New Year '88?
6	A	The old year '87, the New Year '88, right.
7		* * *
8	Q	Did Lisa Piel ever purchase cocaine from you?
9	A	She did not.
10	Q	So you always gave it to her?
11	A	That is correct.
12	Q	Was Gerry Zaremski at the birthday party in 1987?
13	A	I think that would be very likely, yes.
14		* * *
15		JUROR #8: Did you witness Lisa Piel
16		buying cocaine from anyone?
17		WITNESS: I did not.
18		* * *
19		JUROR #10: Do you know or are you aware
20		of Lisa Piel ever having her own cocaine?
21		WITNESS: Not when I used cocaine with
22		her.
23		JUROR #10: You always supplied it to
24		her?
25		WITNESS: Okay.

148

1   * * *

2   -0-

3

4   STATE OF MICHIGAN   )
) ss.
5   COUNTY OF EMMET   )

6   I, Sandra K. Davids, Certified Shorthand

7   Reporter, State of Michigan, do hereby certify that the

8   foregoing pages 1 through 16, inclusive, comprise a

9   full, true and correct transcript of the proceedings

10   and testimony taken in the Multi-County Citizen's Grand

11   Jury on April 10, 1991, of Linda Postle, as edited by

12   the Honorable Richard M. Pajtas, Emmet County Circuit

13   Court Judge.

14

15   _Sandra K Davids_ 10/30/91

16   SANDRA K. DAVIDS, CSR-1033

17

18

19

20

21

22

23

24

25

Editor's note: This commentary was written in the 1990's, signed or unsigned as indicated. Where unsigned it is presumed that Lisa had some part in either writing or relating same to other parties. Each of these accompanying discourses are in rebuttal to the Grand Jury proceedings they follow, attempting to shed more light on issues only partly covered by the questionings. Grand Jury inquisitions are held with indictment potential as outcome and do not of necessity include comprehensive analysis of the panorama of person's lives, only those portions which apply directly to the indictments being sought.

This statement is repeated after each testimony and before each commentary for purposes of index clarification and reiteration of reason for inclusion, with the exception of Julie Woodruff's testimony for which no commentary was found.

- -

No accompanying notes were found with Linda Postle's testimony although there was reference to Postle in the Lora Hinkley (aka Stowe) section. Those portions are reprinted here.

"Hinkley came over to Piel's residence the day she buried her grandmother. She was dressed up and had her son Fredrick Arthur Jr. (F.A.) with her. Postle, Zaremski and Piel were present when she came over to see Postle. Hinkley appeared to be under the influence of something and appeared quite intoxicated. Zaremski asked Hinkley if she could give her a ride somewhere, stating she shouldn't drive. Hinkley declined. Piel and Zaremski left, leaving Postle and Hinkley to visit.

"Hinkley testified Postle picked up an eight ball (3-1/2 grams) at her residence on Blackbird Road, and Piel was present. Piel recalls on one occasion going over to Hinkley's with her, Postle drove. Hinkley had a plastic baggie she retrieved from the freezer. She told Postle they were morel mushrooms her neighbor had picked. Postle loves to cook and cooks gourmet frequently."

This note was unsigned and undated. It does bear the trace of Lisa's semi-official note-taking however and is probably her writing. Linda was a friend of Lisa's but was involved in drug use on a personal basis, causing some rift between them at times.

150

There are some handwritten comments in the transcript itself by unknown parties (which seem like Lisa) to the effect of these answers being untrue or prevaricative. As Postle was forced to testify against her will, and to save herself, one can take both the testimony and the asides as individually perceived.

(Editor)

9

The Grand Jury
And John Rautio

```
1                    STATE OF MICHIGAN

2       IN THE DISTRICT COURT FOR THE COUNTY OF EMMET

3

4   PEOPLE OF THE STATE OF MICHIGAN,
             Plaintiff,

5   vs.

6   LISA PIEL,
             Defendant.

7   _____/

8

9

10

11                TESTIMONY OF JOHN RAUTIO

12          At a session of the Multi-County Grand Jury

13       for the Counties of Cheboygan, Emmet, Luce,

14       Mackinaw, Otsego, Presque Isle, Charlevoix, and

15       Chippewa, on the 22nd day of May, 1991.

16

17  PRESENT:      ROBERT ENGEL, ESQ. (P30437)
                  Emmet County Assistant Prosecuting
18                Attorney

19                GREGORY JUSTIS, ESQ. (P27148)
                  Attorney for Witness
20

21

22

23

24  SANDRA K. DAVIDS
    Certified Shorthand Reporter
25  CSR-1033
```

153

1   MR. ENGEL: First of all, will you

2   stand, both you and your attorney. Mr. Rautio,

3   state your name for the record, and spell your

4   last name.

5   WITNESS: John Michael Rautio,

6   R-A-U-T-I-O.

7   MR. ENGEL: Mr. Justis is your attorney?

8   WITNESS: Yes.

9   MR. ENGEL: Mr. Justis, could you state

10   your name and your location?

11   MR. JUSTIS: Gregory Justis, Petoskey,

12   Michigan.

13   MR. ENGEL: Thank you.

14   (Whereupon, the oath of secrecy and

15   affirmation was administered to the witness by

16   Mr. Engel)

17   (Whereupon, the oath of secrecy was

18   administered to Attorney Gregory Justis by Mr.

19   Engel)

20

21

22   JOHN MICHAEL RAUTIO

23   having been first duly sworn, testified as

24   follows:

25

1	<div align="center">EXAMINATION</div>
2	BY MR. ENGEL:
3	Q Mr. Rautio, where do you live?
4	A 315 Fulton Street, Petoskey.
5	Q Mr. Rautio, through your attorney and yourself
6	and Diane Smith, the Prosecuting Attorney for
7	Emmet County, you have entered into an agreement;
8	did you not?
9	A Yes.
10	Q That agreement was that you would plead guilty to
11	one count of delivery of cocaine under fifty
12	grams, and one count of possession of cocaine
13	under twenty-five grams?
14	A Yes.
15	·Q In return, no other charges will be brought
16	against you as part of the Grand Jury
17	investigation of drug trafficking in the eight
18	county area; is that true?
19	A Yes.
20	Q That charges will not be brought through this
21	Grand Jury indictment, or independently by the
22	office of the Prosecuting Attorney; is that true?
23	A Yes.
24	Q Further, it is part of the agreement that any
25	information disclosed by you during these

1   proceedings will be disclosed to any federal

2   agency?

3   A   That's true.

4   Q   That is to protect yourself from the federal

5   government; is that correct?

6   A   Correct.

7   Q   You understand that if the time comes that the

8   federal court or federal system looks at

9   indicting someone else, they may call upon you to

10   testify, and you might have to work something

11   separately with them at that time?

12 A   Yes.

13   MR. ENGEL: Is that your understanding,

14   Mr. Justis?

15   MR. JUSTIS: To the extent you placed it

16   on the record, and my further understanding is if

17   there comes a time when Mr. Rautio has to

18   testify, that I will be contacted before any

19   disclosure, so we can work out our arrangement

20   with the federal government.

21   MR. ENGEL: I would assume so, and I

22   assume that Mr. Rautio will be contacted by the

23   local level Prosecutor, and that it wouldn't be

24   the feds first.

25   MR. JUSTIS: The intention is that we

1   dispose of any drug charges prior to the date of

2   this testimony in this proceeding.

3   MR. ENGEL: That is my understanding.

4   Mr. Rautio, do you also understand that the

5   Prosecuting Attorney's Office will make no

6   sentencing recommendations in this matter?

7   WITNESS: Yes.

8 BY MR. ENGEL:

9   Q   Is it your understanding, also, that you are here

10   to testify totally and truthfully regarding drug

11   trafficking, before this Grand Jury, and, if

12   needed, at any subsequent proceedings that arise

13   from this Grand Jury?

14   A   Yes.

15   Q   Do you also understand that you are to cooperate

16   fully with the police officers that are

17   investigating these grand jury matters?

18   A   Yes.

19   Q   Do you also understand that your failure to fully

20   cooperate and follow these terms will render this

21   agreement void, and subject you to prosecution

22   for any crimes which you could have been charged?

23   A   Yes.

24   Q   Mr. Rautio, your date of birth?

25   A   August 23, 1953.

1	Q	So, you are thirty-seven at this time?
2	A	Uh-huh.
3	Q	How long have you been using cocaine?
4	A	Since the late '70's.
5	Q	And, you started selling cocaine in the late
6		'70's, did you not?
7	A	Yes.
8		* * *
9	Q	Did you -- at the time you were selling to Alice
10		Waybrandt, did you sell to any of Alice's
11		friends?
12	A	Other than Linda Postle?
13	Q	Did you ever sell to Lisa Piel?
14	A	No, I didn't.
15	Q	Did you ever see Lisa Piel using cocaine?
16	A	One time I seen her touch it. I don't remember
17		ever seeing her use it.
18	Q	Let's talk a little bit about Lisa Piel. Do you
19		know what her employment is?
20	A	She's a city police officer, of Petoskey.
21	Q	Alice Waybrandt used to live with her?
22	A	Yes.
23	Q	Did you ever use cocaine in Lisa Piel's house?
24	A	Several times.
25	Q	Who was present when you would do that?

1	A	Allison, Lisa, and Linda Postle.
2	Q	Did anyone know that cocaine was being used in
3		the house?
4	A	Yeah, there was an understanding. Nobody really
5		watched anyone do it.
6	Q	Where would you do it?
7	A	In the bathroom.
8	Q	Who would set up the lines in the bathroom?
9	A	I did or I would give it to Allison and she
10		would.
11	Q	When the lines were set up in the bathroom,
12		everyone have the opportunity to go in there?
13	A	Yes.
14	Q	Did everyone go in there?
15	A	As far as I know, yes.
16	Q	So, you maybe didn't directly see somebody using
17		it, but you knew?
18	A	It all disappeared.
19	Q	Okay. You set it up in the bathroom?
20	A	Yes.
21	Q	Different people went in the bathroom?
22	A	Uh-huh.
23	Q	Different people came out of the bathroom?
24	A	Uh-huh.
25	Q	And, you'd go back in and it's gone?

```
 1   A    It's gone, yes.

 2   Q    Did everyone appear to be getting the effect that

 3        cocaine has?

 4   A    Yes.  As a matter of fact.  Lisa walked out after

 5        Allison and asked me to set up two lines for her,

 6        and Lisa walked out and sniffed and thanked me.

 7   Q    When was that, approximately?

 8   A    Geez, I don't know.  I would say the winter of

 9        '90, maybe a little in '89 or '90.

10   Q    End of '89?

11   A    Right in the winter of 1990.

12   Q    Winter starting?

13   A    '89 and '90, right in that time.

14   Q    How did it come about that you recall that

15        incident?  Was Lisa working that day?

16   A    She was working, yeah.

17   Q    How do you know that?

18   A    She had a uniform on and a police car parked out

19        front.

20   Q    So she comes home?

21   A    Yes.

22   Q    And, you and Alice Waybrandt --

23   A    Alice and I were in there partying.

24   Q    And, that's when you set some lines up in the

25        bathroom?
```

```
 1   A   Uh-huh.  She asked me to -- Allison did.

 2   Q   Is that before Lisa got there or after Lisa got

 3       there?

 4   A   Lisa was there.

 5   Q   Now, how did Alice say --

 6   A   She asked -- she come up to me and asked me.

 7   Q   Wait until I ask the question, okay?

 8   A   Okay.

 9   Q   Lisa is there?

10   A   Right.

11   Q   Alice is there?

12   A   Right.

13   Q   And, you are there?

14   A   I'm in another room.  Alice came out and asked

15       me, and I laid out a line for Lisa.  And, I got

16       up and walked to the bathroom and put it in

17       there, and I think Alice was with me when I laid

18       them out, and took -- I was assuming she took

19       Lisa in there and did them.

20   Q   You don't have any reason to believe she didn't?

21   A   Lisa came back and sniffed and said, "thank you."

22       I'm assuming she did it.

23   Q   Was there any other occasions in Lisa Piel's home

24       where Lisa was present when cocaine was used?

25   A   Yes, several times.  I can't really recall the
```

1		dates or anything, but there were several times
2		where she was there when we were using it.
3	Q	Would that have been after this occasion?
4	A	Probably some before and some after.
5	Q	And, approximately how much do you believe Lisa
6		Piel would use at that time?
7	A	Maybe quarter gram, at max. Maybe a little --
8		probably close to a quarter gram in each line.
9	Q	Total number of occasions, then, that you believe
10		Lisa Piel used it?
11	A	Probably five.
12	Q	On the day that she came home and she was in
13		uniform, was Alice Waybrandt drinking a wine
14		cooler at the time?
15	A	Yes. Lisa took one drink out of that too, when
16		she walked in.
17	Q	Now, Alice Waybrandt worked for you, did she not?
18	A	Yes.
19	Q	You were in the drywall business at the time?
20	A	Yes.
21	Q	And, you had a job down in the Traverse City
22		area?
23	A	Yup, outside of Acme, right by the Frito-Lay
24		potato chip place. It was a car auction
25		building.

```
1    Q    Did you have some assistance in doing your
2         drywalling down there?
3    A    Yes, I had Alice and Lisa help me.
4    Q    Both came down?
5    A    Yeah.  Alice was working for me and I went over
6         to Lisa's house to pick her up, to take her to
7         work, and they had both been up all night,
8         partying, and Lisa wanted to help too.
9    Q    So, the three of you go down to Traverse City?
10   A    Uh-huh.
11   Q    This is when?
12   A    When was this?  I don't know.  Right around the
13        winter time.  Must have been winter.  I don't
14        know, '89 or '90.  It was in the winter, so I
15        don't really remember.  It was getting cold.
16   Q    Okay.  Well, how many winters ago was it?
17   A    It was --
18   Q    Past winter or winter before?
19   A    A winter before.
20   Q    Winter of '89 and '90?
21   A    '90, yes.
22   Q    And, you are down doing drywall business in the
23        Traverse City area?
24   A    Uh-huh.
25   Q    Lisa and Alice are with you?
```

1	A	Uh-huh.
2	Q	And, was there any cocaine being used at that
3		time?
4	A	Oh, yes. On the job?
5	Q	Yes.
6	A	Uh-huh.
7	Q	Could you tell us about it?
8	A	We were all taking turns doing lines. I gave
9		Allison -- I don't remember if it was the bottom
10		of a grinder or puff or if it was in paper, but I
11		gave it to her and her and Lisa would go around
12		the corner of that building and do a blast.
13	Q	How do you know Lisa was doing something?
14	A	Because Allison would hand it to her and she
15		would disappear.
16	Q	So, Alice had something and Lisa has something
17		and they'd go around the corner?
18	A	Right.
19	Q	And, again this was another white powdery
20		substance?
21	A	Yes.
22	Q	Okay. At that time, when you were down in that
23		area -- first of all, at that location, how many
24		times did this occur?
25	A	I don't really recall, probably two or three,

```
 1              maybe four times.

 2     Q        During the course of a day?

 3     A        Course of a day, yes.

 4     Q        Okay.  Did the time come, then, to stay overnight

 5              down there in Traverse City?

 6     A        Yes.

 7     Q        Was that the same day?

 8     A        Same day, yes.

 9     Q        Where did you stay?

10     A        Points North Inn.

11     Q        Was anyone staying there?

12     A        Yeah, at the beginning -- towards the end, I

13              think they -- Lisa and Allison got in a fight and

14              Lisa left and went to the Waterfront Inn, and

15              Alice took my van and chased her.  I got it back

16              the next day.

17     Q        Did anyone stay at the Holiday Inn?

18     A        I don't think so.  Maybe they said -- the

19              Waterfront is what they told me.

20     Q        Both of them stayed at the what -- Waterfront?

21     A        Yes, after they got in a fight.  It was kind of

22              cloudy after that.

23     Q        Do you know why they got in a fight?

24     A        I have no idea.

25     Q        While you're at your room in the Points North
```

1		Inn, was there cocaine being used there?
2	A	Yes.
3	Q	Can you tell the folks here what happened on that
4		occasion, at the room?
5	A	Alice had a bottom of a puff. She chopped up or
6		ground a bunch -- a few rocks, maybe couple grams
7		of coke, and was coming out of the bathroom area
8		and dropped it on the floor, on the tile floor.
9		And, Lisa was right there and Lisa looked up at
10		me and said, "I guess the cat's out of the bag
11		now", and she helped us pick it up from the
12		floor.
13	Q	Okay.
14	A	I didn't see her do a line, but she helped us
15		pick it up.
16	Q	Okay. Did you know what she meant, "I guess the
17		cat's out of the bag now"?
18	A	I know she touched the cocaine.
19	Q	Lisa's involved?
20	A	Lisa's involved, yes.
21	Q	Do you know how much was dropped on the floor?
22	A	I would assume it was close to two grams. I
23		think I had an eighth or quarter of an ounce with
24		me when we went down there.
25	Q	Did you ever sell cocaine to Alice Waybrandt,

166

1   where she would give to Lisa, other than these

2   times that you mentioned?

3   A   She had stated that a couple of times, that that

4   was going to go to Lisa. Her and Lisa wanted it,

5   you know.

6   Q   What type of quantities are we talking about?

7   A   Maybe an 8-ball, at the most.

8   Q   Okay. Were you aware of any special relationship

9   between Alice and Lisa?

10   A   Well, yeah, they were kind of pretty close.

11   Q   More than just friends?

12   A   More than friends.

13   Q   Well, they were lesbians, as far as you knew?

14   A   Yes.

15   Q   And, they lived together for a period of time in

16   Piel's residence?

17   A   Yes.

18   Q   At some point did Alice move out of Piel's

19   residence?

20   A   I believe she did, yeah. I think right around

21   the time she was -- she went up to the rehab

22   there.

23   Q   Okay.

24   A   I helped her move out once. They got in a fight.

25   Lisa wanted her out of there for some reason. I

1   moved all her stuff out and let her use the van

2   and she moved it all back in the next day.

3 Q Would you know of anyone else that was using the

4   cocaine along with Waybrandt and Piel?

5 A I know -- I believe Lora Hinkley had used it with

6   them before, Linda Postle, and some girl named

7   ***. They called her ***.

8 Q *** ***?

9 A I couldn't tell you. I know they called her ***.

10   I never seen her, but they talked a lot about

11   her. Lisa and Lora Hinkley and all them partied

12   together.

13 Q Did they ever say *** was doing coke too?

14 A Yeah.

15 Q Do you know where they were doing coke at?

16 A Lisa's house, possibly.

17   * * *

18   JUROR #3: Did Alice recently have any

19   conversation with you and Lisa about Grand Jury?

20   WITNESS: She told me that she was going

21   to have to appear in front of it. And, then

22   after she appeared, she came and talked to me and

23   had Lisa in her car and she said Lisa said it

24   would be wise or it might be a good idea if you

25   had left town, or something similar. "It might

1   work better if you left town."

2   JUROR #3:   Was Lisa involved in the

3   conversation?

4   WITNESS: Lisa was out in the car.

5   * * *

6

7   -0-

8

9

STATE OF MICHIGAN   )
10   )   ss.
COUNTY OF EMMET   )

11

12   I, Sandra K. Davids, Certified Shorthand

13   Reporter, State of Michigan, do hereby certify that the

14   foregoing pages 1 through 17, inclusive, comprise a

15   full, true and correct transcript of the proceedings

16   and testimony taken in the Multi-County Citizen's Grand

17   Jury on May 22, 1991, of John Rautio, as edited by the

18   Honorable Richard M. Pajtas, Emmet County Circuit Court

19   Judge.

20

21   ___Sandra K Davids 10/30/9/___

22   SANDRA K. DAVIDS, CSR-1033

23

24

25

169

Editor's note: This commentary was written in the 1990's, signed or unsigned as indicated. Where unsigned it is presumed that Lisa had some part in either writing or relating same to other parties. Each of these accompanying discourses are in rebuttal to the Grand Jury proceedings they follow, attempting to shed more light on issues only partly covered by the questionings. Grand Jury inquisitions are held with indictment potential as outcome and do not of necessity include comprehensive analysis of the panorama of person's lives, only those portions which apply directly to the indictments being sought.

This statement is repeated after each testimony and before each commentary for purposes of index clarification and reiteration of reason for inclusion, with the exception of Julie Woodruff's testimony for which no commentary was found.

- -

"John Rautio was lying to save himself. Also, he was working with police. His brother, Joe Rautio, was a police officer in Petoskey. He, John Rautio, never saw Lisa touch or use drugs. He may have used in Lisa's house but she was not aware of it. That was Alice Waybrant doing, along with Linda Postle. The day she was in uniform, she came home, she saw John Rautio's truck there and told Alicon to tell him to leave. And the winter, 89-90, Lisa was sick with kidney problems. In March, '90, she had a kidney taken out. Lisa went with Alicon to work with drywall on John Rautio's job to make an extra dollar and left after getting there and found out John Rautio went there to party. She had an argument with Alicon. John Rautio was out of his mind with drugs and drunk with booze, went crazy. Anything he said at this time were just lies.

"The time something was dropped on the floor, Lisa was not there. She left long before that. Lisa told Alicon to move out of her house because she could not have her and her friends there anymore, and called Alicon's parents to have them get her in rehab. If Lisa was a lesbian or not, that had nothing to do with this matter. Engel brought that up because in small towns they have small minds, and they would think that being a lesbian, she

170

must be guilty. The name with the three stars is Spag: Sandy Spagnola. She works at the Sheriff's office. I heard she was involved in helping police arrest and fire one of her co-workers who later tried to kill herself. Spag was guilty as the other girls. Lisa knows they, the police, were after her for years. So why would she not keep herself clean as she could, being it is hard to pick and keep friends.

Lisa was wrong in the eyes of the law for not turning in people she knew that were involved in drugs. Lisa told her superior officers that John Rautio was ind rugs. They told her to mind her own business. She did not tell on one of her superior officers, named Ken Burke, who was in sales of drugs. But we found out later, he said, Burke, that is, he would kill Lisa if she ever told on him. He also was the town drunk who drove city-owned cars drunk and out of town. Joe Rautio went home to his mother's most every day for lunch where John Rautio was with Alicon doing drugs and was very high, told to me, Art Piel, by Alicon. John Rautio also got drugs from his mother's house keeper who took drugs from a doctor she cleaned for."

– As told to me by Lisa.

(signed, Art Piel)

(dated, 5-31-97)

"Question: why did robert Engel, Prosecuting Attorney, not spell out the name that was dashed out? Who I believe was Spag, short for, Sandy Spagnola who works in the Sheriff's office. Then why, again, is the Sheriff's office hiding her? As John Raution said, 'They call her ＿＿＿ ＿＿＿ .' "

(addenda by Art Piel, Jan. 1998)

10

The Grand Jury
and Kathy Boyer

```
1                    STATE OF MICHIGAN

2        IN THE DISTRICT COURT FOR THE COUNTY OF EMMET

3
   PEOPLE OF THE STATE OF MICHIGAN,
4             Plaintiff,

5    vs.

6    LISA PIEL,
              Defendant.
7    _____/

8

9

10

11                  TESTIMONY OF KATHY BOYER

12             At a session of the Multi-County Grand Jury

13         for the Counties of Cheboygan, Emmet, Luce,

14         Mackinaw, Otsego, Presque Isle, Charlevoix, and

15         Chippewa, on the 21st day of May, 1991.

16

17   PRESENT:        DIANE M. SMITH, ESQ. (P32402)
                     Emmet County Prosecuting Attorney
18
                     STEVEN GRAHAM, JR. (P41935)
19                   Attorney for Witness

20

21

22

23

24   SANDRA K. DAVIDS
     Certified Shorthand Reporter
25   CSR-1033
```

1   (Whereupon, the oath of secrecy and

2   affirmation was administered to the witness by

3   Ms. Smith)

4   (Whereupon, the oath of secrecy was

5   administered to Attorney Steven Graham, Jr., by

6   Ms. Smith)

7   MR. GRAHAM: I do, so long as it does

8   not conflict with my duty to my client.

9   MS. SMITH: Thank you. You may be

10   seated.

11

12

13   KATHY BOYER

14   having been first duly sworn, testified as

15   follows:

16

17   EXAMINATION

18   BY MS. SMITH:

19   Q   Would you state your full name for the record,

20   please?

21   A   Kathy Ann Boyer.

22   Q   Was your name at one time Kathy Burke?

23   A   Yes.

24   Q   Do you have an agreement with the Emmet

25   Prosecutor's office with regard to your testimony

```
 1         here today?
 2    A    Yes, I do.
 3    Q    Is it your understanding that you will plead
 4         guilty to one count of delivery of cocaine under
 5         fifty grams?
 6    A    Yes.
 7    Q    And, is it your understanding that you are also
 8         to cooperate with the Straits Area Narcotic
 9         investigation team?
10    A    Right.
11    Q    Is it further your understanding that the
12         Prosecution, in exchange for that, will not bring
13         any other charges against you through this Grand
14         Jury or through the Prosecutor's office, for any
15         activity up to today's date?
16    A    Yes.
17    Q    Is it also your understanding that as part of
18         this agreement, you are to testify totally and
19         truthfully to anything that you know about drug
20         trafficking in northern Michigan before this
21         Grand Jury?
22    A    Yes.
23    Q    And, also any subsequent proceeding that you may
24         be subpoenaed to testify to?
25    A    Yes.
```

1   Q   Do you also understand that failure to fully

2   cooperate and follow these terms could render

3   this agreement null and void and you could be

4   charged with any other crimes that you may have

5   committed?

6   A   Yes.

7   Q   Any questions about the agreement?

8   A   No.

9   Q   You had a chance to discuss that with your

10   attorney?

11   A   Uh-huh.

12   MR. GRAHAM: You have to say yes or no,

13   so the record can pick it up.

14   WITNESS: Yeah.

15 BY MS. SMITH:

16   Q   For the record, your attorney is Steve Graham,

17   Jr., today?

18   A   Today, yes.

19   MR. GRAHAM: So it is clear, for the

20   record, I'm filling in, on behalf of the other

21   Steve Graham, this afternoon.

22   MS. SMITH: Thank you.

23 BY MS. SMITH:

24   Q   Kathy, at some point in your life did you become

25   involved in the use of cocaine?

1	A	Yes, I did.
2	Q	When was that?
3	A	The fall of '89.
4	Q	How did it come about that you got involved?
5	A	I had friends that did it. I used it
6		occasionally.
7		* * *
8	Q	Did you get some effect from it?
9	A	Yes.
10	Q	What was the effect?
11	A	You get a speedy high, basically.
12	Q	Then did you use it again after that party?
13	A	Occasionally.
14	Q	Did you come to a point where you started using
15		it quite a bit?
16	A	Later, yeah, in the fall. Not a lot, just
17		occasionally.
18	Q	In the fall of what year?
19	A	'89.
20	Q	You used it more during that time?
21	A	More than before, but still not a lot.
22	Q	How much were you using at that time?
23	A	Maybe a gram a week.
24	Q	Where were you getting it?
25	A	From Ann Arbor.

```
1                          * * *

2    Q    Did you ever deliver cocaine to her, or with her,

3         to Lisa Piehl's?

4    A    They bought it from me for her.

5    Q    Can you tell us about that?

6    A    In the bar, at Crooked Lake Club, she was sitting

7         at the table and they took the money from --

8    Q    Who, Julie, are are you talking about?

9    A    Linda Postle.

10   Q    Okay?

11   A    And, went in the bathroom and I sold it to Linda

12        Postle, left the bathroom and told me to send

13        Lisa in.

14   Q    She told you what?

15   A    To send Lisa in the bathroom.

16   Q    So, Lisa was in there?

17   A    She went in the bathroom, into the stall, with

18        Linda.

19   Q    Did you actually see any of them use cocaine?

20   A    No.  I have seen Linda use it.

21   Q    Did -- was that bathroom at that facility

22        normally used for cocaine?

23   A    Yes.

24   Q    Did you use any yourself on that particular

25        occasion?
```

178

1	A	No
2	Q	How long were they in there?
3	A	Maybe ten or fifteen minutes.
4	Q	Did you have any conversation with them
5		afterward?
6	A	No. I left.
7	Q	Would you have noticed whether they seemed
8		different or had any effect from possibly using
9		cocaine?
10	A	Well, yeah. I have seen them both when they have
11		done it and, both, when they haven't done it.
12	Q	When have you seen them, both, when they were
13		doing it?
14	A	At parties.
15	Q	Where?
16	A	Out at Lori Jewell's and Julie Keller's house.
17	Q	What have you observed about them after they used
18		it?
19	A	They talk more. They're friendlier.
20	Q	Is that a pretty common reaction for people who
21		use cocaine?
22	A	Yes.
23	Q	How often have you seen Lisa Piehl change, after
24		you felt she was using cocaine?
25	A	Two or three, probably.

(handwritten: NEVEL - EVER - THERE)
(handwritten: Lived there 4 yes ago.)

179

1	Q	Now, at these parties, where was cocaine used?
2	A	Usually in the bathroom.
3	Q	Did you see her in the bathroom?
4	A	Yes.
5	Q	With who?
6	A	Usually with Lori Jewell or Linda Postle or
7		Woodruff or all above, together.
8	Q	Do you know who had cocaine available?
9	A	Usually Lori Jewell.
10	Q	Did you ever actually see Lisa Piehl using
11		cocaine?
12	A	No.
13	Q	Is Julie Woodruff a friend of Lisa Piehl's?
14	A	Yes.
15	Q	Lori Jewell -- is she a friend of Lisa Piehl's?
16	A	Yes.
17	Q	Have either of those two people indicated to you
18		that they have used cocaine with Lisa Piehl?
19	A	Yes.
20	Q	What have they told you?
21	A	They just use to sit and joke about it all the
22		time, because Linda and Lisa would get it at
23		night, and either Lori or Julie would deliver it.
24	Q	To, to their --
25	A	To their house, on Arlington.

1	Q	Did they live together there?
2	A	Yes.
3	Q	Do you know who would place the calls?
4	A	Sometimes Linda, sometimes Lisa. *(NEVER)*
5		* * *
6	Q	At the Crooked Lake Club, when you went into the
7		bathroom, did you stay in the bathroom while Lisa
8		and Linda were in the stalls? Did you go into
9		the stall to use cocaine or just the bathroom
10		area?
11	A	They went into the stalls.
12	Q	Did you stay in the bathroom?
13	A	At first I stayed in there and did a line with
14		Linda, went out -- and I'm trying to remember --
15		went out, told Lisa to go back in, and I went
16		back in. And, then I left, like, ten or fifteen
17		minutes after we all came out of the bathroom. I
18		didn't stay. It was earlier in the evening.
19	Q	Did you go into a stall, yourself, when you used
20		it?
21	A	Yes.
22	Q	Did Linda and Lisa go in the same stall or
23		separate stalls?
24	A	In the same stall.
25	Q	Would that be unusual if someone was actually

```
 1        going to use the bathroom, that they would go in

 2        the same stall?

 3    A   I would think so.

 4    Q   Where is Lori Jewell now?  Do you know?

 5    A   I don't know.  I know the last couple of years

 6        she moved back and forth between Florida and

 7        Harbor, but I'm not sure where she is now.

 8        Usually in the summer she works at that Pine Hill

 9        Golf Course, up in Brutus.

10    Q   Did you, personally, take any cocaine to Lisa

11        Piehl's house?

12    A   I stayed in the car.

13    Q   Who went with you?

14    A   Julie Woodruff.

15    Q   What did Julie do?

16    A   She took it in the house.

17    Q   You never went in?

18    A   No.

19    Q   Did you know how much cocaine she took in?

20    A   A gram.

21    Q   Did she say who was home or who was there?

22    A   Linda and Lisa.

23    Q   Did she say who she gave it to?

24    A   No.

25                        *  *  *
```

1

2

3   -0-

4

5

6   STATE OF MICHIGAN   )
)   ss.
7   COUNTY OF EMMET   )

8   I, Sandra K. Davids, Certified Shorthand

9   Reporter, State of Michigan, do hereby certify that the

10 foregoing pages 1 through 11, inclusive, comprise a

11 full, true and correct transcript of the proceedings

12 and testimony taken in the Multi-County Citizen's Grand

13 Jury on May 21, 1991, of Kathy Boyer, as edited by the

14 Honorable Richard M. Pajtas, Emmet County Circuit Court

15 Judge.

16

17 ___Sandra K Davids___ 10/30/91

18 SANDRA K. DAVIDS, CSR-1033

19

20

21

22

23

24

25

Editor's note: This commentary was written in the 1990's, signed or unsigned as indicated. Where unsigned it is presumed that Lisa had some part in either writing or relating same to other parties. Each of these accompanying discourses are in rebuttal to the Grand Jury proceedings they follow, attempting to shed more light on issues only partly covered by the questionings. Grand Jury inquisitions are held with indictment potential as outcome and do not of necessity include comprehensive analysis of the panorama of person's lives, only those portions which apply directly to the indictments being sought.

This statement is repeated after each testimony and before each commentary for purposes of index clarification and reiteration of reason for inclusion, with the exception of Julie Woodruff's testimony for which no commentary was found.

- -

"KATHY BOYER: aka: Burke

"Father: Edmund Burke - retired Sgt. Michigan State Police, Petoskey.

"Kathy Boyer: married with one child, grade school, born out of wedlock.

"Husband: James Boyer, currently serving a prison sentence for one count of delivery of cocaine under 50 grams, plea bargain with prosecutor's office. Prior conviction: larceny from a motor vehicle 12/87, arrested by Piel, Petoskey Police Department.

"Kathy Boyer received through plea bargain one count of delivery of cocaine, sentenced: life probation.

"Boyer testified she became involved with cocaine in the fall of 1989, also stating Piel was involved in buying and use at the Crooked Lake Club at or around this time. Records indicate that the Inland House, home of the Crooked Lake Club, burnt down March 7th, 1989 (copy of News-Review sent to attorney Abood dated March 16, 1989). Boyer testified she saw Piel at parties out at Lori Jewell's and Julie Keller's house. Piel was never at Jewell/Keller's residence. Jewell lived with Keller on Quick and Hedrick Roads in Harbor Springs. This was over four years ago, and moved out after Keller's baby was born and she had remarried.

"Lori Jewell was called in to the Michigan State Police Post in Petoskey by SANE officers Breed and Croton after Piel's arrest. She was granted immunity for information concerning the grand jury. Steve Graham, Jewell's attorney, was present. Jewell told Piel that 'they only wanted you, bad.' She told them she never saw Lisa Piel snort cocaine and did not remember the incident at the Crooked Lake Club.

"Piel only recalls seeing Boyer at the Sensational Tanning Salon on the Harbor-Petoskey Road (M-119) when she was with her brother, Dean. This was the fall of 1988 when he was quite ill, between hospital visits. Piel knew Boyer's father from work and had small talk with Boyer while waiting for her brother to tan. Small talk included her father's health, her son; she even showed Piel a photo of her father with her son. End of any contact with Boyer, who was then Kathy Burke.

"Gerri Zaremski worked at the Crooked Lake Club in the Spring/Summer of 1988. Zaremski told Piel she came to work one day in July and sent home along with other employees because the place was closed down; the owners failed to renew the liquor license. Zaremski showed Piel a copy of her final paycheck, dated July 30, 1988. Zaremski worked as a bartender; the bar faced the restrooms Boyer testified about."

(unsigned, undated)

185

11

The Grand Jury
And Alice Waybrant
- 2

STATE OF MICHIGAN

IN THE DISTRICT COURT FOR THE COUNTY OF EMMET

PEOPLE OF THE STATE OF MICHIGAN,
            Plaintiff,

vs.

LISA PIEL,
            Defendant.
_____/

TESTIMONY OF ALICE WAYBRANDT

            At a session of the Multi-County Grand Jury

        for the Counties of Cheboygan, Emmet, Luce,

        Mackinaw, Otsego, Presque Isle, Charlevoix, and

        Chippewa, on the 22nd day of May, 1991.

PRESENT: ROBERT ENGEL, ESQ. (P30437)
           Emmet County Assistant Prosecuting Attorney

ALSO PRESENT: DAN DOWDELL, ESQ. (P37676)
                Attorney for Witness

SANDRA K. DAVIDS
Certified Shorthand Reporter
CSR-1033

1   MR. ENGEL: First of all, can we have

2   you identify who you are, starting with Miss

3   Waybrandt.

4   WITNESS: Alice Waybrandt.

5   MR. ENGEL: How do you spell your last

6   name?

7   WITNESS: · W-A-Y-B-R-A-N-D-T.

8   MR. ENGEL: And, you have an attorney

9   here with you today, do you not?

10   WITNESS: Yes, I do.

11   MR. ENGEL: And, who are you?

12   MR. DOWDELL: Dan Dowdell,

13   D-O-W-D-E-L-L, from Cedarville, Michigan,

14   representing Miss Waybrandt today.

15   MR. ENGEL: Thank you. First of all,

16   Miss Waybrandt, raise your right hand. I'm going

17   to put you under oath at this time.

18   (Whereupon, the oath of secrecy and

19   affirmation was administered to the witness by

20   Mr. Engel.)

21   (Whereupon, the oath of secrecy was

22   administered to Attorney Dowdell by Mr. Engel.)

23

24

25

```
1                    ALICE WAYBRANDT

2         having been first duly sworn, testified as

3         follows:

4

5                     EXAMINATION

6    BY MR. ENGEL:

7    Q    Miss Waybrandt, you previously appeared before

8         the Grand Jury on January 29, 1991, did you not?

9    A    Yes, I did.

10   Q    And, at that time you had testified regarding

11        certain drug trafficking issues that were

12        presented to, the Grand Jury?

13   A    Yes.

14   Q    You were represented by an attorney by the name

15        of Jack Feldman, at that time?

16   A    Felton.

17   Q    Excuse me, from Gaylord, I believe?

18   A    Yes.

19   Q    You were placed under oath at that time,

20        regarding the oath of a witness, in regard to

21        testifying truthfully and also in keeping the

22        matter secret, the matters that occurred here; is

23        that correct?

24   A    Yes.

25   Q    And, you entered into a plea agreement with the
```

```
 1          Prosecuting Attorney's office, with both Ms.

 2          Diane Smith, and on behalf of the Prosecutor's

 3          office; is that correct?

 4    A     Yes.

 5    Q     And, as part of that plea agreement, you

 6          understand you were to testify truthfully and

 7          fully to all you know regarding drug trafficking

 8          before the Grand Jury, and any and all subsequent

 9          relating proceedings; is that correct?

10    A     Yes.

11                          *  *  *

12    Q     Now, you were asked at the last hearing if you

13          knew a subject by the name of Lisa Piel.  Do you

14          know Lisa?

15    A     Yes.

16    Q     And, do you know what her occupation is?

17    A     Yes.

18    Q     What is that?

19    A     She's a police officer.

20    Q     You are a friend of Lisa's?

21    A     Yes.

22    Q     Was there a time when you lived with Lisa?

23    A     Yes.

24    Q     How long ago was that?

25    A     How long ago since when?
```

1	Q	Since you lived with Lisa?
2	A	Since I moved out?
3	Q	Yes.
4	A	Probably about a month.
5	Q	Month ago from now?
6	A	Yeah.
7	Q	And --
8	A	I stayed there off and on since I lived there,
9		but I went into rehab and I stayed there off and
10		on since I got out.
11	Q	Have you ever seen cocaine in Lisa Piel's house?
12	A	Yes.
13	Q	Okay. Whose cocaine was it?
14	A	Mine.
15	Q	Did Lisa Piel know you had cocaine in the house?
16	A	Not to my knowledge.
17	Q	Did you ever use cocaine in Lisa Piel's house?
18	A	Yes.
19	Q	Was she present at any time when you used cocaine
20		in her house?
21	A	Yes.
22	Q	Did she know you were using cocaine in her house?
23	A	Not to my knowledge.
24	Q	Did you ever sell any cocaine to Lisa Piel?
25	A	No.

1 Q Did you ever give any cocaine to Lisa Piel?

2 A No.

3 Q Do you know John Rautio?

4 A Yes.

5 Q Was there an occasion when you and Lisa Piel and

6   John Rautio went down to the Traverse City area

7   because John was doing a drywall job?

8 A Yes.

9 Q Was that in the spring of 1990, a year ago?

10 A I don't remember when it was.

11 Q Was it before you went into the hospital?

12 A Yes.

13 Q Where was this drywall job being done at?

14 A I think Acme.

15 Q Acme is in Grand Traverse -- that is near the

16   Grand Traverse Resort, the tall hill there, the

17   tall building?

18 A I know where the Grand Traverse Resort is. The

19   job was --

20 Q Outside of Acme?

21 A Outside of Traverse City.

22 Q Did you stay at the motel down·there, at that

23   time?

24 A Yes.

25 Q Do you know what motel it was?

```
 1   A    Holiday Inn.

 2   Q    Did you ever stay at the motel called the Points

 3        North?

 4   A    John got a room there.

 5   Q    That's where John's room was?

 6   A    Yup.  We were all together -- we were all going

 7        to stay, and we left.

 8   Q    You left for where?

 9   A    Went and stayed at another motel.

10   Q    What motel did you go and stay at?

11   A    I believe the Holiday Inn.  John stayed there.

12   Q    John stayed where?

13   A    Points North.

14   Q    Was there anyone else there besides you and Lisa

15        Piel and John Rautio?

16   A    No.

17   Q    Did you ever go to Mr. Rautio's room at Points

18        North Inn?

19   A    Yeah.

20   Q    Do you recall an occasion in the bathroom of Mr.

21        Rautio's room, at the Points North, where you

22        were coming out of the bathroom and you dumped

23        cocaine on the floor?

24   A    I dumped some in the bathroom.

25   Q    Spilled it, I assume that it wasn't intentionally
```

1   done?

2   A   It was in the bathroom.

3   Q   Who was in the bathroom when you dumped it or

4   spilled it?

5   A   No one.

6   Q   How much cocaine did you spill?

7   A   Just a little bit that John gave me. I was

8   trying to hide it, and knocked it off the

9   counter.

10 Q   Where was Lisa when that happened?

11 A   In the other room.

12 Q   With John?

13 A   Yeah.

14 Q   Was the cocaine just sitting on the countertop,

15   or whatever, in the bathroom?

16 A   I had it in my pocket and took it out, and it was

17   already shake and stuff and I knocked it off and

18   I called John in there and said, "look what I

19   just did!" and we cleaned it up.

20 Q   You say we. Who is we?

21 A   John and I.

22 Q   Lisa Piel helped to clean it up?

23 A   No.

24 Q   Lisa Piel -- did she make a statement to the

25   effect of, "I guess the cat's out of the bag

1   now", after you spilled the cocaine?

2   A   Not that I remember.

3   Q   Is it possible that she said that?

4   A   Said it to me?

5   Q   Said it to anyone that was in the room, either

6   you or Mr. Rautio or said it in general?

7   A   It is possible. I don't know.

8   Q   Do you recall telling John Rautio that you

9   purchased cocaine for Lisa Piel?

10   A   No.

11   Q   Did you ever tell him that?

12   A   No.

13   Q   Do you remember a time when Lisa Piel was -- this

14   would be like the end of 1989, where Lisa was on

15   duty and she came home during the course of her

16   duty and she was in uniform, and at that time you

17   had a wine cooler and she took a few sips of the

18   wine cooler?

19   A   No. I don't remember that.

20   Q   Do you recall that lines were laid out in the

21   bathroom, lines of cocaine had been laid out, and

22   she went into the bathroom?

23   A   I don't remember a time of that, no.

24   Q   Is it possible that that happened?

25   A   That I would have put it out in the bathroom?

1	Q	Somebody put it out, either you or John Rautio?
2	A	We did it in the bathroom.
3	Q	Who is we?
4	A	John and I.
5	Q	At -- the time I'm talking about is the end of
6		1989, when Lisa was in uniform and Mr. Rautio was
7		over at Lisa's residence?
8	A	Okay.
9	Q	Did John Rautio come over to the residence very
10		often?
11	A	Not very often. He picked me up. We made
12		Christmas cookies once.
13	Q	Lisa came home in her uniform, at that time, and
14		she goes in the bathroom, where the lines are
15		laid out, and she comes out of the bathroom a
16		short time and looks at Rautio and says, "thank
17		you", and leaves the residence. Do you recall
18		that?
19	A	No, I don't.
20	Q	Is that not true?
21	A	Not to my knowledge, no.
22	Q	You consider yourself a very good friend of Lisa
23		Piel's; do you not?
24	A	Yes.
25	Q	You still are, even though you moved out of her

```
 1        residence?

 2   A    Uh-huh.

 3   Q    In fact, you go over to her residence regularly,

 4        even though you have moved out?

 5   A    I have been over there a couple of times since I

 6        moved out.

 7   Q    Have you been over there since you were

 8        subpoenaed for today?

 9   A    Uh-huh.

10   Q    When were you subpoenaed for today?

11   A    I think it was Friday.

12   Q    Were you there over the weekend and saw Lisa?

13   A    I stayed there one night.  I don't remember what

14        night it was, and my car was there Sunday.  I was

15        getting ready for the country show down there.

16   Q    Lisa was working at the time and stopped at the

17        house in her patrol car?

18   A    Yeah.

19   Q    Did you use any cocaine at that time?

20   A    No.

21   Q    Now, a motel room is not very big; is it?

22   A    This one was.

23   Q    Okay.  You dropped the cocaine -- going back to

24        Traverse City, again -- the cocaine gets dropped

25        on the floor, and you say "Mr. Rautio" -- you say
```

197

1   to Mr. Rautio -- "come in." Are you saying --

2   are you telling this Grand Jury that Lisa knew

3   nothing about the cocaine?

4   A   I don't know if she did or not.

5   Q   She never said anything to you about the cocaine?

6   A   No.

7   Q   You didn't think it would bother her if she knew

8   you were using cocaine in that bathroom?

9   A   Yeah, I think she would have gotten mad.

10   Q   Miss Waybrandt, going back to when you went down

11   to the drywall site, were you and Lisa Piel

12   helping John Rautio in some way?

13   A   Yeah.

14   Q   What were you doing?

15   A   Drywall.

16   Q   The drywall was up and you were filling in the

17   cracks and stuff?

18   A   Uh-huh.

19   Q   At that time, when you were doing that, did you

20   and Lisa Piel use cocaine at the work site?

21   A   I did.

22   Q   Was Lisa with you?

23   A   No.

24   Q   Do you know if John Rautio was giving Lisa Piel

25   any cocaine?

```
1   A    I don't know.

2   Q    Do you know if he was selling any cocaine to her?

3   A    I don't think so, but I don't know.

4   Q    Okay. Now, after you testified at the Grand Jury

5        hearing, back at the end of January, did you

6        leave her and go to the Riverside Bar in Alanson?

7   A    Yes, I think so.

8   Q    And, you went to the Riverside Bar in Alanson,

9        and were you telling people that you had been to

10       the Grand Jury and testified?

11  A    People knew.

12  Q    How was it that they knew?

13  A    The bar owner walked up to me and said "you too?"

14  Q    Who is the bar owner?

15  A    I don't know. His last name is Allen.

16  Q    Allen? What does he look like?

17  A    Curly, reddish hair.

18  Q    How old?

19  A    Pardon me?

20  Q    How old?

21  A    I don't know how old he is.

22  Q    Is he older than me, younger than me, same age as

23       me?

24  A    Probably about your age.

25  Q    How big?
```

1	A	Maybe about Matt's size.
2	Q	The detective's size?
3	A	Yes, maybe about that size, except he has got a
4		stomach on him, a little scrawnier than Matt is.
5	Q	What did you say regarding your testimony?
6	A	I don't remember what I said.
7	Q	I'm not asking you for specifics. I mean, it is
8		pretty hard to get a quote from you, but what was
9		the general discussion?
10	A	I really don't remember. I remember stopping
11		there. My nerves were a wreck. I used their
12		bathroom and the only person I ever talked to is
13		Allen. I know there were other people in there,
14		that I knew, but --
15	Q	Did you talk about your testimony at the Grand
16		Jury?
17	A	I admitted that I just got back from there.
18	Q	Did you tell anyone what you said there?
19	A	Not that I remember, no.
20	Q	Did you have an opportunity, after you were done
21		testifying here, to talk to John Rautio?
22	A	Yup.
23	Q	Who was with you?
24	A	What do you mean?
25	Q	Who was with you when you went to talk to John

200

1   Rautio?

2 A No one. His wife was there.

3 Q Where did you meet John Rautio?

4 A I drove to his house.

5 Q Was anyone with you in the car, when you went to

6   the house?

7 A Lisa was in the car.

8 Q Would you have told Lisa at that point what you

9   had testified about at the Grand Jury?

10 A I told her that I felt bad that I had to tell on

11   John.

12 Q In fact, that is one thing that you were going to

13   John Rautio about, was to tell him that you

14   testified against him; is that correct?

15 A Yes.

16 Q Did not Lisa Piel tell you that she thought that

17   John Rautio should leave town, after your

18   testimony?

19 A Yeah.

20 Q And, that is what, in fact, you went and told

21   John Rautio, that he should leave town?

22 A I don't remember saying that, no.

23 Q Something to that effect?

24 A I started crying and said, "what are you going to

25   do?" I said I was sorry, but I didn't feel I had

```
 1        a choice, and I told him that I got it from him

 2        and he told me his thoughts on the matter and I

 3        left.

 4   Q    So, prior to going in and talking to John Rautio,

 5        you told Lisa that you had testified at the Grand

 6        Jury?

 7   A    Uh-huh.

 8   Q    And, you told Lisa that you had testified against

 9        John Rautio?

10   A    (Nodding head.)

11   Q    Yes or no?

12   A    Yes.

13   Q    Lisa told you she thought it would be best if he

14        would leave town?

15   A    Something like that, yeah.

16   Q    Based on what you had told her?

17   A    I just said that I think he's going down and she

18        said, God, it's too bad that he just couldn't get

19        out of here, or something to that effect.

20   Q    Now, you say you knew Linda Postle?

21   A    Yes.

22   Q    Do you know where Linda Postle lives?

23   A    Texas.

24   Q    Did you call Linda Postle recently?

25   A    Yeah.
```

1 Q   Did you call Linda Postle and complain about her

2   testifying in the Grand Jury?

3 A   Yes.

4 Q   What did you tell her?

5 A   She had called and left a message for me, so I

6   returned her call and she said she was just

7   thinking about me and asked me if I heard

8   anything on what was going on, and I said that I

9   felt like she was making up stories, to save her

10   ownself, and I thought it was ignorant, and we

11   all did what we did and should be willing to take

12   the blame for our own action. I didn't like what

13   she was doing.

14 Q   When you talked to Linda Postle, did you

15   specifically talk about Lisa Piel?

16 A   Uh-huh.

17 Q   How Lisa may be involved in dealing with drugs or

18   using drugs, cocaine?

19 A   I don't understand what you are saying.

20 Q   Did you discuss with Linda Postle the fact that

21   Lisa Piel possessed or used cocaine?

22 A   I said that I felt they were after Lisa and that

23   I also believed that she had came in here and

24   told them something that wasn't true, and I

25   didn't think it was right.

```
 1   Q   Back to the trip down to Traverse City, where

 2       John Rautio had the room at Points North, --

 3   A   Uh-huh.

 4   Q   -- in that room, either based on your own

 5       observation or what was told by anyone else, or

 6       what you had seen, did Lisa Piel ever use

 7       cocaine?

 8   A   No.

 9   Q   Did she possess cocaine?

10   A   I didn't see her, no.

11   Q   Besides seeing her, did anyone tell you or did

12       John Rautio or Lisa Piel tell you that she either

13       used or possessed cocaine?

14   A   No.

15   Q   Has Lisa Piel ever told you, at any time, that

16       she just had used or possessed cocaine?

17   A   No.

18   Q   Has anyone else ever told you that they were told

19       or saw Lisa Piel using or possessing cocaine?

20           MR. DOWDELL:  Excuse me one minute,

21       please.  May I?

22           MR. ENGEL:  Yes.  I'm sorry.

23           (Whereupon, there was a discussion

24       between the witness and her attorney.)

25           WITNESS:  What was the question, please?
```

1 MR. ENGEL:

2 Q   Okay. The last question .is, have you heard from

3   anyone else that they either saw or knew Lisa

4   Piel to either possess or use cocaine?

5 A   Suspected that she used?

6 Q   That's fine?

7 A   Yeah.

8 Q   Who?

9 A   You and him, and I'm gathering from Linda Postle

10   that she thinks Lisa has done it, and when I

11   first moved out here, to go to school and got to

12   be friends with Lisa, I heard things about her.

13 Q   From whom?

14 A   Hearsay. Andy Sanford told me a long time ago

15   that she was a vindictive cop and she used drugs

16   and stuff.

17 Q   Has there ever been an occasion where you and her

18   were in the bathroom or kitchen or some other

19   room, in either a house or motel room, and lines

20   of cocaine were laid out, and maybe you used some

21   yourself, and maybe you walked out of that

22   bathroom or kitchen, or whatever room it was, and

23   left the lines of cocaine there, that you didn't

24   use, and then Lisa Piel would go into the room?

25 A   No.

```
1   Q    You are sure?

2   A    Yeah.

3   Q    Has there ever been an occasion where lines would

4        be laid out and Lisa Piel could have access to

5        those lines, and then the lines are missing a

6        short time later?

7   A    There has been times when, like, Linda and I, or

8        someone had done it there.  I mean, lots of time

9        there could have been things taken, whether they

10       were or not, I don't know.  But, I mean it was

11       accessible.  It was in the house.

12  Q    Were you -- when you were at the motel in

13       Traverse City, did you also use the hot tub

14       there?

15  A    Yes.

16  Q    Who else was using the hot tub?

17  A    John and Lisa.

18  Q    Was there any cocaine used by anyone in the area

19       of the hot tub?

20  A    No.

21  Q    You are sure?

22  A    Yeah.

23  Q    Not ever by you or John Rautio?

24  A    No.

25  Q    Definitely not Lisa Piel?
```

1	A	Definitely not.
2	Q	Let me ask you about the -- about a person named
3		Julie Woodruff. Have you ever heard of her?
4	A	Uh-huh.
5	Q	How do you know Julie Woodruff?
6	A	Friend of Linda's.
7	Q	Have you ever been involved with any kind of drug
8		trafficking with either possession, use, or sale
9		or delivery of cocaine with her?
10	A	I have done it with her.
11	Q	You done cocaine with Julie Woodruff?
12	A	Uh-huh.
13	Q	Where?
14	A	At Linda's and Woody's apartment, Julie Woodruff.
15	Q	That's her nickname, Julie's nickname, which is
16		Woody?
17	A	Yes.
18	Q	Do you know how she got the cocaine on that
19		occasion?
20	A	From Linda, I assume.
21	Q	You don't know, though?
22	A	(Shaking head.)
23	Q	It wasn't from you?
24	A	I don't remember ever giving it to her, no.
25	Q	Approximately when would that have been?

```
 1    A     Anytime during the duration of my addiction, when

 2          I was using it.

 3    Q     Sometime in 1989, to the early part of 1990,

 4          then?

 5    A     Yeah.

 6    Q     I just have a couple more questions to ask you,

 7          Miss Waybrandt.  Have you ever seen or heard of

 8          Lisa Piel either possess or use cocaine?

 9    A     Heard?

10    Q     Other than what you have testified so far today

11          about?

12    A     Seen or heard?

13    Q     Yes.

14    A     I have heard.

15    Q     Other than what you have just testified about

16          here today, from the police officer and from Andy

17          Sanford?

18    A     No.

19    Q     Have you ever seen her do it?

20    A     Nothing, other than what I have talked about in

21          here today.

22    Q     Okay.

23    A     Is that what you are asking me?

24    Q     Yes.

25    A     No.
```

1	Q	Nothing other than what you have said here today,
2		correct?
3	A	No. No, I haven't.
4	Q	Have you ever been in a position where you may
5		not directly have seen Lisa Piel use cocaine? I
6		mean, you weren't in the same room with her when
7		she was using it, but it was set up as such and
8		she could go in the room and use cocaine and
9		leave the room, without you actually seeing it?
10	A	Without me knowing about it?
11	Q	Without you actually seeing it, first of all?
12	A	Yeah. She could have been in another room, I
13		suppose.
14	Q	In her own house?
15	A	Possibly.
16	Q	In the bathroom of her own house, and lines could
17		have been set out and you walked out of the room
18		and whatever she does in there, you know, and you
19		come back in and the lines are gone? Is that
20		right?
21	A	I don't think I was that careless with it.
22		MR. ENGEL: Okay. I have no other
23		questions to ask this witness at this time. I
24		would offer her to the Grand Jury, if they have
25		any questions.

1   JUROR #12: Where did you store the

2   cocaine that you had at Lisa Piel's?

3   WITNESS: Usually in the bathroom.

4   JUROR #12: Where, in the bathroom?

5   WITNESS: I turned on the water and

6   pretended I was running the water. I would do it

7   right on the counter.

8   JUROR #12: But, you must have had a

9   quantity. How much did you have?

10   WITNESS: Just a little package.

11   JUROR #12: So, did you carry it with

12   you?

13   WITNESS: Yeah.

14   JUROR #12: You had it there, stored in

15   the bathroom?

16   WITNESS: I always -- if I had more than

17   a little bit, I would put it in a small package

18   or something and carry it in my pocket.

19   JUROR #12: How much cocaine did you

20   have in your possession when you were at that

21   motel in Traverse City, where you spilled it?

22   What was the total amount that you had that day?

23   WITNESS: Just a little bit, probably

24   about a gram. It was in a red container.

25   JUROR #12: Could you give us some

1   dimensions?

2   WITNESS: How much a gram is?

3   JUROR #12: What kind of container is

4   it?

5   WITNESS: Just a little red container,

6   about that big.

7   JUROR #12: Something like a film

8   bottle?

9   WITNESS: No. This goes to an object

10   called a derring. It's about that high.

11   JUROR #12: Like a little --

12   WITNESS: Something like -- it's about

13   that big around and has a top that twists off.

14   JUROR #12: Thank you.

15   JUROR #3: How long did you live with

16   Lisa Piel?

17   WITNESS: About two years, off and on.

18   JUROR #3: Did you have any kind of a

19   relationship with her or were you just roommates?

20   WITNESS: Just roommates.

21   JUROR #3: And, you really knew her

22   pretty well, then?

23   WITNESS: I think so.

24   JUROR #3: Again, you are saying, and

25   you are testifying in front of this Grand Jury,

1   that you don't know whether she ever used

2   cocaine?

3   WITNESS: No, I don't.

4   JUROR #3: Or ever had it in her

5   possession?

6   WITNESS: I don't know.

7   JUROR #3: You were -- you are aware of

8   the penalties for perjury?

9   WITNESS: Yes, I am.

10   JUROR #3: Okay.

11   * * *

12   JUROR #10: Did you and her and Lisa

13   Piel ever do coke together?

14   WITNESS: No.

15   JUROR #10: You mentioned you went to

16   John Rautio's house after you left here the last

17   time?

18   WITNESS: Uh-huh.

19   JUROR #10: You told him a few things

20   and then you said that John Rautio told you his

21   thoughts?

22   WITNESS: Uh-huh.

23   JUROR #10: What were his thoughts?

24   WITNESS: That he had his own game plan

25   and he didn't think that there was -- that

nothing -- that there was nothing to do, but John
-- let's see. Just that he was going to play
hardball. He was -- if they wanted him that bad,
that he was going to make it hard, make them take
it to the limits. He thought it was funny,
because everyone thought he was buying from him,
that he was a supplier, and he said he got all
the stuff from Lora Hinkley.

JUROR #17: In all the times that you
lived with Lisa Piel, on and off, she did not
know that you were using it and that you had it
in your possession?

WITNESS: I used the drug for about five
months and after awhile it got really apparent
that something I was -- that I was doing
something, because I was losing a lot of weight
and I didn't come home or go to bed at night.
Lisa would get up in the morning and I would
still be out in the living room, or passed out on
the couch, and when she finally found out that
that's what I -- what my problem was, when I got
down to eighty-nine pounds, she called my mom and
dad and told them that I had a problem with
cocaine, and she helped them put me in the
Marquette General Hospital.

1   JUROR #17: And, you have not used since

2   that time?

3   WITNESS: No.

4   JUROR #12: Did Lisa Piel --did you ever

5   see her use the controlled substance of

6   marijuana?

7   WITNESS: No.

8   JUROR #7: You say Lisa was in the car

9   when you went to John Rautio's house, after you

10   were her?

11   WITNESS: Uh-huh.

12   JUROR #7: Was she aware of the secrecy

13   oath that you had taken?

14   WITNESS: Yeah.

15   JUROR #7: Did she not feel that you

16   should not be doing that or did she advise you in

17   any way?

18   WITNESS: We were coming home from the

19   bar and I said I wanted to go down to John's, and

20   I felt bad, and she said she didn't think I

21   should do that, and I was asking for more

22   problems, and I said I felt that I -- that was --

23   it was my decision and that I felt really bad

24   about it, and I wanted to be the one to tell him

25   that I told. I didn't want him to walk in here

1   and hear it from somebody else. I wanted to go

2   straight to him and tell him that I was sorry,

3   but --

4   JUROR #7: But, that was against the

5   secrecy oath that you had took?

6   WITNESS: Yeah, I guess it was.

7   JUROR #7: Okay.

8   JUROR #4: When you were here in

9   January, you led us to believe that you were

10   afraid of John Rautio, and then you go right from

11   here to his house?

12   WITNESS: I gave you an instance of

13   where I felt threatened by him. Other than that,

14   I said I thought he was a nice man. Do your

15   notes also say that?

16   JUROR #4: You said --

17   WITNESS: He was a good friend.

18   JUROR #4: Yes.

19   WITNESS: Yeah. I remember saying that.

20   JUROR #4: You said he had big friends.

21   Do you remember saying that?

22   WITNESS: I remember saying that.

23   JUROR #4: You said that you were afraid

24   of him?

25   WITNESS: At one point I also said that

1   I thought he was a nice man, and I felt bad for

2   what is happening. I also stated that I felt I

3   provoked his actions.

4   JUROR #3: Earlier you were talking

5   about Joyce Cruickshank and talking about selling

6   her drugs. What was she doing with them, using

7   them herself or reselling them?

8   WITNESS: I think she was using all of

9   them. She went into rehab too. She had quite a

10   problem, herself, too.

11   JUROR #3: Do you know if she sold any

12   of them at all?

13   WITNESS: I don't know that for a fact,

14   no.

15   JUROR #10: When you went to John

16   Rautio's with Lisa, did Lisa drive or did you

17   drive?

18   WITNESS: I drove.

19   JUROR #10: She was present?

20   WITNESS: She was in the car. Actually,

21   she left me there. She didn't think that I

22   should be there.

23   JUROR #10: She knew what you were doing

24   there?

25   WITNESS: Uh-huh.

1   JUROR #10: She knew John Rautio was

2   selling you drugs?

3   WITNESS: In the past, yes.

4   JUROR #10: But prior to that?

5   WITNESS: Yeah.

6   JUROR #10: When you were living

7   together, she knew?

8   WITNESS: No. She didn't know at the

9   time.

10   JUROR #10: Did she find out that John

11   was selling you drugs?

12   WITNESS: When she found out I had a

13   problem with them, when she found out what my

14   problem was, she kept asking me what was wrong

15   and what are you doing to yourself, what are you

16   doing to yourself, and I finally got so bad, and

17   I just told her that I was doing coke. So, she

18   called my dad and my mom.

19   JUROR #3: You said -- you just said

20   that you drove but that she left you?

21   WITNESS: She took my car and left me

22   there.

23   JUROR #3: When did she -- did she come

24   back and get you?

25   WITNESS: She didn't. I walked.

1   JUROR #12: What kind of car did you

2   have?

3   WITNESS: A red Daytona.

4   JUROR #3: Were you working then?

5   WITNESS: I don't remember. I switched

6   jobs.

7   JUROR #3: What have you done for the

8   last few years, by way of employment?

9   WITNESS: The last few years?

10   JUROR #3: Yes, last couple or three

11   years?

12   WITNESS: Waitress. I worked for John

13   doing drywall, finishing work. I worked at a

14   deli, worked at cutting wood, worked at emptying

15   out the old K-Mart store. I don't remember what

16   else. I worked as a cashier.

17   JUROR #12: Did you purchase that car

18   yourself or was it given to you?

19   WITNESS: It was a loan through Chrysler

20   Credit.

21   JUROR #2: Did Miss Piel have a

22   boyfriend?

23   WITNESS: Pardon me?

24   JUROR #2: Did she have a boyfriend,

25   this Lisa Piel?

don't know if she has a

are were a couple of people

h now and then, but I don't

ds.

ave you seen any of them

use?

.

No?

only met one. One guy I met

e was Woody, something, and

It's not like that. She goes

ith him. I don't know who he

You say you lived with her

s, and you don't know who any

I mean, this is a little

ell, the only friends that I

have was, when I met her,

gnuola, and her parents and a

ly, and a friend named Norman.

Is it your intention to talk

t your testimony today like

me?

Editor's Note: these two pages were found copied together and this is the only copy existent.

S: No.

#12:   You mentioned that you lived

.   What type of employment are you

:   I was working at a deli and

started working on the

t, there is a partial owner. One

a friend of mine, David, that I

will be working with David,

off that, and putting new siding

12:   And, your friend, do you pay

:   Not right now. He's letting

hat's pretty much why I moved.

2:   Did you pay rent when you

iel?

In the beginning I did, as

That's why I had to move.

t afford it. I don't make

fford to help pay half of her

rtgage payments or whatever.

:   When was the last time that

tion with John Rautio?

That day I went over.

1   JUROR #3: You haven't talked to him or

2   seen him since then?

3   WITNESS: He drove by and I waved at him

4   the other day.

5   JUROR #3: You had no conversation or

6   anything with him since that day?

7   WITNESS: Just the night I went over.

8   JUROR #3: What about Lisa?

9   WITNESS: I talked to her yesterday.

10   * * *

11   MR. ENGEL: Now, isn't it true that

12   everyone in Petoskey, in the Petoskey area, knew

13   that John Rautio was selling drugs?

14   WITNESS: Pardon me?

15   MR. ENGEL: It was common knowledge that

16   John Rautio was selling drugs in Petoskey, the

17   Petoskey area; isn't it true?

18   WITNESS: Common knowledge?

19   MR. ENGEL: Yes.

20   WITNESS: Well --

21   MR. ENGEL: I mean, if somebody wanted

22   to buy drugs, John Rautio was the person to go

23   see? Is that right?

24   WITNESS: I don't know. I haven't been

25   in Petoskey that long. I never heard his name

1   until I came into the Perry one day.

2   MR. ENGEL: But, you got to know John a

3   little bit, obviously?

4   WITNESS: Yes.

5   MR. ENGEL: Because he was supplying you

6   with drugs?

7   WITNESS: Yeah.

8   MR. ENGEL: And, you knew other people

9   were buying from John Rautio?

10   WITNESS: Uh-huh, I assumed others were,

11   yes.

12   MR. ENGEL: And, it was generally felt

13   by people that if you needed some cocaine, the

14   person to contact was John Rautio? Is that true?

15   WITNESS: Not really.

16   MR. ENGEL: Wouldn't you think Lisa

17   Piel, as a police officer, would know there was

18   drug activity around in the area?

19   WITNESS: Yeah.

20   MR. ENGEL: Did she have him over to her

21   house, ever?

22   WITNESS: She didn't invite him there

23   and didn't appreciate him there. When he gave me

24   a job, supposedly helping him doing the drywall,

25   she said if I was going to be living there that

1   she didn't want me working for him, and at that

2   time I really didn't understand why. Then she

3   told me that rumor had it that he was into that

4   and she didn't need it and I said that I didn't

5   think that was fair of her to tell me that I

6   couldn't stay there if I worked for him, and it

7   pretty much was a decision of my own.

8   MR. ENGEL: But, yet the three of you

9   ended up in Traverse City doing a drywall job,

10   correct?

11   WITNESS: Yeah.

12   MR. ENGEL: And, you ended up going to

13   his motel room, the three of you, in his motel

14   room?

15   WITNESS: Uh-huh.

16   MR. ENGEL: Where cocaine was being used

17   in his motel room?

18   WITNESS: Spilled, yes.

19   MR. ENGEL: And, she doesn't know

20   anything about the cocaine being spilled?

21   WITNESS: I don't know if she caught on

22   or not. Nothing was said.

23   MR. ENGEL: And, you used a hot tub --

24   the three of you were in the hot tub together?

25   WITNESS: Uh-huh.

1   MR. ENGEL: And, yet you say she doesn't

2   like this person, doesn't like to hang around

3   with this person? Does that make any sense to

4   you?

5   WITNESS: Yeah. When he gave me a job,

6   she said that she didn't think I should be

7   working for him. She heard the rumor. And, he

8   came over and Lisa got to know him. I told her

9   it was my choice, that if he was doing that, it

10   didn't mean that I had to do it, so she had a

11   weekend off or something, and we were working

12   over there and I asked her if she wanted to come

13   and help out.

14   MR. ENGEL: Why would Lisa Piel suggest

15   that John Rautio leave town?

16   WITNESS: It was just a passing comment.

17   It wasn't like, "God, go tell him to leave

18   town."

19   MR. ENGEL: But that's what, in fact,

20   you did?

21   WITNESS: You're misinterpreting the

22   statement.

23   MR. ENGEL: You did tell John Rautio

24   that maybe he should leave town?

25   WITNESS: Yeah, I said "what are you

1   doing here?"

2   MR. ENGEL: I don't have anymore

3   questions. Do any of the grand jurors have any

4   further questions?

5   JUROR #10: In going back to this motel

6   room, this is kind of mind-boggling here. The

7   motel room, you say, is very big. I have never

8   seen a big motel room, unless you stay at the

9   Rockafeller's or something, but Lisa Piel was

10   your friend?

11   WITNESS: Uh-huh.

12   JUROR #10: Good friend?

13   WITNESS: Yeah.

14   JUROR #10: Best friend?

15   WITNESS: Not necessarily.

16   JUROR #10: One of your best friends?

17   WITNESS: Yeah.

18   JUROR #10: If you were in the motel

19   room, in the bathroom, and you needed help,

20   wouldn't you call your friend?

21   WITNESS: I just said "John, come here

22   for a minute."

23   JUROR #10: Wouldn't you think it was

24   unusual that you were calling John to come in the

25   bathroom?

1   WITNESS: I don't know.

2   JUROR #10: I mean, I'm not -- I can't

3 believe that you are that naive or I'm that

4 stupid, that she didn't come and take a peek or

5 something?

6   WITNESS: If you call for someone to

7 come here, specifically, I think the other person

8 would get the impression that meant that you

9 wanted to talk to them in private about something

10 else, or you would have said, everyone just come

11 here. I don't think that's odd.

12   JUROR #10: When there is a pretty good

13 relationship, one calls another one in the

14 bathroom and I would want to know what is going

15 on. I mean, you are friends, best friends or

16 whatever?

17   WITNESS: Well, I don't know.

18   JUROR #12: I would think you would be

19 very excited that you spilled that cocaine since

20 cocaine costs, and I would think that would make

21 your voice be more perceptive, or make her want

22 to come and see why you called him in there?

23   WITNESS: Perhaps.

24   JUROR #17: Is anyone living with Lisa

25 Piel now?

1   WITNESS: No. I don't think so.

2   JUROR #12: Did you, John, and Lisa

3 Piel, ever go to the Riverside Bar together, or

4 just you and Lisa?

5   WITNESS: Yeah. I used to play in a

6 band there. She would come and listen to me.

7   JUROR #12: During that period of time,

8 did you ever do cocaine there?

9   WITNESS: I don't know of any specific

10 time, but I have done it in the Riverside

11 bathroom before.

12   JUROR #12: Don't you think that Lisa

13 would wonder what was going on?

14   WITNESS: That I would go to the

15 bathroom?

16   JUROR #12: Well, wouldn't you

17 frequently use the bathroom and do cocaine?

18   WITNESS: I don't know, because we were

19 playing -- if you are playing in a band, you get

20 breaks. You play for like forty-five minutes and

21 you get a break.

22   JUROR #12: Did you do it together with

23 somebody else?

24   WITNESS: No.

25   JUROR #12: Just alone, you are saying?

1   WITNESS: I was only -- I was the only

2   female in the band. I would get off the stage

3   and go in the bathroom.

4   JUROR #12: Nobody else went in there

5   with you?

6   WITNESS: Rachelle, maybe, sometimes.

7   JUROR #12: Where would you do it in the

8   bathroom?

9   WITNESS: You open the door and there's

10   a curtain and stall behind it. I would dump some

11   in the top of the container and do it.

12   JUROR #12: You both would go in

13   together, at the same time?

14   WITNESS: Both of who?

15   JUROR #12: You and Rachelle?

16   WITNESS: No. I would give the other

17   person the package.

18   JUROR #12: After you came out?

19   WITNESS: Yes. I would open the curtain

20   and exchange it and then the other person would

21   go in.

22   JUROR #3: You really are aware of what

23   the penalties are for not telling the truth to

24   this Grand Jury is? I mean, any of the

25   agreements that you have made are all null and

227

```
1       void by not telling the truth.  Do you realize

2       that?

3                    WITNESS:  Uh-huh.

4                    JUROR #3:  You really understand what

5       you are doing here?

6                    WITNESS:  Yeah.

7                    JUROR #3:  Okay.  I just wanted to make

8       that very, very clear, real clear, because we are

9       seeing a lot of conflicts in your testimony.

10                   JUROR #10:  That was part of my

11      question.  Are you aware of the penalties and

12      what can happen to you --

13                   WITNESS:  Some --

14                   JUROR #10:  -- for sitting here and not

15      telling the truth.  Are you willing to give that

16      up, sacrifice everything?  Is that registering

17      with you?

18                   JUROR #3:  Are you willing to -- do you

19      want to talk to your attorney a little bit before

20      we end this session?  I'm serious about this.

21                   MR. DOWDELL:  When you indicated there

22      were conflicts in her testimony I don't know if

23      you mean conflicts between her previous testimony

24      here or what some other individuals who may have

25      been sitting here, in this chair, said.
```

1   JUROR #10: Many witnesses. You want to

2   challenge that?

3   MR. DOWDELL: We don't know what the

4   other witnesses have said.

5   MR. ENGEL: Mr. Foreman, I think we had

6   an opportunity to discuss it with her attorney

7   and her before we started here.

8   JUROR #10: Is she aware?

9   MR. ENGEL: She was present when we

10   discussed it, so I don't think we really are

11   going to gain anything by going any further with

12   that line. I think your questions that you have

13   asked her about, that there has been an adequate

14   response by her, as to her knowledge about what

15   possibly could happen. Are there any other

16   questions?

17   JUROR #10: None.

18   MR. ENGEL: Do you have anything you

19   want to change, Miss Waybrandt, in your

20   testimony?

21   WITNESS: No.

22   MR. ENGEL: Miss Waybrandt, you do

23   understand that you are under oath?

24   WITNESS: Yes.

25   MR. ENGEL: Okay. Do you also

1   understand that you are under the oath of

2   secrecy?

3   WITNESS: Yes.

4   MR. DOWDELL: Absolutely.

5   MR. ENGEL: Miss Waybrandt?

6   WITNESS: Yeah.

7   MR. ENGEL: You cannot go out of here

8   and talk to anyone about what's occurred here.

9   Do you understand that?

10   WITNESS: Yes.

11   MR. ENGEL: And, you can't do like you

12   did last time, go and talk to people, and if any

13   people ask you about being at the Grand Jury, you

14   can't talk to them about it. Do you understand

15   that?

16   WITNESS: Yes.

17   MR. ENGEL: It is part of your oath of

18   secrecy.

19   WITNESS: Yes.

20   MR. ENGEL: Do you also understand that

21   a violation of that oath of secrecy could make

22   you subject to criminal penalties, which, I

23   believe, are a misdemeanor, up to a year in the

24   county jail for violating the oath of secrecy?

25   WITNESS: Yes.

1   MR. ENGEL: Do you understand that?

2   WITNESS: Yes.

3   MR. ENGEL: I think we are finished with

4   this witness. You are free to leave.

5   MR. DOWDELL: Thank you.

6

7   -0-

8

STATE OF MICHIGAN   )
9   ) ss.
COUNTY OF EMMET   )
10

11   I, Sandra K. Davids, Certified Shorthand

12   Reporter, State of Michigan, do hereby certify that the

13   foregoing pages 1 through 46, inclusive, comprise a

14   full, true and correct transcript of the proceedings

15   and testimony taken in the Multi-County Citizen's Grand

16   Jury on May 22, 1991, of Alice Waybrandt, as edited by

17   the Honorable Richard M. Pajtas, Emmet County Circuit

18   Court Judge.

19

20   _Sandra K Davids_ _10/30/91_____

21   SANDRA K. DAVIDS, CSR-1033

22

23

24

25

231

Editor's note: This commentary was written in the 1990's, signed or unsigned as indicated. Where unsigned it is presumed that Lisa had some part in either writing or relating same to other parties. Each of these accompanying discourses are in rebuttal to the Grand Jury proceedings they follow, attempting to shed more light on issues only partly covered by the questionings. Grand Jury inquisitions are held with indictment potential as outcome and do not of necessity include comprehensive analysis of the panorama of person's lives, only those portions which apply directly to the indictments being sought.

This statement is repeated after each testimony and before each commentary for purposes of index clarification and reiteration of reason for inclusion, with the exception of Julie Woodruff's testimony for which no commentary was found.

- -

"Before Alice Waybrant was called to the grand jury, she had been off drugs for a year or so with the help of Lisa Piel, who found out she was doing drugs, and helped to get her in the rehab.

As Engle was saying on page 36 (wouldn't you think Lisa Piel, as a police officer, would know there was drug activity around in the area?). Yes, she did, and so did all the other police officers, and Joe Rautio, John's brother, who saw John at his mother's house while he was doing drugs. He or the other officers should have turned him in."

(signed) Art Piel
(dated) 6-10-97

"After Waybrant testified a second time, May 22, 1991, she was told they did not believe her, and there would be no deals made through the prosecutor's office. Waybrant now had a different attorney, Dan Dowell from Cedarville. She (Waybrant) advised Piel she feared going to prison as the SANE officers told her she would, and was thinking of requesting the grand jury to hear her again. She called Piel from her parents' house where she was now living and asked her to come to Cedarville ASAP, that her attorney wanted to talk with her. Piel did as requested and met with

Dowell at his office. Upon Piel's arrival Dowell sent Waybrant away, requesting to talk with Piel alone. They/He discussed the grand jury investigation, Waybrant's testimony, the investigators and the grand jury's feeling towards Piel. Stating, "they want you bad," Dowell told Piel Waybrant was a bad witness and he was very embarassed by her testimony. He further stated Waybrant could very well receive prison time if she did bot testify against her, and could still possibly do some time as they were not happy with her. The meeting lasted over an hour or so, as Waybrant joined in the latter part. Piel got the impression Dowell was asking Piel permission to let Waybrant testify against her. Piel expressed her concern with losing her job of 13 years, having to sell her house and relocate with no references to back her when trying to find another job. She advised them that Waybrant should, "do what she had to do, and she would do the same." Dowell stated he got the impression from them that they had enough to nail Piel anyway, and that he would instruct Waybrant that she observed Piel doing cocaine several times. Piel advised Dowell she would most probably fight any charges brought against her as she had just too much to lose. Again, Dowell assured her Waybrant was a bad witness and could easily be discredited."

(unsigned, undated)

233

Lisa's Great Grandfather, Henry W. Piel, at 17,
driving a mail car, 1890's.

Lisa's Great Grandfather, Henry W. Piel, early 1940's.

I

Lisa's Great Grandfather, Henry W. Piel, early 1920's, first one to drive a police car in Detroit.

Lisa's Great Grandfather, Henry W. Piel,
Chief of Detectives, Grosse Pointe, 1940's.

Lisa's Grandfather, Raymond D. Piel, 1930's.

Chief Henry W. Piel, 1930's.

Henry W. Piel, driving one of
the first police cars, 1920's.

Lisa's Grandfather, Raymond D. Piel, 1930's.

Lisa's Grandfather, Raymond D. Piel,
Detroit Police Department, 1935/6.

Lisa's Grandfather, Raymond D. Piel,
Detroit Auto Recovery, 1940's.

Lisa Michele Piel, 1 year, 1958.

VIII

Lisa, 13 years, 1970.

Lisa's 16th birthday, 1973.

Lisa, off to Grand Valley College for police training, 1978.

Lisa, first year on the force, 1979.

Lisa, on the job, 1980's.

Lisa, on the job, late 1980's.

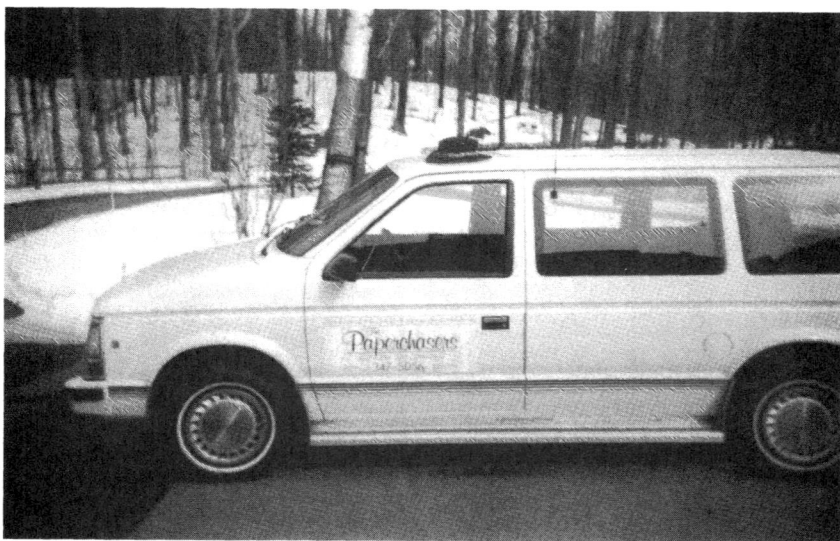

Lisa, on a new job, 1994.

Lisa and brother, Skip, 1988.

Lisa and family, 1988:
Skip, Dad, Lisa, Mom, Denise, Renee and Steven.

XIII

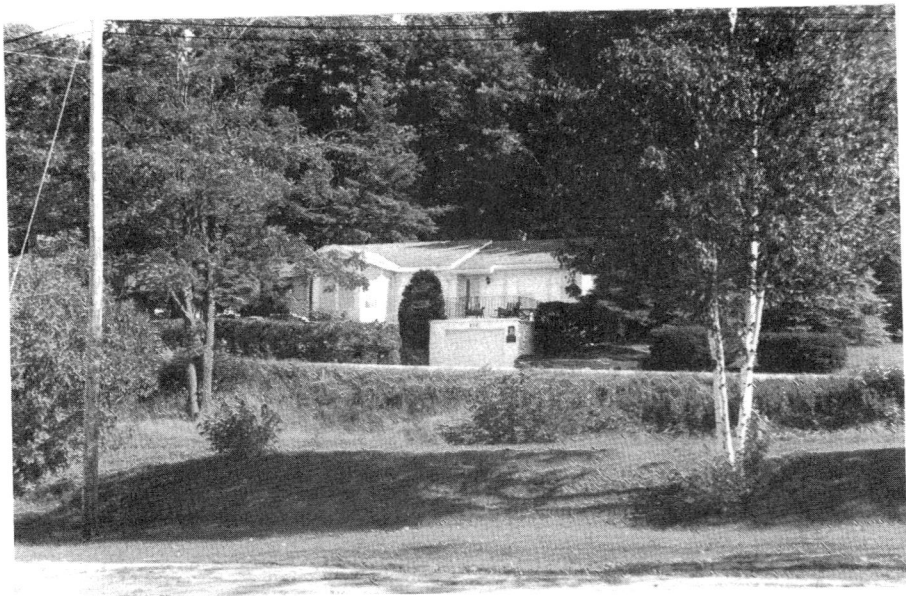

Lisa's house overlooking Lake Michigan.

Lisa with friends Nancy Simon and Gerri Zaremski, 1988.

Lisa, mid 1980's.

Lisa with friend, Bob Ryan, 1988.

Lisa at time of "resignation," 1992.

XVI

Lisa, 1994.

Lisa, 1994.

XVII

Lisa's 1985 Mazda XR7
"LITTLE LISA" lettered on the hood.

Lisa and Dad, Father's Day, 1994.

```
CHECKR   LORRAINE
NUMBER   54

CAT CHOW            TC D        .99
FINESSE            TC D       2.69
BAR SOAP           TC D       3.27
BATHTISSUE         TC D        .89
WHISKER LKH.       TC D       1.13
S/8 POTATOES        Z D       1.59
DT.RR SQUIRT        Z D       1.00
.40 DEPOSIT         F          .40
MILK                Z D       1.45
THE WORKS          TC D       1.55
LIQUOR                       10.97
BREAD               Z D       1.65
APPLE JUICE         Z D        .85
8 CT PRK CHP        Z D       1.88
MEAT                Z D       3.96
MEAT                Z D       3.74
STIR FRY            Z D       1.79
    0.66 LB  8       .59    /  LB
YLLW ONIONS         Z D        .39
YOPLAIT             Z D        .59
YOPLAIT             Z D        .52
YOPLAIT F.F.        Z D        .63
YOPLAIT YOG.        Z D        .83
BABY LOTION        TC D       2.39
BARBASOL BNS       TC D       1.19
SPAGHETTI           Z D        .99
    0.37 LB  8      1.09    /  LB
TOMATOES            Z D        .40
LIGHT IMPERI        Z D        .59
GREEN BEANS         Z D        .73
    1 QTY 2/ $1.00
ONELB CARRTS        Z 9        .50
NEWS-REVIEW                    .50

SUB TL                       :58.70
             VN CPN  Z D       -.50
             STRCPN
GROCERY              Z D       -.50
             VN CPN  Z D       -.20
             STRCPN
GROCERY              Z D       -.20
             VN CPN  Z D       -.55
             VN CPN  TZ D     -1.00
             VN CPN  TZ D      -.50
             STRCPN
TXBL GROCERY         TC D      -.50
             VN CPN  TZ D      -.55
             VN CPN  Z D       -.25
             STRCPN
GROCERY              Z D       -.25
             VN CPN  Z D       -.55
             VN CPN  Z D       -.20
             STRCPN
GROCERY              Z D       -.20

SLSTAX                         .31
TOTAL                       $44.28

CASH                        $50.00
CHANGE                       $5.40

COUPON    32C
                  ITEMS  56

VCPN         9                -4.30
                              ..07

       2-0002 2619   7:45PM  10/ 7/9/  FST
```

PURCHASES LIS
MADE 10/7

Lisa's last shopping receipt, the night before she died, 10-7-1994.

XIX

Lisa's Memorial Plaque, placed by Art Piel, 1994/5.

12

The Grand Jury
And Alice Waybrant
- 3

```
1              STATE OF MICHIGAN

2       IN THE DISTRICT COURT FOR THE COUNTY OF EMMET

3

PEOPLE OF THE STATE OF MICHIGAN,
4             Plaintiff,

5    vs.

6    LISA PIEL,
              Defendant.
7    _____/

8

9

10

11              TESTIMONY OF ALICE WAYBRANDT

12           At a session of the Multi-County Grand Jury

13       for the Counties of Cheboygan, Emmet, Luce,

14      Mackinaw, Otsego, Presque Isle, Charlevoix, and

15      Chippewa, on the 29th day of May, 1991.

16

17   PRESENT:        ROBERT ENGEL, ESQ. (P30437)
                     Emmet County Assistant Prosecuting
18                   Attorney

19                   DAN J. DOWDELL, ESQ. (P37676)
                     Attorney for Witness
20

21

22

23

24   SANDRA K. DAVIDS
     Certified Shorthand Reporter
25   CSR-1033
```

235

1   MR. ENGEL: Please come right up. For

2 the record Mrs. Waybrandt, state your name for

3 the record and spell your last name, please?

4   WITNESS: Alice Jane Waybrandt,

5 W-A-Y-B-R-A-N-D-T.

6   MR. ENGEL: Miss Waybrandt, you are

7 represented by counsel, are you not?

8   WITNESS: Yes.

9   MR. ENGEL: Counsel, could you put your

10 name on the record and your address?

11   MR. DOWDELL: Dan Dowdel, P.O., Box 39,

12 Cedarville, Michigan.

13   MR. ENGEL: First of all, Miss

14 Waybrandt, I need to put you under oath.

15

16   (Whereupon, the oath of secrecy and

17 affirmation was administered to the witness by

18 Mr. Engel)

19

20   (Whereupon, the oath of secrecy was

21 administered to Attorney Dan Dowdell by Mr.

22 Engel)

23

24

25

1   ALICE WAYBRANDT

2   having been first duly sworn, testified as

3   follows:

4

5   EXAMINATION

6   BY MR. ENGEL:

7   Q   Please be seated, both of you. Miss Waybrandt,

8   you appeared before the Grand Jury on two

9   occasions, have you not?

10   A   Yes.

11   Q   Okay. The first one I think was January 29th,

12   1991, approximately?

13   A   Yeah.

14   Q   And, then you appeared here last Wednesday, May

15   22, 1991, did you not?

16   A   Yes.

17   Q   After testifying at the last proceeding, on May

18   22, 1991, you subsequently have, through your

19   attorney, contacted the law enforcement officers.

20   and you wish to come back in and wish to correct

21   some testimony: is that correct?

22   A   Yes.

23   Q   Okay. First of all, all your testimony that you

24   gave at the prior proceeding has not been

25   truthful?

1   A   That's right.

2   Q   Any particular reason?

3   A   Because I had hoped that I could keep some people

4   that I care about out of this.

5   Q   Is that your only reason?

6   A   Yeah.

7   Q   What people did you want to keep out of it, out

8   of trouble?

9   A   Linda Postle and Lisa Piel.

10   Q   In regards to testimony you previously have

11   given, which people do you wish to change your

12   testimony about, at this time?

13   A   Lisa Piel and Linda Postle, and I guess there are

14   some things to clarify about John Rautio.

15   Q   Well let's start with Lisa Piel, then. Have you

16   ever used or done cocaine with Lisa Piel?

17   A   Yes, I have.

18   Q   How many occasions?

19   A   Several.

20   Q   Where would this take place?

21   A   Over at Linda Postle's house or at Lisa's,

22   sometimes.

23   Q   What period of time did this start?

24   A   When I got into it.

25   Q   When was that?

```
 1   A   I can never remember the date.

 2   Q   Approximately how long ago?

 3   A   Around November, I guess, of '89.

 4   Q   November of '89?  Is that what you are saying?

 5   A   I'm not -- I went into the rehab in April, and I

 6       was into it for about five months, so that was

 7       around November.

 8   Q   I believe you testified, orginally, it was around

 9       August or September of 1989.  Do you recall that?

10   A   I don't remember.

11   Q   So, sometime in 1989, last half of the year?

12   A   Yes.

13   Q   Okay.  When was the first time you did cocaine

14       with Lisa Piel?

15   A   I don't really remember the very first time that

16       I did it when she was present or vice versa.

17       She'd hide it from me and I'd hide it from her,

18       for quite awhile, before we actually sat down and

19       did it together.

20   Q   You'd hide it, did you say, or --

21   A   Hide it, tried to keep it from one another.

22   Q   Keep it so the other person wouldn't know?

23   A   Wouldn't see.

24   Q   So, you had some cocaine and Lisa had cocaine?

25   A   No.  Linda would bring -- this is how it all
```

239

started, is Linda always had it and she was at

Lisa's house one day and brought it out and was

trying to hide it from me and I caught them and

they -- I got mad because at that time I didn't

do any drugs at all. I had seen a friend of mine

get pretty messed up on it and I was against it,

and I got angry and said that, you know, if they

only understood what it could do, and if they

wanted me -- wanted to have me sit there and

watch them ruin their lives, they could sit there

and watch me ruin mine, and Linda said that I was

like a kid, you know, and how could I judge

something that wasn't a problem, who -- I would

-- I never ever done it, so she took me

downstairs.

Q   Excuse me. Where were you at when this occurred?

A   At Lisa's.

Q   You went downstairs at Lisa's, you and Linda

     Postle?

A   Yeah.

Q   Go on.

A   Linda put some out downstairs and showed me how

     to do it and I tried it. And, then, from that

     point on Linda just always brought it around and

     gave it to me and gave it to Lisa, but Lisa never

```
 1              wanted me to actually see her do it.  So, it was
 2              done in a different room or something.
 3     Q        So, on this first occasion, this was the first
 4              time you used cocaine?
 5     A        Yeah.
 6     Q        How was it presented to you?
 7     A        She had a package and she poured out a line.
 8     Q        What did it look like?
 9     A        White, powdery substance.
10     Q        Okay.  What did you do with that white, powdery
11              substance?
12     A        Snorted it.
13     Q        Snorted it through the nose?
14     A        Yes.
15     Q        Did it give you any effect?
16     A        I didn't like the taste of it and I don't really
17              -- after I while, I kept doing it, then, with
18              Linda and I got jittery and nervous and felt
19              energetic, like I wanted to get up and do
20              something.
21     Q        Would it cause numbness in your nose, when you
22              would use it?
23     A        Yeah.
24     Q        So, this was the first time that you did it, was
25              Linda Postle took you downstairs at Lisa Piel's
```

1   residence?

2 A   Yeah, but in my testimony before I said the first

3   time I did it was with Andy Sanford. That

4   happened -- the incident I told you happened

5   after this one.

6 Q   The incident with Andy Sanford was at a later

7   time?

8 A   Yes.

9 Q   That was an incident that you talked about at the

10   Riverside Bar?

11 A   Yeah.

12 Q   So, prior to the Riverside Bar, you already used

13   cocaine with Linda Postle?

14 A   Yes.

15 Q   Talking about that day, then, at Lisa Piel's

16   residence, is that her house in Petoskey?

17 A   Yeah.

18 Q   Overlooking the bay?

19 A   Yeah.

20 Q   Now, you say you caught Linda and Lisa using

21   cocaine, at that time, when you came home?

22 A   I didn't see anyone actually doing it. Linda was

23   getting ready to put some out and I blew up at

24   her then. But, at that time I saw Linda do it

25   after that because she did some with me, but when

```
 1            I came into the room, I didn't actually see
 2            anyone doing it.  I just saw the drug itself.
 3      Q     Now, did Lisa ever tell you prior to that date
 4            she was using cocaine?
 5      A     No.
 6      Q     Did you know she was using cocaine?
 7      A     I suspected on a couple of occasions, because
 8            Linda did use it.
 9      Q     Well, did Linda and Lisa kind of go off somewhere
10            together on those occasions?
11      A     No, it was usually Linda and Lisa and I chummed
12            around a lot together, and we used to go out to
13            her apartment and I would always fall asleep and
14            find, like, a mirror under the couch or
15            something, with smear markings on it, so it was
16            kind of obvious, I guess, in the morning.
17      Q     On this first occasion when you were using
18            cocaine with Linda Postle, did you then use
19            cocaine with Lisa that day?
20      A     Not on that day.  Lisa was mad that Linda got me
21            involved in it.
22      Q     Subsequent to that, when was the first time that
23            you recall using cocaine with Lisa Piel?
24      A     I don't remember the first time.  I honestly
25            don't.
```

1   Q   Well, I mean, how long after the first time you

2   used cocaine, approximately?

3   A   Maybe a couple of weeks, but not actually sitting

4   down with her. Linda would set people up in

5   different rooms. Like, one person would go in

6   and do it. We were all doing it together, but

7   not in front of each other. Do you know what I

8   mean?

9   Q   What room would you use?

10 A   Linda had like a laundry room in her apartment,

11   that she kept her stuff in, scales and stuff like

12   that. She'd usually take it in there, in the

13   room.

14 Q   Approximately how many occasions did you use

15   cocaine with Lisa Piel?

16 A   I couldn't count. Several times.

17 Q   Five? Ten? Just approximate numbers.

18 A   I have no idea. A lot of times.

19 Q   A lot of times?

20 A   A lot of times.

21 Q   Did Lisa ever have her own cocaine?

22 A   No.

23 Q   Every time that she used it, that you knew about,

24   is because someone brought it to her? Is that

25   what you are telling this Grand Jury?

244

1	A	Either Linda or I would just share it and give it
2		to her. We were doing it -- put some out.
3	Q	Was Lisa ever on duty when she did cocaine?
4	A	Not that I remember.
5	Q	The times that you saw Lisa -- knowing that
6		Lisa's was doing cocaine -- she would go into
7		another room -- you are saying in those
8		situations Linda would lay out the cocaine in
9		this room?
10	A	(Nodding head).
11	Q	Then you knew Lisa would go in the room?
12	A	Yeah.
13	Q	And, then the cocaine would be gone?
14	A	Yes.
15	Q	Did you ever see any effect of Lisa from using
16		cocaine? What did it do to her?
17	A	I don't really understand.
18	Q	What effect did the cocaine have on Lisa?
19	A	I don't know how she felt.
20	Q	You didn't notice anything, if she was acting any
21		differently?
22	A	I don't know. I was on it myself. I don't know
23		if I ever noticed anything.
24	Q	Now, you said that you, sometimes, did -- used
25		cocaine at Linda Postle's house?

1	A	Yeah.
2	Q	Where was that?
3	A	On Conway.
4	Q	That's in Emmet County?
5	A	Is it?
6	Q	You don't know?
7	A	No.
8		* * *
9	Q	Let's talk a little bit about drywall finishing.
10		Did there come a time when Lisa, John, and you
11		went to Traverse City, to do drywall?
12	A	Yes.
13	Q	Down in the Traverse City area; is that correct?
14	A	Yes.
15	Q	And, at the time that you went down there, there
16		was a room rented at Pointes North, or some
17		similar hotel, in the Traverse City area?
18	A	Yes.
19	Q	During the time that you were there was cocaine
20		-- was it ever seen or used?
21	A	Yes.
22	Q	Tell us about that.
23	A	I had some at the job site, and Lisa and I would
24		go around the corner, or whatever, in a different
25		part -- it was a big building -- and do some, and

1   then we got to -- I don't know how we decided

2   that we would get a room and stuff and stay, but

3   we did, and then we didn't have very much at that

4   time.

5   Q   Who supplied you with the cocaine at that work

6   site?

7   A   I already had it. I had got it from John, like,

8   the day before or something, but I already had

9   some of my own.

10 Q   So, you and Lisa would go around the corner, away

11   from John, to use the cocaine?

12 A   Yes.

13 Q   How would you use it, then?

14 A   Same way, snorting it.

15 Q   Approximately when would this have been? If you

16   went in rehab, let's say, March of 1990, how much

17   sooner before that did this occur?

18 A   I don't remember. I don't remember if it was

19   winter or not.

20 Q   Okay. It was sometime after you started using

21   cocaine in the fall of 1989, before you went into

22   rehab in 1990; is that correct?

23 A   Yes.

24 Q   And, that time, when you were down in Traverse

25   City, approximately how many occasions did you

```
1           and Lisa Piel snort cocaine?

2    A      I don't remember how many times.

3    Q      More than once?

4    A      Yes.

5    Q      More than twice?

6    A      Yes.

7    Q      More than five times?

8    A      Probably around five or ten times.

9    Q      Now, did there come an occasion, when you were at

10          the motel room, that some cocaine was spilled?

11   A      Yes.

12   Q      Who spilled it?

13   A      I did.

14   Q      What happened then?

15   A      I screamed, and they wanted to know what I did

16          and I told them, and Lisa didn't want John to

17          know that she was doing it, and that's when she

18          said, "looks, like the cat's out of the bag",

19          because then he knew that she knew.

20   Q      Was there a time when you and John Rautio were at

21          Lisa Piel's house, toward the latter part of

22          1989, when Lisa came home while she was on duty?

23   A      Yeah.

24   Q      And, you were sipping a wine cooler on that

25          occasion, weren't you?
```

```
 1   A    I don't remember.

 2   Q    Did Lisa Piel come in on that occasion and use

 3        cocaine?

 4   A    I don't remember her ever using it.  There was a

 5        day -- it was a day that we made cookies and --

 6        as a matter of fact, I don't even think I was

 7        using it that day.

 8   Q    Okay.  Are you saying that if someone else were

 9        to testify along that line, that Lisa came into

10        her house on that occasion, that she took a

11        couple swiggs off a wine cooler, that you were

12        drinking, that she then went into the bathroom,

13        where a line had been set up, and came out a

14        short time later and said, "thank you for that",

15        that that didn't happen?

16   A    I don't remember that happening, no.

17   Q    On the times that you used cocaine with Lisa

18        Piel, where did you generally use the cocaine?

19        What location?

20   A    Sometimes at Linda Postle's house, or apartment,

21        or at Lisa's house.

22   Q    Were you living with Lisa at that time?

23   A    Yeah.

24   Q    Was anyone else ever present when you would do

25        cocaine with Lisa, other than Linda Postle or
```

```
1        John Rautio?

2    A   Yes.

3    Q   Who else?

4    A   Julie Woodruff.

5    Q   Tell me about Julie Woodruff a little bit.  Did

6        she use cocaine?

7    A   Yes.

8    Q   Did she deal cocaine?

9    A   I don't know.  I never bought anything from her.

10   Q   Well, did you hear whether or not she was dealing

11       cocaine?

12   A   Not really.  She was Linda's friend, living with

13       Linda.  I don't think she --I think she used it

14       when it was around.  I don't think she was ever

15       involved.  I don't know for sure what she did, or

16       if she was involved in that in any way.

17   Q   Did Julie Woodruff ever supply you with cocaine?

18   A   Not that I remember.

19   Q   You are not sure?

20   A   I can't think of a time, no.

21   Q   Approximately how many occasions were you around

22       when Julie Woodruff used cocaine?

23   A   I don't remember how many times.  Quite a few

24       times.  But, --

25   Q   Did Lisa Piel ever say anything about being a
```

```
 1          police officer and using cocaine?  Would you like
 2          me to reask the question in a little different
 3          sense?  You were -- Lisa was a police officer; is
 4          that right?
 5     A    Yeah.  I don't remember, ever, her saying
 6          anything about being a cop, when we were doing
 7          that.
 8     Q    I mean, like, for instance, did you ever have
 9          occasion to hear Lisa say, "I'm a police officer.
10          You can't be telling anyone I'm doing this stuff
11          because it will get me in trouble"?
12     A    Not really that.  I never heard -- no.
13     Q    Not really that.  What do you mean?
14     A    I said no, but she did -- when I started getting
15          into it heavy and stuff, she said, "you know, I
16          can't have you doing it here.  I can't have you
17          here, period, if you are going to do that",
18          because she was a cop.  She, in fact, kicked me
19          out of her house.
20     Q    Anyone else that you did cocaine with, in the
21          presence of Lisa Piel, other than the ones you
22          mentioned here: Linda Postle, John Rautio, and
23          Julie Woodruff?
24     A    I never done it with John and Lisa at the same
25          time, no.
```

1   Q   You done it in the same house, haven't you?

2   Maybe not in the same room, at the same time, but

3   in the same house?

4   A   I guess, yeah.

5   Q   On these occasions would sometimes occur at Lisa

6   house, did they not, where John would lay out

7   lines in the bathroom, and you and Lisa would

8   have an opportunity to snort up the lines? John

9   may not have been present in the bathroom, but he

10   was in the house and laid them out for you?

11   A   I don't think, to my knowledge, John ever put

12   lines out for Lisa. I did, but I don't think he

13   ever did. He'd only been there a couple of

14   times, a few times.

15   Q   Okay.

16   A   And, she didn't trust him.

17   Q   Now, when you put the lines out for Lisa, did you

18   ever see Lisa actually ever snort the cocaine?

19   A   When?

20   Q   On any occasion?

21   A   Yeah.

22   Q   Let's talk about Traverse City, the time you said

23   you did between five and ten times, possibly.

24   Did you actually see Lisa snorting cocaine on

25   those occasions?

```
 1   A    Yes.

 2   Q    At Lisa house, did you ever see her snort the

 3        cocaine?

 4   A    Yes.

 5   Q    At Linda Postle's house, did you ever see her

 6        snort the cocaine?

 7   A    Yes.

 8   Q    Did you ever use cocaine in Lisa's car, or RX7

 9        that she had?

10   A    I don't remember ever doing that, no.

11   Q    Any other places that you used cocaine with Lisa

12        Piel, other than those you mentioned here?

13   A    Not that I remember, no.

14   Q    Did you ever use cocaine in any other vehicles

15        that Lisa Piel was driving or owned?

16   A    No.

17   Q    Like her Jeep?

18   A    No.

19                         *  *  *

20   Q    At times that Lisa Piel was doing cocaine, did it

21        ever occur shortly before she would go on duty?

22   A    I don't know.  You have to understand the kind of

23        shape I was in.

24   Q    Sure, I understand.

25   A    I don't remember a lot of specifics.
```

```
 1    Q    Would it be unusual -- let me put it that way --
 2         for Lisa to have done cocaine shortly before
 3         going on duty?
 4    A    I'm sure it could have taken place.
 5    Q    Could have taken place?
 6    A    Yeah, but I can't say for sure.  I don't remember
 7         any particular time.
 8    Q    Is there anything else in your testimony that you
 9         have given in these proceedings that you wish to
10         correct?  This is your time to correct it.  You
11         don't get another chance.
12    A    I'm trying to think if this is a correction or
13         not.  I can't think of anything else.
14    Q    Have you testified truthfully and completely
15         about everything regarding drug trafficking, that
16         you know about?
17    A    Here today?  Yes, I have.
18    Q    Is there anything else that you recall, involving
19         other people than the names that have been
20         mentioned here today, where you would testify
21         truthfully and completely, from drug trafficking,
22         that may have been different from something you
23         said before?
24    A    I can't think of anything.
25    Q    Okay.  Did you talk to Lisa Piel after the last
```

254

```
 1              time you testified here, last week?

 2     A        I saw her yesterday.

 3     Q        Before yesterday?

 4     A        Yeah.

 5     Q        You talked to her after you got done testifying

 6              at these proceedings, didn't you?

 7     A        Uh-huh.

 8     Q        Told her what you said?

 9     A        No.

10     Q        Did you tell her who else was here to testify?

11     A        I told her I saw John outside.

12     Q        John Rautio?

13     A        Yeah.

14     Q        What did Lisa say?

15     A        Not much.  I just told her I didn't think I had a

16              choice but to tell the truth.

17     Q        Well, did you tell her that you had not testified

18              truthfully, then, last week, to cover for her?

19     A        Yeah.

20     Q        I'm sorry?

21     A        Yes.

22     Q        And, somewhere along the line, after you saw Mr.

23              Rautio here, that's when you had second thoughts

24              about your prior testimony?

25     A        I guess that and watching what this is doing to
```

255

1   my parents. It seems like a losing battle.

2 Q   Then you talked to Lisa and told her you were

3   going to come back and change your testimony, to

4   what is supposed to be the truth; is that

5   correct?

6 A   Yes.

7 Q   What was Lisa response?

8 A   That there is nothing I could do.

9   MR. ENGEL: I don't believe I have any

10   other questions. I will open it up to the Grand

11   Jury.

12   * * *

13   JUROR #10: You don't know of Lisa Piel

14   buying cocaine directly from John Rautio?

15   WITNESS: Not for a fact.

16   JUROR #10: But did you, yourself, buy

17   cocaine from John Rautio, that was specifically

18   for Lisa?

19   WITNESS: No.

20   JUROR #10: Did she give you money and

21   say, "will you get me coke from John Rautio"?

22   WITNESS: No. I never knew her to spend

23   a dime on it, to tell you the truth. She would

24   rather walk away from it.

25   JUROR #4: You don't take this oath of

1   silence very seriously, do you?

2   WITNESS: Yeah, I do. But --

3   JUROR #4: Twice you ran out and went

4   and told people. Are you going to go out after

5   you leave here and tell Lisa or anyone what went

6   on?

7   WITNESS: No. The first time I came in

8   here, I talked about it. I find this very hard

9   to keep from the people that I care about,

10   especially when they're either involved or

11   they're my parents.

12   JUROR #4: But that's not what the oath

13   says.

14   WITNESS: I know that.

15   MR. DOWDELL: Am I entitled to make a

16   point at all?

17   MR. ENGEL: I don't think so, sorry.

18   Any other questions from the grand jurors? Thank

19   you very much. Then we conclude this witness at

20   this particular time.

21

22   -0-

23

24

25

1 STATE OF MICHIGAN   )
) ss.

2 COUNTY OF EMMET   )

3   I, Sandra K. Davids, Certified Shorthand

4 Reporter, State of Michigan, do hereby certify that the

5 foregoing pages 1 through 9, inclusive, comprise a

6 full, true and correct transcript of the proceedings

7 and testimony taken in the Multi-County Citizen's Grand

8 Jury on   May 29, 1991, of Alice Waybrandt, as edited

9 by the Honorable Richard M. Pajtas, Emmet County

10 Circuit Court Judge.

11

12   _____Sandra K David_____10/30/91

13 SANDRA K. DAVIDS, CSR-1033

14

15

16

17

18

19

20

21

22

23

24

25

Editor's note: This commentary was written in the 1990's, signed or unsigned as indicated. Where unsigned it is presumed that Lisa had some part in either writing or relating same to other parties. Each of these accompanying discourses are in rebuttal to the Grand Jury proceedings they follow, attempting to shed more light on issues only partly covered by the questionings. Grand Jury inquisitions are held with indictment potential as outcome and do not of necessity include comprehensive analysis of the panorama of person's lives, only those portions which apply directly to the indictments being sought.

This statement is repeated after each testimony and before each commentary for purposes of index clarification and reiteration of reason for inclusion, with the exception of Julie Woodruff's testimony for which no commentary was found.

- -

"On May 29, 1991, Waybrant testified in front of the grand jury after Dowell contacted Croton and advised him Waybrant wanted to change her story. No subpoena was issued this time."

(unsigned, undated)

"WAYBRANT, history told to Piel:

Waybrant told Piel she was sexually assaulted by her uncle on several occasions when she was about twelve. This went to court, where he was found guilty and went to jail for one year. She received counselling until her counsellor moved. At sixteen years she attempted suicide by taking an overdose of tylenol. She was put in Lockwood Hospital, psychiatric unit, following that attempt. She was there two months and was transferred to a half-way house per her doctor's orders, down in Pontiac, Michigan. She was there only an hour and requested her mother sign her out, and she left against her doctor's orders. She was on mood stabilizers but did not continue to take them as prescribed.

"Waybrant is a song writer and plays many instruments. Many of her songs have been copywritten and she spends as much time as her budget will allow in the recording studio.

(Ed. note: much of this is repetitive but was found in different writings, presumably by Lisa, or transcribed from conversation)

"After meeting up with John Rautio in mid-December, 1989, she was taking large doses of valium, xanax, halicon, and liquid demerol, which was given to her in sample pack form by Rautio. He also gave her a white powder he called cocaine which made her have bowel movements after sniffing and made her feel like she drank a lot of coffee. She would sometimes stay up two-three days at a time without sleep. She admitted to Piel she hallucinated and heard things. On one occasion she shaved her body and did not realize it till she awoke the next morning.

"Waybrant also told Piel that Rautio made her perform oral sex on him when she could not afford the drugs he provided. She lost a lot of her belongings to pay for drugs.

"As Waybrant's problems progressed and became more noticable, Piel asked her to find another place to live. This happened on several occasions and Waybrant would beg for another chance, stating she'd change. A verbal fight would break out and Waybrant would start hauling her belongings out with no direction. Piel first noticed Waybrant's involvement with Rautio when she again asked her to move. Piel was working and saw Rautio's van in her driveway. She called the house and told Waybrant to get him out. Another incident, Waybrant put minor slits in her wrist. Still another, she slit her neck (photo showing same enclosed) (Ed. note: no photos were found accompanying this writing), after Piel once again asked her to leave. This went on and on. Another occasion, Rautio put her up at the Best Western for several days until Piel told her to get out of there, this is not what she meant by moving out and that she was killing herself.

"Finally Piel realized she could not help Waybrant and she needed professional help with her never-ending problems she could no longer deal with. Piel called Waybrant's parents advising them of her drug problem and the self-destructive course she was on. Piel advised them their daughter needed professional help ASAP.

260

From there Alicon agreed to go into a rehab and stayed for approximately one month with Piel's support.

"In summary, the girl is very insecure and unstable!"

(unsigned, undated)

"On December 2nd or 3rd (1991) Waybrant advised Piel she received her subpoena for the pre-lim set for December 13 at 3:30 p.m.

"On December 4, 1991 Waybrant told Piel that Dan Dowell had contacted her at her aunt's house in Bay City where she is now living and going to school. Dowell told her he had received a call from Diane Smith requesting any information he had regarding Waybrant's testimony for the upcoming pre-lim December 13th. She further advised him she received information from Mr. Hopkins, who is in charge of Waybrant's probation file, that she may perjure herself, and her office was fully prepared to prosecute at that time. Dowell said he told Smith he had not talked with Waybrant.

"On Saturday, December 7th, Waybrant told Piel she received another call from her attorney, Dowell, at a friend's in Cedarville. She stated Dowell was quite excited, stating SANE officer Breed had called him advising the State Police wanted to subpoena him for the upcoming pre-lim Friday. They wanted to know if he had talked with Piel; he stated he did. Dowell said they advised him to advise his little client if she screws up the case, they would definitely prosecute her for perjury. Again, Waybrant stated he was quite upset and wanted to know what she was going to do. He was planning to run for prosecutor in Mackinaw County and did not need this. Waybrant advised him she was very upset about a letter that was sent to the judge requesting her psychologist send . . . her review, stating 3/4 was incorrect (Ed. ?). She told him she did not trust him, he was not her attorney anymore, and he was on his own."

(unsigned, undated)

13

The Grand Jury
And Julie Woodruff

1   STATE OF MICHIGAN

2   IN THE DISTRICT COURT FOR THE COUNTY OF EMMET

3

PEOPLE OF THE STATE OF MICHIGAN,
4   Plaintiff,

5   vs.

6   LISA PIEL,
             Defendant.
7   _____/

8

9

10

11   TESTIMONY OF JULIE WOODRUFF

12   At a session of the Multi-County Grand Jury

13   for the Counties of Cheboygan, Emmet, Luce,

14   Mackinaw, Otsego, Presque Isle, Charlevoix, and

15   Chippewa, on the 21st day of August, 1991.

16

17

18   PRESENT: ROBERT ENGEL, ESQ. (P30437)
                   Emmet County Assistant Prosecuting
19   Attorney

20   RONALD POWERS, ESQ. (P19059)
                   Attorney for Witness
21

22

23

24   SANDRA K. DAVIDS
     Certified Shorthand Reporter
25   CSR-1033

```
 1              MR. ENGEL:  Before we start, I have to
 2         put both of you under oath.  We will start with
 3         you, Julie.
 4              (Whereupon, the oath of secrecy and
 5         affirmation was administered to the witness by
 6         Mr. Engel)
 7              (Whereupon, the oath of secrecy  was
 8         administered to Attorney Ronald Powers by Mr.
 9         Engel)
10
11
12              JULIE WOODRUFF
13         having been first duly sworn, testified as
14         follows:
15
16              EXAMINATION
17    BY MR. ENGEL:
18    Q    Julie, first of all, could you state your name
19         for the record?
20    A    Julie Ann Woodruff.
21    Q    How do you spell your last name?
22    A    W-O-O-D-R-U-F-F.
23    Q    You tend to have a fairly deep voice.  You will
24         have to speak up so everyone can hear.  Julie,
25         where do you live?
```

1   A   Austin, Texas.

2   Q   Are you formerly from the Petoskey area?

3   A   Yes, sir.

4   Q   When is it that you moved to Austin, Texas?

5   A   April of '90.

6   Q   Little over a year ago?

7   A   Right.

8   Q   When -- prior to moving to Austin, Texas, did you

9   spend most of your time in the Emmet and

10   Charlevoix areas?

11 A   Yes, sir.

12 Q   Julie, you have been involved to some extent with

13   discussions with some police officers today, have

14   you not?

15 A   Yes, sir.

16 Q   Prior to coming in here for the Grand Jury you

17   entered into a plea agreement, did you not?

18 A   Yes, sir.

19 Q   And, the substance of that is that you would

20   plead guilty to one count of use of cocaine?

21 A   Yes, sir.

22 Q   And, in return the Emmet County Prosecuting

23   Attorney's office or other prosecutors in this

24   area, dealing with this Grand Jury, will not

25   charge you with any other drug offenses arising

1   out of the Grand Jury, committed prior to today's

2   date?

3 A   Yes, sir.

4 Q   You agree to cooperate completely with the police

5   officers, investigating and prosecution of people

6   within the juridiction of the Grand Jury?

7 A   Yes, sir.

8 Q   Do you agree -- and, you also agree to testify

9   truthfully and completely regarding drug

10   trafficking in the eight-county Grand Jury

11   jurisdiction, and at any and all subsequent

12   proceedings arising from this Grand Jury?

13 A   Yes. sir.

14 Q   And. you understand that should you fail to

15   follow these terms and conditions, in your full

16   cooperation and truthful testimony, this

17   agreement is void and null and that you may then

18   be subject to any charges with which could be

19   brought?

20 A   Yes, sir.

21 Q   That is the extent of our agreement, is it not?

22 A   Yes.

23 Q   No other promises have been made to you?

24 A   No.

25 Q   Julie, I want to talk to you a little bit about

1   when you first became involved with the use of

2   the controlled substance cocaine. Could you tell

3   the Grand Jury when that occurred?

4   A March of '88.

5   Q March of '88?

6   A Yup, or '89 -- excuse me, '89.

7   Q Let's back up. You left to go to Austin, Texas

8   in 1990?

9   A Yes.

10 Q A little over a year ago?

11 A Right.

12 Q How many years have you been involved with

13   cocaine prior to that?

14 A About a year or year and a half.

15 Q I thought when you were talking with us a little

16   earlier, you first started -- would have been on

17   your birthday, in March of '87. Did I make my

18   notes wrong?

19 A It wasn't '87. It was the year before I left.

20   It was my birthday of '89.

21 Q Okay. How is it that you became involved with

22   cocaine on your birthday, in '89?

23 A Linda Postle brought it over to my house.

24 Q To your house?

25 A Yes.

```
1    Q    And, where was your house at that time?

2    A    I was living with my parents, in Oden.

3    Q    You have to speak up a little bit louder.

4    A    Sorry.

5    Q    And, how much did Linda Postle bring over at that

6         time?

7    A    She brought three and a half grams over.

8    Q    Who used the cocaine on that occasion?

9    A    Linda Postle and myself.

10   Q    Did you pay Linda Postle anything for any of the

11        cocaine?

12   A    No. sir; I didn't.

13   Q    How did you use the cocaine?  What manner did you

14        take it and use it?

15   A    With a straw.

16   Q    Okay.  How was it laid out for you?

17   A    In lines.

18   Q    On what?

19   A    The kitchen table.

20   Q    Who laid out the lines?

21   A    Linda Postle.

22   Q    What did it look like?

23   A    It was white.

24   Q    What kind of white?  White what?  Liquid or

25        solid?
```

1   A   Solid powder.

2   Q   Powder?

3   A   Uh-huh.

4   Q   And, you said that you used a straw with it?

5   A   Yes, sir.

6   Q   How did you use the cocaine with a straw? Where

7   did it go?

8   A   In the nose.

9   Q   You snorted it?

10 A   Yes, sir.

11 Q   Did you get any effect from it?

12 A   Yes, sir.

13 Q   What type of effect did you get from this white

14   powdery substance, that you believe to be

15   cocaine?

16 A   Speedy feeling.

17 Q   Okay. Made you a little high or more active or

18   whatever?

19 A   Right.

20 Q   Any other effects?

21 A   Then the next day I would wake up and my head

22   would be stuffy and I couldn't breathe.

23 Q   And, did you get that effect from the first time

24   you used it?

25 A   Pretty close.

1	Q	After -- did you and Linda use the entire three
2		and a half grams of it on that occasion?
3	A	No, sir. We did a gram of it.
4	Q	Between the two of you or gram each?
5	A	Between the two of us, sir.
6	Q	After that first occasion in using cocaine, did
7		you ever use it again?
8	A	Yes, sir.
9	Q	Approximately how many times would you say that
10		you have used cocaine, from that first time up to
11		today's date?
12	A	Maybe --
13	Q	Proximately?
14	A	Approximately twenty times.
15	Q	Who have you used cocaine with in the past?
16	A	Linda Postle, Alice Waybrandt, Joyce Cruickshank.
17	Q	You weren't sure of the last name until someone
18		said what it was and then you were sure who it
19		was. Where is Joyce from, if you know?
20	A	Cedarville.
21	Q	Who else?
22	A	Rajean Swalding, Lora Hinkley, Tina Voss, and
23		Lisa Piel.
24	Q	Now, were any of these people within your circle
25		of friends?

1 A   Pardon me?

2 Q   Were any of these people within your circle of

3   friends? People that you associate with on

4   somewhat of a regular basis? Were these people

5   that you hang out with?

6 A   That I do stuff with, yeah.

7 Q   How long had you known Linda Postle?

8 A   Since high school.

9 Q   How long have you known Alice Waybrandt?

10 A   About two years.

11 Q   How did you meet Alice Waybrandt?

12 A   I met Allison over at Lisa Piel's house.

13 Q   Was it through the use of cocaine, basically,

14   that it occurred, that you met her?

15 A   Not at that time, no.

16 Q   How did you know Lisa Piel?

17 A   I have just known her for a few years.

18 Q   Now, this list of people that you have given us

19   are people that you used cocaine with. Did you

20   ever sell or deliver cocaine to any of these

21   people or other people?

22 A   To Tina Voss and to her sister, Sheryl.

23 Q   Have you sold or delivered to any other people?

24 A   Not that I can recall, sir.

25 Q   You say not that you recall. Selling or

1   delivering cocaine to somebody is simply

2   something that you will probably remember. Are

3   you saying you just don't have a memory or are

4   you saying that you didn't do it to anyone else

5   but these two people?

6 A   That's all I remember doing it to, sir.

7   * * *.

8 Q   You say that you have used cocaine with Lisa Piel

9   before. How many occasions?

10 A   Once.

11 Q   Where was that?

12 A   It was at Linda Postle's apartment.

13 Q   Where was that?

14 A   On North Conway Road.

15 Q   That North Conway Road would be, like, between

16   Petoskey and Alanson?

17 A   Right, Conway and Alanson.

18 Q   But, in Emmet County?

19 A   Right.

20 Q   On that occasion who was at that apartment?

21 A   Linda Postle, and Alice Waybrandt.

22 Q   And, who else?

23 A   Lisa Piel and myself.

24 Q   So, four, altogether?

25 A   Right.

```
 1   Q   How was it that cocaine was used at that
 2       apartment by Lisa Piel?
 3   A   With a straw.
 4   Q   Well, first of all, where was the cocaine?
 5   A   Under the couch, on a mirror.
 6   Q   Okay.  You put your hands out.  Approximately
 7       what size mirror?  Describe it in inches or
 8       something for me, just approximately.
 9   A   Probably, dinner plate size.
10   Q   Dinner plate size?
11   A   Yes, sir.
12   Q   How was the cocaine on that minor?
13   A   Laid in lines.
14   Q   How many lines?
15   A   There were four.
16   Q   What did it look like?
17   A   It was a white, powdery substance.
18   Q   And, you said that a straw was used by Lisa?
19   A   Yes, sir.
20   Q   Did you also take any of the lines?
21   A   I took one.
22   Q   How many did Lisa take?
23   A   Two.
24   Q   How was it ingested, then?  You used a straw, and
25       where did it, the cocaine, go?
```

273

```
 1    A    It went up the nose and down my throat.

 2    Q    Up the nose, like you usually use cocaine?

 3    A    Right.

 4    Q    Did you receive some kind of effect from this

 5         substance on this occasion?

 6    A    Yes.  I had a speedy effect from it.

 7    Q    Did you get the complications the next day that

 8         you say you get from cocaine?

 9    A    Yes, sir; I did.

10    Q    Did you have any doubt in your mind it was

11         cocaine that you were using?

12    A    No, sir.

13    Q    Do you know who provided the cocaine on that

14         occasion?

15    A    It was probably Linda Postle.

16    Q    Because it was her apartment?

17    A    Right.

18    Q    Where was Linda Postle and Allison Waybrandt, at

19         that time?

20    A    They were in the bedroom.

21    Q    What were they doing in the bedroom?

22    A    I believe they were doing cocaine in there.

23    Q    Had there been lines set up in the bedroom, for

24         use of cocaine?

25    A    Yes, sir.
```

```
1    Q    Where would that be in the bedroom?

2    A    On Linda's dresser.

3    Q    Did Lisa ever go back to the room, bedroom?

4    A    I believe she did, sir.

5    Q    I'm talking about that occasion when you were

6         there, talking about bringing it out from

7         underneath the couch?

8    A    Right.

9    Q    Do you know if Lisa went back in the bedroom with

10        the purpose of using cocaine?

11   A    I believe she did.

12   Q    You didn't actually see it?

13   A    Right.  I didn't see her go into the bedroom, but

14        she went back in that area.  The bathroom is also

15        located there.

16   Q    But, it was common knowledge among the four of

17        you that cocaine was back there, in the bedroom?

18   A    Right.

19   Q    Approximately when was this that this occurred?

20   A    Approximately?

21   Q    Proximate date?

22   A    It was right around Christmas, December of '39.

23   Q    Before or after Christmas?

24   A    I believe it was after, sir.

25   Q    Has there been any other occasions where you were
```

1   present when Lisa used cocaine in your presence?

2   A   No, sir.

3   Q   Have there been other occasions when you were in

4   a residence, where cocaine was available, that

5   Lisa would have used the cocaine, even though no

6   in your presence?

7   A   Yes, sir.

8   Q   And, approximately how many times?

9   A   I believe, four.

10   Q   Four times? Whose house would it be?

11   A   At Linda Postle's apartment.

12   Q   Every time?

13   A   (Nodding head).

14   Q   You have to say yes or no.

15   A   Yes. I'm sorry.

16   Q   That's the one on North Conway Road, that you

17   talked about?

18   A   Yes, sir.

19   Q   How do you know there was cocaine available on

20   those occasions?

21   A   Because I saw it, sir.

22   Q   Where was the cocaine?

23   A   It was in Linda's bedroom, on the dresser, or in

24   the bathroom.

25   Q   Was it laid out?

276

```
 1   A    Yes, sir.

 2   Q    How was it laid out?

 3   A    Into lines.

 4   Q    Did you use any of the cocaine on any of those

 5        occasions?

 6   A    A couple of them.

 7   Q    Could you see where lines had already been used,

 8        of cocaine?

 9   A    Yes, sir.

10   Q    Would Lisa have already been back in the bedroom

11        area prior to when you'd go in to use the

12        cocaine?

13   A    She may have.

14   Q    When is the -- let's try to get some dates on

15        these times.  Do you recall any of the dates for

16        any of these occasions that Lisa would have been

17        able to go back in the bedroom, at Linda Postle's

18        residence, to use the cocaine?

19   A    Once would have been on Linda's birthday.

20   Q    Linda Postle's birthday?

21   A    Right, of '89, and then April of '90.

22   Q    Linda Postle's birthday is in what month of the

23        year?

24   A    November.

25   Q    And, you said the earlier part of April, of '90?
```

```
 1    A    Yes.

 2    Q    Why do you remember these two particular dates?

 3         Just because Linda's birthday is the one?

 4    A    And, the one was right before we were leaving, to

 5         move to Texas.

 6    Q    Any other occasion that you remember cocaine

 7         being used by Lisa Piel, either directly in your

 8         sight, or indirectly?

 9    A    Not that I can remember, sir.

10    Q    You are familiar with where Lisa Piel lives in

11         Petoskey?

12    A    Yes, sir.

13    Q    Have you ever been to her residence?

14    A    Yes, sir.

15    Q    Have you ever seen cocaine at her residence?

16    A    Yes, sir.

17    Q    How many occasions?

18    A    Once.

19    Q    Whose cocaine was that?

20    A    Linda Postle's.

21    Q    Was Lisa Piel present at that time?

22    A    No, she was not.

23    Q    Were you aware of any other time of anyone else

24         having cocaine at Lisa Piel's residence?

25    A    Yes.
```

1   Q   And, who would that have been?

2   A   Alice Waybrandt.

3   Q   Did Alice used to live with Lisa.

4   Q   Yes, sir; she did.

5   Q   Was it Alice that told you that she kept cocaine

6   there? How did you know?

7   A   Yes, sir; Alice did.

8   Q   Alice told you. Did you ever see it when Alice

9   was there?

10   A   Yes, but Lisa was never there.

11   Q   Did you get use of cocaine, ever, at Lisa's

12   place, even though she was not there?

13   A   Not with Allison, just with Linda.

14   Q   With Linda?

15   A   Yes.

16   Q   How many occasions?

17   A   Once.

18   Q   Now, being a friend of Lisa Piel's, have you ever

19   talked to her about getting high from coke or

20   using coke?

21   A   No. We didn't talk about it.

22   Q   Have you ever had any conversations with her,

23   where she told you she'd been at a party and used

24   some coke and gotten high or anything?

25   A   No.

1	Q	Did she ever tell you she'd been somewhere and
2		done some lines or anything?
3	A	No.
4	Q	Now, you say you moved to Austin, Texas, back
5		last year. After you moved to Austin, Texas,
6		have you ever had any contact with Lisa Piel?
7	A	She came to visit last October.
8	Q	At that time was there any discussions regarding
9		the up-coming Grand Jury -- what, at that time,
10		was the up-coming Grand Jury?
11	A	Yes, sir. We talked about it.
12	Q	What, if anything, was said about the Grand Jury?
13	A	That nothing -- basically, they were going to be
14		having one and it was going to be bigger than
15		Charlevoix's.
16	Q	Anything else regarding Grand Jury, at that time,
17		when she was in Texas?
18	A	Not really.
19	Q	Subsequent to that personal visit by Lisa Piel to
20		Texas, had you any conversations with Lisa Piel
21		regarding the Grand Jury?
22	A	She called me.
23	Q	Approximately, when was that?
24	A	Approximately, two months ago.
25	Q	You were in Texas at the time?

1   A   Yes, sir.

2   Q   Did you and her have some kind of conversation

3   regarding the Grand Jury?

4   A   Yes, sir.

5   Q   Could you tell the Grand Jury what the

6   conversation was?

7   A   She had asked me if I had been contacted, and I

8   told her that I had, and that, and she asked me

9   what I was going to do, and I said I got to

10   decide, and I said I have to decide if I was

11   going to come back or not.

12 Q   She asked you if you were going to come back?

13 A   Right.

14 Q   Were you aware, at that time, that Linda Postle

15   had already been here and testified?

16 A   Yes, sir.

17 Q   In fact, you -- it was you and Linda that moved

18   to Texas together?

19 A   Correct.

20 Q   So, you were familiar with Linda having already

21   come up here and testified?

22 A   Right.

23 Q   Did Lisa ever talk with Linda Postle about the

24   Grand Jury and about whether or not she had

25   testified?

```
 1    A    Yes, sir.

 2    Q    Did Linda tell you that?

 3    A    That she -- that she had, yes.

 4    Q    Did Linda Postle tell you about what she had said

 5         about the Grand Jury?

 6    A    No, sir; she didn't.

 7    Q    Did Lisa ask you to say anything in particular,

 8         or to tell anything in particular, if you did

 9         appear before the Grand Jury?

10    A    No, sir.

11    Q    Now, you know Lisa was a police officer?

12    A    Yes, sir.

13    Q    Or, is a police officer, I guess I should say.

14         Being she's a police officer, being involved with

15         drugs would be something illegal, right?

16    A    Yes.

17    Q    Not good for a police officer, right?

18    A    Right.

19    Q    The fact that you used cocaine with her on

20         several occasions, or on at least one occasion

21         knew she was using, and probably on other

22         occasions, did she ever say anything about her

23         use of cocaine?

24    A    Not that I really recall.

25    Q    Did she ever tell you anything about what would
```

1		happen if she got caught, or it was found out she
2		had been using cocaine?
3	A	She never said anything, but, you know, I assumed
4		she would-lose her job.
5	Q	Did she ever say to you, in some fashion, similar
6		to the words not to tell anyone if anyone ever
7		asked?
8	A	Well, it wouldn't be something that I would
9		volunteer.
10	Q	Well --
11	A	I mean, if you asked me on the street, I would
12		say no.
13	Q	I mean, did Lisa ever say anything to you, look,
14		this is something illegal, don't tell anyone what
15		we're doing?
16	A	I don't believe she would ever have to say that.
17	Q	Do you have any doubt about the time that Alice
18		Waybrandt was living there, that Lisa knew that
19		Alice was selling cocaine?
20	A	No.
21	Q	Did Alice ever tell you that or did Linda ever
22		tell you that, or anything about that Alice was
23		selling cocaine?
24	A	I knew Allison was selling cocaine.
25	Q	And, Alice was living with Lisa at that time; is

```
 1         that right?

 2    A    Right.

 3    Q    Do you think that Lisa would not have known that

 4         there was any cocaine being sold or used at her

 5         residence?

 6    A    I really couldn't say, but I don't believe that

 7         cocaine was sold from her residence.  I believe

 8         that it was sold up in the Riverside Bar, in

 9         Alanson.

10    Q    I'm going to change directions a little bit now.

11         Marijuana -- did you ever use marijuana with Lisa

12         Piel?

13    A    Never.

14    Q    Did you ever see Lisa Piel use marijuana?

15    A    No, sir.

16    Q    Other than the one time that you were right

17         there, when Lisa Piel used cocaine at Linda

18         Postle's apartment, and the four times that you

19         described that also occurred, where you believe

20         was set up in the bedroom and she'd go in there

21         --

22    A    Right.

23    Q    -- do you have any other knowledge of Lisa Piel

24         using cocaine?

25    A    Not that I can think of, sir.
```

284

1 Q   Did anyone ever tell you that Lisa Piel had used

2   cocaine with them?

3 A   No, sir.

4 Q   Linda Postle never told you?

5 A   Well, Linda, but I mean --

6 Q   Okay. How many times did Linda Postle say she

7   used cocaine with Lisa?

8 A   Maybe ten times or fifteen times.

9 Q   And, this would be spread out during that time

10   period?

11 A   Right.

12 Q   Again, what time period are we talking about

13   here?

14 A   Well, I'm talking from April of '89 -- March of

15   '89 to April of '90.

16 Q   Okay. From the time you first started cocaine

17   until you went to Texas?

18 A   Right.

19 Q   Approximately -- then what you are saying is ten

20   occasions, in conversations with Linda Postle,

21   she had said that she and Lisa used cocaine ten

22   different times? Do you want me to rephrase it?

23   It looks like you're a little lost.

24 A   I'm kind of.

25 Q   You said Linda told you that she and Lisa had

1   used cocaine and it had been used on ten

2   different occasions?

3 A   She told me that one time.

4 Q   She told you one time that she and Lisa had done

5   cocaine on about ten different occasions?

6 A   Right.

7 Q   Would you say -- would she say where she had done

8   the cocaine?

9 A   No.

10 Q   Just a few more questions. Was Lori Jewell

11   friends with Lisa Piel?

12 A   They knew each other. I mean, I guess they were

13   friends.

14 Q   Did you ever see them party together or get

15   together?

16 A   No.

17   * * *

18 Q   Talking about the time when you and Lisa did the

19   cocaine, there in Linda Postle apartment, where

20   she pulled it from underneath the couch, what was

21   said by Lisa?

22 A   I don't remember what she said at that point,

23   sir.

24 Q   Was there anything said, first of all?

25 A   Sir, we had been drinking quite a bit. doing

1   shots, and to be honest with you, I can't

2   remember.

3   Q   Did Lisa seem surprised by finding cocaine there?

4   A   I really don't remember, sir.

5   Q   And, it wasn't an occasion, oh, my God, what's

6   this stuff, or anything like that was it?

7   A. No.

8   Q   So, kind of in summary, then, Mrs. Woodruff, you

9   used cocaine with Lisa Piel on one occasion at

10   Linda Postle's apartment, around Christmas time,

11   1989?

12   A   Yes, sir.

13   Q   And, she used two lines at that time and you used

14   one line?

15   A   Right.

16   Q   And, you know of about four other occasions where

17   cocaine was available at Linda Postle's

18   apartment, and she could have used cocaine on any

19   of those occasions?

20   A   Right.

21   Q   Because it was all available for anyone to go in

22   the bedroom, whenever they wanted to?

23   A   Correct.

24   Q   You have no reason to believe that Lisa wouldn't

25   have gone back there?

1 A Would not have gone back there? Right.

2 Q Other than the names that you already talked

3 about in the beginning, about people you used

4 cocaine with, who you bought the cocaine from,

5 and you sold cocaine to, is there anyone else,

6 other than those from whom you received drugs,

7 either coke, marijuana or whatever, in the last

8 three years?

9 A No, sir.

10 Q Is there anyone else, other than what you already

11 mentioned here, where you saw someone deliver

12 drugs to other people?

13 A Yes.

14 Q And, who would that be?

15 A That would be Linda Postle.

16 Q Delivering to who?

17 A Allison, and I think Joyce, I saw once, too.

18 Q Joyce Cruickshank?

19 A Yes.

20 Q Anyone else?

21 A Tina Voss.

22 Q Anyone else?

23 A That's all I can think of right now, sir.

24 Q Okay. That's all the questions I have for you.

25 The members of the Grand Jury may wish to ask

1   questions of you at this time.

2   * * *

3   JUROR #8: Did Linda Postle live with

4   Lisa Piel at one time?

5   WITNESS: Yes, she did.

6   JUROR #8: How long a time did they live

7   together?

8   WITNESS: I really don't know. I could

9   guess maybe three years.

10   JUROR #9: It is my understanding, is

11   this right, that Lisa Piel is a police officer?

12   WITNESS: Yes, sir.

13   JUROR #9: Do you know where she got her

14   drugs?

15   WITNESS: To my knowledge she never had

16   any herself. Linda Postle would -- I can only

17   speculate on that.

18   JUROR #9: Thank you.

19   JUROR #10: You mentioned Allison

20   Waybrandt lived with Lisa Piel?

21   WITNESS: Right.

22   JUROR #10: And, Linda Postle lived with

23   Lisa Piel?

24   WITNESS: Right.

25   JUROR #10: Is there anyone else of

1 these people, that you know, that lived with Lisa

2 Piel?

3 WITNESS: No.

4 JUROR #15: The drugs that you sold to

5 Tina Voss and her sister, Sheryl, where did you

6 get those?

7 WITNESS: They were Linda Postle's.

8 JUROR #9: This supply of drugs seems to

9 be rather uninterrupted?

10 WITNESS: You mean, did they --

11 JUROR #9: In other words, they didn't

12 have long periods where they didn't have any

13 drugs?

14 WITNESS: No.

15 JUROR #12: Who mostly supplied the

16 money for the supply of the cocaine? Did you

17 pool it together or did you help -- did you help

18 support some of that?

19 WITNESS: No, Linda Postle.

20 JUROR #12: Linda Postle?

21 WITNESS: Right.

22 JUROR #12: Thank you.

23 JUROR #3: Did you ever attend a party

24 with John Rautio and Lisa and Alice Waybrandt?

25 WITNESS: There was an occasion on New

1   Year's day, of 1990, that they were all at Linda

2   Postle's house, when Linda Postle came to pick me

3   up. When I got back, John Rautio left, so I was

4   never there -- I mean for a brief second, but

5   that's it.

6   JUROR #7: You said you observed Linda

7   delivering drugs to Alice Waybrandt. Do you know

8   the last time that she did that, approximately?

9   WITNESS: I would -- I really couldn't

10   say.

11   JUROR #7: Was it within that '89 and

12   '90?

13   WITNESS: Yeah. It would have been

14   probably, like, from October to April, of that

15   time.

16   JUROR #2: Did Linda Piel ever have a

17   boyfriend?

18   WITNESS: There is no Linda Piel.

19   JUROR #2: Lisa Piel -- excuse me.

20   WITNESS: Not that I know of for sure.

21   JUROR #14: When you used cocaine with

22   Lisa Piel, you know she was a police officer and

23   it never bothered you that you did that?

24   WITNESS: No, ma'am. At that point, it

25   didn't.

```
1              JUROR #14:  Thank you.

2              JUROR #9:  You mentioned that someone

3        obtained drugs from a man's name.  What was that

4        name?

5              WITNESS:  John Rautio.

6              JUROR #9:  Did Lisa Piel know John

7        Rautio?

8              WITNESS:  I think she knew -- I don't

9        know if she knew him, but she knew of him, at

10       that point.  But, when Allison got involved with

11       him, then she would bring him over to Lisa's

12       house while Lisa was working.

13             JUROR #9:  Thank you.

14             MR. ENGEL:  Okay.  If you folks don't

15       have any other questions, I have a couple

16       follow-ups.  So, if somebody thinks of something

17             --

18  BY MR. ENGEL:

19  Q    Mrs. Woodruff, speaking of John Rautio, then, did

20       you know John Rautio as being a drug dealer?

21  A    Yes.

22  Q    That was pretty common knowledge, wasn't it?

23  A    Yes.

24  Q    It would be very difficult to expect a police

25       officer not to know he's a drug dealer?
```

```
 1    A    That's right.

 2    Q    You are talking about this one time that you were

 3         supposed to meet up with Lisa and Linda and John,

 4         and something happened that you didn't get to

 5         meet up with him.  Maybe I misunderstood what you

 6         were saying a few minutes ago?

 7    A    It was on a New Year's day, and they were at

 8         Linda's apartment.  When Linda came to get me,

 9         then when she got back, John left.

10    Q    Who was all at Linda's apartment?

11    A    Allison, Lisa, and Linda, and John.

12    Q    And, John?

13    A    Uh-huh.

14    Q    Was there cocaine being used at that time?

15    A    I don't know, sir.  I wasn't there.  When I got

16         back, I went to the bedroom.  When I came back,

17         John had left.

18    Q    Had anyone mentioned they were going to be using

19         cocaine at a party, or whatever was going on?

20    A    They drank after that, quite heavily, but there

21         was no cocaine there, unless they done it before

22         I arrived.  I don't know.

23    Q    Nobody mentioned anything?

24    A    No.

25    Q    That would have been on New Year's of 1990?
```

1   A   Yes, sir.

2   Q   Regarding Tina Voss, do you know if she was a

3   friend of Lisa's?

4   A   No, she wasn't.

5   MR. ENGEL: That's all I have, unless

6   one of the grand jurors have a question. Okay.

7   Thank you very much, Miss Woodruff. I want to

8   remind you of the oath of secrecy that you have

9   taken. We take that very seriously. So,

10   anything that has been said here shall not go out

11   of here.

12   WITNESS: Right.

13   MR. ENGEL: I need to see you and your

14   attorney outside for just a minute, to go over

15   procedural things. Please wait outside, if you

16   would.

17   -0-

18

19

20

21

22

23

24

25

```
 1    STATE OF MICHIGAN    )
                           )  ss.
 2    COUNTY OF EMMET      )

 3               I, Sandra K. Davids, Certified Shorthand

 4    Reporter, State of Michigan, do hereby certify that the

 5    foregoing pages 1 through 33, inclusive, comprise a

 6    full, true and correct transcript of the proceedings

 7    and testimony taken in the Multi-County Citizen's Grand

 8    Jury on August 21, 1991, of Julie Woodruff, as edited

 9    by the Honorable Richard M. Pajtas, Emmet County

10    Circuit Court Judge.

11    _____ Sandra K David 10/30/91
12    SANDRA K. DAVIDS, CSR-1033

13

14

15

16

17

18

19

20

21

22

23

24

25
```

LISA'S STORY

'I'm so tired,
tired of it all''

14

Resignation

T he headline read, "Petoskey police officer resigns." This by John Charles Robbins, News-Review staff writer. Lisa's photo, apparently taken at the time of her final court indictment on December 19, 1991, shows not a resigned person in demeanor but rather one contemplating the rules of "justice" she supposedly served for more than thirteen years.

"This was a "deal" all the way. A plea bargain, as it is termed. After the Grand Jury proceedings the city figured it had enough of a case and, as aforesaid, prosecuted.

Lisa, herself, as a friend later described it, was, "tired of it all." That is the look that may be discerned on the almost side view of Lisa on that day, as may be seen in the photograph section in the center of this book.

The Grand Jury took its toll. All the subpoenaed persons questioned were plainly led to their testimonies by the inquisitive prosecutors, all of them being intimidated by threat of actual jail time if their testimonies did not conclude with the prosecuting allegations. It has always been a curious premise that persons who testify under duress of conviction themselves are taken quite so literally as to condemnation of former friends and associates.

The plea bargain had been negotiated by attorneys Mark Blumer of the Attorney General's Office and Richard Abood of Lansing for the defence–Lisa. Lisa had signed a letter of resignation just prior to this final court appearance, this being a "key condition to the plea agreement," according to Mark Blumer. Her lawyer, Richard Abood informed the court that this had already been signed and delivered.

This process, duly reported and made to sound like legal house-cleaning, was actually the end result of a syndrome known to lawyers (and hence politicians) as subornation. To suborn is to induce through underhanded means someone to do some improper or unlawful thing, such as commit perjury. Sadly, this is a mainstay of police and prosecutorial work in making the sought charges stick.

Since the 1960's when criminal activity was seen as a societal ill rather than as a heinous and deliberate action or reaction, the public cry for more legislation has resulted in such post-civil rights tactics as subornation in attempt to level the playing field once again to more early American "law and order"–which in itself was a hodge-podge of ethnic inequity but in retrospect seemed to get the job done more expeditiously. Perhaps this accounts for the moral double standard of police work and courtroom jurisprudence, often knowing what's right while doing what's wrong. The inversionary stratagem of bending the rules to benefit the desired result is seen most glaringly in "plea bargaining."

The Grand Jury witness testimonies, in particular those of Alice Waybrandt, would seem to be forced and drawn out, digging for inferences that were hardly or not there. Why else would this witness be constrained to testify on three separate occasions? And, as seen in the various commentaries following each witness' testimony, there was no doubt more to the story than implicated felons guided to repentance by turning on their own kind. Any issues but for those that condemned Lisa Piel were occluded, dismissed and totally disregarded.

Any bare reference to Lisa's realistically harboring intent to use drugs or distribute them in any way are vague and in legal terms, "hear-say" only. No "hard evidence" existed at any time, only the inevitable "allegations." This, in fact, is one of the purposes of this compilation of events: to throw the replicate of allegations back in the faces of the one-sided accusational body perpetrating the sequences of probable malfeasance that so malignly disrupted the career of one law officer whose only admitted misdeed was based in not revealing a potential drug abuser.

Even the casual observer of these transcripts might well perceive the oppressive demeanor of that court of inquisition. And "Inquisition" it apparently was, with closed doors and supposed secrecy prevailing, even though the paper-thin walls of the little public building were afterward said to be a joke as to covertness, and as each witness saw each other witness in the hallway outside waiting, hardly approached the clandestine tribunal that it claimed to be. There may even be, as had been suggested thereafter, some illegality to those proceedings in terms of their pre-emptive and exclusionary manner and the rural setting in the very small town of Topinabee where secrecy cannot and does not exist.

As Art Piel, Lisa's father, suggested in one of his written critiques of the jury, the Northern Michigan community is unaccustomed to variances in societal input, changes of cultural acceptance, and very insulated as to opinion, with aberrant behavior suggestions being anathematic and repugnant to them and hence conducive to condemnation. This anthropological synusia, though in flux in latter years, still is found to be the bastion of "normalcy" in the North and is bolstered by the courts and the press, furtively backed by the private clubs and orders of influence.

The City of Petoskey, Emmet County, and contiguous areas surrounding conspired to bring such an onslaught of charges down upon Lisa that to cope with them some compromise was needed. This is not an unusual tactic in these times. Many charges are brought, some overlapping others, acts are broken up into fragmented parts, all in expectation of the almighty plea bargain that usually precludes any change of an outright acquittal of the defendant. In other words, pile on enough accusations to where the accused says, "alright, alright, what does it take to get out of this?", and then police and prosecutor take credit for yet another "bust" for justice, the American way, and such propaganda as furthers justification for more funds allocated and political careers to be furthered.

There is a minor drug problem in North Michigan and it is not the purpose of this writing to belittle attempts at curtailing hard drug activities–those which tend to lead to blatant criminal actions–nor suggest that all legal procedures are based on discriminatory precedent. This book is about one instance of misconduct over a thirteen-plus-year span of time that ended up taking the life of the individual involved. Drugs, however, are the most expedient means of arrest and conviction in all areas of the country. A tiny package of dope can be easily "found" anywhere, in anyone's car, clothing upon searching, hidden in any closet or bathroom of a suspected user or dealer, or anyone who just

300

happens to be disliked by the authorities. This is true, and, much more significantly, it happens.

In Lisa's case, the mere suggestion (spelled allegation) of drugs was, with the added allusion of homosexuality,. more than enough to tip the weighted dice of indictment to a predictable landing of predisposition of guilt. The wearisome enactment of Grand Jury question and answer sessions led Lisa to her exasperated stance of, "I'm so tired, tired of it all"–this after thirteen-plus years as chronicled herein. The wear-you-down style vindictiveness finally worked its excoriating way to the heart and soul of Lisa Piel. She succumbed–but only to the one charge of compassion for a friend involved helplessly in illegal substance use. The other charges were unfounded and spurious.

There remain only scanty recollections of this period of Lisa's life previous to the Grand Jury sessions. The "late March of 1988" inference to drug knowledge indicates that someone was watching her, that someone being the Straights Area Narcotics Enforcement squad of course. So, it is presumable that forces of conspiracy were becoming more subtle and clandestine than merely trying to infer illegal coffee breaks. Lisa's younger acquaintance, Alice Waybrant, came to town in late 1988 and met Lisa in 1989; As it is known that Alice became involved with drugs, due to being a musician and their availability henceforth, soon after her arrival in Petoskey, it seems that this was most likely the tie-in with Lisa that promulgated the watch by SANE, no doubt aided by the local constabulary. Alice Waybrant became one of Lisa's roommates as had others named as witnesses in the indictment of Lisa. It seems in retrospect that there was drug activity surrounding the house on Arlington Street due to Lisa's roommates and the appearance at times of John Rautio–who later served one year in jail for drug violations. A curious and very telling, though barely noticeable, inclusion in the report of agreement to follow is the signature of Joseph T. Rautio on this form as Union Representative. Joe is, of course, the brother of John.

The "SETTLEMENT AGREEMENT AND RELEASE," as it is titled, signed on February 12th and 14th, is carefully worded by the cooperation of both lawyers involved. There are, however, several observations to be made that reveal the potential impropriety of such an agreement. It is absolute lawyer talk in its attempts at bipartisan absolutism, but discrepancies are there for the perspicacious eye. The first discrepancy is in letter (c) under number 2., which states, "To the extent permitted by law, decline to release the contents of Piel's personnel file or this Settlement Agreement and Release to third parties not signatory . . .", suggests a definitive paranoia of the parts of the authorities much in keeping with the manner of subterfuge employed heretofore, as if any scrutiny and publicity might be embarrassing or likely to cause reversals of this agreement. Then under issue number 3. (2) "Piel agrees to immediately withdraw her grievance filed under the collective bargaining agreement between the City and the Fraternal Order of Police.", there seems to have been some squirming underlying this clause.

The most salient revelation to leap forth from these pages is issue number 5, which states in full: "Nothing in this Settlement Agreement and Release is an admission or confession of liability or wrongdoing by Piel, the City or the City's agents, officers, employees, servants and representatives; nor shall this settlement Agreement and Release or the settlement itself be interpreted or construed to be such an admission or confession." No wonder they didn't want anybody else reading this!! If there was no wrongdoing, what the hell was this thing all about in the first place?

The article on Lisa Piel's resignation reads like a Dick Tracy Crimestoppers comic strip blurb as reported by Robbins of the Petoskey News-Review. There is no in-depth "All Things Considered" therein; it's chopped-up allusions to factual material which comes across much like 1950's newsreels, disjointed and surreal. John Robbins makes Lisa's resignation seem like a real drug bust, a "bad cop," a small town taking revenge against an evil-doer, when in fact no deed was done by her but rather to her. This failure of the local press is no doubt contingent to the overall workings of the Political landscape/cityscape attending the inhibited small-town atmosphere of Northwestern Lower Michigan. To read this particular article one might assume that a truly bad cop had been found out and might wonder what other depravities this lady had sunk to. Such is the attempted moral stance of the small-town bureaucracy in collusion with the local business population, not to omit those church-going adjuncts who allow these travesties of justice to be promulgated in the name of peace and brotherhood. No one would take Lisa's side in this matter. No one but her family, a few close friends, and one rather mysterious man who was to play a curious part in events to come. That man is J. D. Reed. Watch for his involvement to surface and evolve.

For purpose of reference the complete Settlement Agreement is reprinted here:

"SETTLEMENT AGREEMENT AND RELEASE

"This Settlement Agreement and Release is made and executed by and between the City of Petoskey (the "City") and Lisa M. Piel "Piel"), on the date set forth below. In consideration of the promises described below, the parties agree as follows:

"1. The City has employed Piel in its Police and Public Safety Department from September 25, 1978 to the present. For reasons unique to each party and the current circumstances, the City has agreed to accept Piel's resignation in exchange for this Settlement Agreement and Release.

"2. Upon execution of this Settlement Agreement and Release, the City agrees to:

"(a) Reduce Piel's pending unpaid suspension by one week and pay her through September 6, 1991, which amount equals gross pay of $551.20 ($23.78 per hour x 40 hours), subject to all tax and payroll withholdings.

"(b) Provide Piel the opportunity to continue her health care insurance coverage pursuant to COBRA, 42 USC S 300bb etseq.

"(c) To the extent permitted by law, decline to release the contents of Piel's personnel file or this

Settlement Agreement and Release to third parties not signatory to this Settlement Agreement and Release, except as to those individuals employed by the City or working under its control and direction on a "need to know" basis.

"(d) In accordance with the pertinent plan documents, Piel will be eligible to receive any accrued pension benefits under the MERS plan and benefits under the deferred compensation plan.

"(e) Pay Piel within eight (8) days of the execution of this Settlement Agreement and Release, 160 hours of accrued vacation pay totalling $2,204.80 ($13.78 per hour x 160 hours) subject to all tax and withholdings.

"3. In exchange for the promises set forth in Paragraph 2 of this Settlement Agreement and Release, Piel agrees to immediately resign from her employment with the City. This resignation will be effective upon execution of this Settlement Agreement and Release. In addition, (1) in light of her resignation, Piel agrees that she is not eligible for unemployment benefits under the Michigan Employment Security Act; and (2) Piel agrees to immediately withdraw her grievance filed under the collective bargaining agreement between the City and the Fraternal Order of Police.

"4. In further consideration for the promises of the City set forth in Paragraph 2 of this Settlement Agreement and Release and except for claims under the Age Discrimination and Employment Act, 29 U.S.C. S 621, Piel voluntarily agrees to and hereby does knowingly, fully and completely waive any and all claims, demands, causes of action, damages, costs, expenses, compensation, and sums of money, including but not limited to: any claim for wrongful discharge, just cause dismissal, breach of contract, breach of the collective bargaining agreement, negligence, defamation, fraud or misrepresentation, invasion of privacy, violation of ERISA, 29 U.S.C. S 1002 et seq, for any and all state and federal employment discrimination (including sex, race, religion, creed, national origin, height, weight, age and handicap), under Title VII of the Civil Rights Act, 42 U.S.C. S 2000 et seq, Equal Pay Act, 29 U.S.C. S 206, Rehabilitation Act, 29 U.S.C. S 701 et seq, Americans With Disabilities Act, 42 U.S.C. S 12101 et. seq, Michigan's Elliot-Larsen Civil Rights Act, MCL 37.2101 et. seq, and Michigan's Handicappers' Civil Rights Act, MCL 37.1101 et seq that has been asserted or might hereafter be asserted arising out of or in any way connected with her employment at or the termination of her employment with the city. This waiver includes, but shall not be limited to the right to initiate, proceed with or participate in any state or federal lawsuit, any administrative complaints, statutory or common law claims, or civil rights charges, that she has or may have against the City, its officers, agents, servants and employees, as well as any predecessor or successor and assigns to them, that has been asserted or might hereafter be asserted arising out of or in any way connected with her employment at or the termination of her employment with the City.

"5. Nothing in this Settlement Agreement and Release is an admission or confession of liability or wrongdoing by Piel, the city or the City's agents, officers, employees, servants and representatives; nor shall this Settlement Agreement and Release or the settlement itself be interpreted or construed to be such an admission or confession.

"6. This Settlement Agreement and Release constitutes the entire understanding between the parties. No prior contemporaneous, oral or written, express or implied agreement shall have any effect.

305

Further, this Settlement Agreement and Release may not be modified or amended except in writing by both of the parties.

"7. The terms of this Settlement Agreement are to be interpreted, construed, enforced and performed under the laws of the State of Michigan.

"8. This Settlement Agreement and Release shall be binding upon the heirs, representatives, successors and assigns to each party.

"9. Piel further acknowledges that she has carefully read each provision of the Settlement Agreement and Release, that she understands its contents, that she has been allowed the opportunity to consider its contents, that she has been allowed the opportunity to consider its terms and consult with an attorney before executing this Settlement Agreement and Release, and she, accordingly, knowingly signs this Settlement Agreement and Release as her own free and voluntary act and deed.

"10. The parties have executed this Settlement Agreement and Release on this day and year indicated below.

Date: __2-14-92__ (signed) Lisa M. Piel
                 Lisa M. Piel
Date: __2-14-92__ (signed) Richard J. Abood
                 Witness
Date: __2-12-92__ (signed) George Korthauer
                 George Korthauer, City Manager, Petoskey
Date: __2-14-92__ (signed) Joseph T. Rautio
                 Union Representative"

After such rhetorical and nomenclatural redundancy, it might easily be supposed that anyone would sign just to avoid any more of that.

And this is indeed the prosecutorial manner of business employed in "criminal justice." Lawyers essentially run this country, from the White House to the recording industry. The handshake, with all the personal honor it implied, is gone, and with it went access to the whole truth behind any given circumstance. "The truth, the whole truth, and nothing but the truth" is an anachronism now, a rhetorical chant not at all intended to comply with its wording. Supersedence of format has allowed this to happen, circumvention of issues by clever or innovative linguistics, one side against the other, constant rewriting and reinterpreting of statutes, Supreme Court decisions, retrospectives and public opinion have all added up to, at best, a collage of objectives that are hubristically called "justice," but which when seen in long-term overview are but constrained visions of attitudes of the constantly changing era. In this case in particular, once again, so much for justice.

Lisa Piel was now officially unemployed as of February 1992. It is uncertain but it appears that she had no roommates subsequent to the Grand Jury sessions since some of her roommates, past and present, had testified. She had a little money from the settlement and momentarily settled in to her home sans distractions to contemplate a thirteen-year career abruptly terminated. What next?

As J. C. Robbins has so aptly reported, the Agreement provided that,

> "Piel would resign from the police department.
>
> "Piel would plead guilty to willful neglect of duty, a misdemeanor offense. The plea was offered on the condition Piel receive a six-month deferred sentence.
>
> "Three felony charges would be dismissed without prejudice; meaning they can be brought again. These include cocaine possession and misconduct in public office.
>
> "If she violates probation in the next six months, the felony charges can be immediately re-issued against her.

"Judge Harvey C. Varnum granted Piel a six-month deferred sentence. Piel has only to remain lawful, report monthly to the district court probation agent, and pay $15 a month in probation oversight fees. No court costs were assessed and no fine was imposed against Piel."

In a parallel editorial Mr. Robbins journalized the City's comments as to the outcome of this litigation, stating, "Local officials voiced satisfaction with the outcome of Lisa Piel's criminal case. . . . The judge, Harvey Varnum, said, 'My learned opinion is the agreement serves the ends of justice . . . and the needs of this community.' "

"He (the judge) congratulated attorneys Mark Blumer of the Attorney General's office and Richard Abood of Lansing for working out the agreement. Late Friday city manager George Korthauer told the News-Review, 'The City had nothing whatsoever to say about the criminal portion of the matter';" and "As for the plea bargain, Korthauer said, 'I'm well satisfied by the outcome of it;' adding, 'the City, the city staff and the public are well-served by her resignation.'

"Public Safety Director Tom Postelnick told the News-Review today, 'I'm satisfied with the plea agreement because it includes Lisa Piel's resignation from the police department . . . If not for the grand jury, and SANE, and the excellent police work of the officers involved in the investigation, this matter may never have been resolved.'

"Asked how the public may react to the plea bargain and disposition of Piel's case, Postelnick said, 'I think the punishment of losing a 14-year career is quite substantial.' –(signed) John Charles Robbins"

308

The 21st of August, 1991 marked the end of the Grand Jury proceedings against Lisa. The 30th of that month signified the date of her arrest and suspension. No time wasted there. To recap the charges held against Lisa, it again falls to the reportage of John Charles Robbins who elucidated thus:

> "Count I of the indictment alleged Piel 'did knowingly or intentionally' possess cocaine from the fall of 1989 through early April 1988.
>
> "Count II of the indictment alleged Piel possessed cocaine from the fall of 1988 through the spring of 1990. Possession of less than 25 grams of cocaine is a felony punishable by up to four years in prison and/or a $25,000 fine.
>
> "Count III of the indictment alleged Piel 'did, while a public officer or employee charged with enforcement of the criminal laws of the State of Michigan, commit the crime of Misconduct in Office . . .' from the fall of 1989 through the spring 1990, according to the court file. The misconduct charge is a felony punishable by up to five years in prison and/or a $10,000 fine.
>
> "Count IV of the indictment is the misdemeanor charge Piel pleaded guilty to: willful neglect of duty."

Robbins concludes with, "The grand jury investigated drug trafficking during 1991, and shut down on January 8, 1992. Piel is one of 22 people indicted by the multi-county grand jury, stemming from Emmet County cases."

As perceived from the leap of logic between allegations and the severity of the potential punishments, it seems not only possible but somewhat probable that Lisa Piel might have even received some jail time or fine or both from these charges had she decided to fight them as she had originally planned to do. With the many forces against her, her own friends forced to testify—some dubiously—the entire department decidedly not in her favor, and the public mood discernibly disposed toward lynching, any outcome imaginable might have transpired from a lengthy and drawn-out jury trial of the quagmire of charges, witnesses, political ambitions, animosities and public sentiment prevalent at the time. These sentiments and proclivities seem not to have softened or changed in the ensuing years 1992 to 1997.

Lisa paid her $15. a month in "oversight probation fees," retired to her home overlooking Lake Michigan's beautiful Little Traverse Bay, and meditated on the now-inevitable conclusions to her tenure in police work.

On June 12, 1992, she successfully completed a training program in INTRODUCTION TO COMPUTERS at North Central Michigan College in Petoskey. On October 9, 1992, a copy of a letter of cover exists indicating seeking of work in the private sector as an investigator.

> "HUNTINGTON RESEARCH ASSOCIATE Ltd.
> 225 South Main, Royal Oak, MI
> "Re: Investigator Position
>
> Dear Mr. Conway:
>
> "Thank you for considering me as a possible candidate for a position with your firm.
>
> "As requested, enclosed is a copy of a report dictated by me involving a fatal fire. Please note this occured in 1984. Since then the format has changed along with my experience and abilities, prior to my resignation from the police department in February of this year.
>
> "I know I could be an asset to your agency and look forward to hearing form you in the near future.
>
> Very Truly Yours,
>
> (signed) Lisa M. Piel"

A local attorney, Michael Buckingham, was retained in October of 1992 to attempt to expunge records from Lisa's police file. His initial letter of October 26, 1992 is as follows:

"Mark E. Blumer
Assistant Attorney General
P.O. Box 30218
Lansing, Michigan 48908
"Re: People v Lisa Piel
File No. 92-118-FY

"Dear Mr. Blumer:

"Please be advised that I represent Lisa Piel in the above captioned matter. While the case has been dismissed, there is a small housekeeping matter which needs to be finished: return of all arrest cards; fingerprints; photographs; and the elimination of any evidence of my client's arrest.

"Enclosed please find: my appearance; a proposed Order; and a copy of the plea and sentence transcript. If the enclosed Order meets with your approval, please sign the same and return it to my office. I will see that it is filed with the court and provide you with a true copy of the same.

"Thank you for your anticipated cooperation,

"Very truly yours,

(signed)

Michael B. Buckingham"

The only other relevant data preserved on this matter is this brief form dated October 26, 1992 as well, and apparently submitted to judge Harvey C. Varnum (whose signature does not appear above his typed name) stating:

"It is further ordered that any person(s) or agencies having caused any criminal history lien by way of example CCH to indicate Defendant's arrest regarding these matters shall promptly see that said criminal history lien or CCH shall not show evidence of Defendant's arrest."

Buckingham's signature appears below but not Mark Blumer's whose name is also indicated in type and underline.

It is not known to what extent this request was granted, but as previously suggested, these records may still exist intact.

Lisa later rented a room to an acquaintance, Jennifer Novenske, to help make ends meet, she being unemployed. Ultimately she decided upon the wallpapering business as her next trade. A photo of her mini van is show in the picture section herein.

She received some help in this venture by the aforementioned J. D. Reed who is a local resident and businessman–and enigmatic figure. Dave Reed helped Lisa with promotion and similar expertise for her wallpapering concern which was called "Paper Chasers." For a new business she did well enough and it promised to be a fulfilling venture in the long run. Self-employment seemed to suit her well. She would hire her friends occasionally to help on jobs.

Dave Reed, as he goes by, is a married man, or at least was at that time, 1992. He was known to have had some affiliation with Jennifer Novenske but this is sketchy. Reed had had two drunk driving busts in California from his younger days but had yet remained unencumbered by legal complications in Petoskey, though these would soon be garnered, as will be shown. He is a corporate executive for a local business, as reported by John Charles Robbins in the News-Review paper.

Jennifer Novenske, of whom little is known, evidently liked to enjoy herself, and some even commented on her being a "party animal." This was to become a problem later for Lisa when she herself became overindulgent with alcohol for a time and subsequently "dried out" at a rehab center.

As Lisa's world grew smaller she may have relied too heavily on the few friends and acquaintances she had. She had a supportive family, of course, but they were few. She had always entertained at her home, always her house was a welcome stopover for any friend passing by. On a few occasions certain persons were actually told to leave the premises by passing officers in cruisers. The harassment by the city continued in petty ways.

It is still not totally known what was the impetus toward such a torrent of hatred as was directed at Lisa. There were political ambitions to be sure, there were gender-based animosities, there were innuendoes of homosexual leanings, and there were the ubiquitous drug insinuations. Nothing of legal basis was ever proven substantially. Nothing of social origin ever stood up as aberrant behavior. She was singled out because she was the first and only police woman in town. Through constant rumor the insinuations eventually stuck until now in 1997 she is still alluded to by some local residents as "the lesbian cop." Why? Because local prejudice dies hard and slowly.

Apart from the drug use by Lisa's friends not much seems to have interrupted her existence during this time period that could cause any abnormal stress. She probably, by all accounts, did not know about most of this drug use since it seems to have been effectively hidden from her. After the Grand Jury indictments, the resignation, and Lisa's finding a potential of a new career, most aspects of her life seem to have quieted down. She was drinking a little more heavily, it is true. The aftermath of depression would rise and she drank to attempt to ease her mind. It was a gregarious time though, all in all, with enough camaraderie to belie the penultimate events to follow.

Sometime in 1994 Lisa voluntarily went to an alcohol detoxification and rehabilitation center. She had determined that she was losing control of that fine line between casual/social drinking and compulsive drunkenness. Most of her friends and roommates drank, her relatively new friend, Dave Reed drank, and the atmosphere at Lisa's home never having been against alcohol, it may have posed some problems for her in sobriety. Friends can be a detriment at moments like this, if they are accustomed to the "party" aspect of a person and place. Lisa was known to have been in the company of Dave Reed and Jennifer Novenske, the latter who had said to a mutual friend that she "wasn't going to change her lifestyle for Lisa," where alcohol was present–Lisa was not drinking. She was a person of strong character who, when something was perceived as needing to be done, did it. This character trait is probably what allowed her to exist so long under adverse conditions at the police department, served her well in abstinence from drink, but ultimately her sense of dramatic sincerity might have been the catalyst which led her over the precipice. But this is only conjecture since events to come are, as usual, ambiguous. As it is said, truth is stranger than fiction, these penultimate segments next raise perhaps more questions than answers.

The only blatant hint of events to follow comes as an account of Jennifer Novenske's having taken Lisa's hand gun when moving out of Lisa's house, apparently after an altercation between the two. Lisa thereupon is said to have gone to the domicile where Jennifer was staying, broken into her car—a task she was experienced in—and retrieved her pistol. This sinister-sounding statement certainly seems "loaded" with potential for tragedy. It is not known how much, if any, drinking might have played a part in this sequence.

15

The Wrong Hand
On The Gun

1 994 concluded the second year of Bill Clinton's inaugural advent. After Maya Angelou's moving and poetic eulogy to this promised return to decent politics began to wear thin, and Clinton himself began to exhibit certain inconsistencies, a certain let-down feeling pervaded the country's atmosphere. Lisa Piel must have certainly felt this herself for her career ended at the time Bill Clinton was elected. Diane Smith, the County Prosecutor and political opportunist–and hence, her nemesis–lost her bid for judgeship locally at about this time. Lisa at more than two years into her life after police work, felt the conflicting thoughts of ending/beginning and tenuous feelings of foraging for direction and balance within a basically unbalanced society.

The National Debt was running rampant, which caused more uncertainty in investment and monetary matters in general, an uneasiness that spilled over into even the most picayune decisions of finance. With the Soviet Union's collapse and promise of Democracy looming, the democratic world, which is largely the U.S.A., had a lot to live up to. This image of example was not exemplary. Still, as in Russia, the "party" goes on. In comfortable, as opposed to abject, poverty, the growing strata of poor still ate and slept well enough, while in replicate the "outerclass" of political/economic turmoil here turned to homelessness to point out that while democracy was welcome in Russia it did not provide the automatic fix that was presupposed.

Lisa had a house to run. A nice house, as said, overlooking the magnificent bay of Lake Michigan apparent from her every north portal and capacious front deck. Many congenial gatherings were held on this deck.

Jennifer Novenske was Lisa's roommate that summer and fall. They reportedly were "fighting a lot," but about what is not known. By October of 1994 Jennifer had moved out, Dave Reed had ensconced himself as a friend of Lisa's, her wallpapering business seems to have been paying for itself and there were no apparent indications that she was feeling suicidal.

- -

The Autopsy Report read, "CAUSE OF DEATH: Gunshot wound to heart, MANNER OF DEATH: Suicide, DATE/HOUR OF DEATH: October 8, 1994, approximately 10:00 a.m."

Lisa Piel was found dead in her own bed by her own gun at thirty-seven years of age. This breviloquent statement of summation of course requires much expounding. Why, what, where, who, how, when? The what and when and where and how of the autopsy report are much too brief and official to impart any more than the normal police data gathered at the scene. The pathologist report is rudimentary. "Who" is succinctly addressed simply as "self." "Why" is left to conjecture.

It is perhaps best at this juncture to turn a belated methodology of investigation over to an attorney by name of Ross Hickman who was contacted by Art Piel several months later, and who subsequently wrote to, still, prosecutor, Diane Smith with some pertinent questions and observations as to the investigation and aftermath of Lisa's death.

> "Diane Smith
> Emmet County Prosecuting Attorney
> Emmet County Building
> 200 Division Street
> Petoskey, MI 49770
> Re: Lisa Piel
> January 8, 1996
>
> Dear Ms. Smith,
> "Please be advised that I have been retained by Art Piel to look into the circumstances surrounding his daughter's untimely death. As you know, Mr. Piel has some doubt that his daughter's death was a suicide.
> "The material that he provided seems incomplete and numerous questions remain unanswered. Could you check your records to determine whether he was provided the entire file? If you determine that he was not provided the entire file please forward the missing reports to my attention as soon as possible.

317

I am particularly interested in knowing whether any tests were performed to determine whether Lisa actually fired the gun. Was the gun dusted for fingerprints? If so, were the prints Lisa's? Was there any powder residue on her hands? The gun was found near her left hand. Did the investigation determine that Lisa was right handed?

"I would also like to know whether any attempt was made to confirm the information that was provided by Jennifer Novenske and Dave Reed. Was either of their whereabouts at the time of Lisa's death confirmed by other sources?

"Attached to the report that I reviewed is a letter to Pete Castillo from Dave Reed. This letter makes reference to Mr. Castillo's apparent belief that Mr. Reed was responsible for Lisa's death. Was Mr. Castille ever interviewed by the police? The letter also states:

'In addition certain notes, documents, tapes, photos, chronicle of events and personal details and insights complete with documentation and substantiation have been assembled and secured away from my home to be released to the Piel family and the authorities in the event of any harm to me.'

Were any of these notes, documents, tapes, photos, chronology of events and personal details obtained and reviewed by you?

"A review of the information that I was provided by Mr. Piel would lead one to believe that it was assumed from the beginning of the investigation that Lisa's death was suicide and nothing was done to dispel this assumption.

"It is my understanding that it is standard procedure to treat all shooting deaths as a homicide until the investigation determines otherwise. It is for this reason that I have assured Mr. Piel that there must be additional information that is not in his possession.

"Mr. Piel is not a wealthy man but he is determined to do whatever it takes to determine the cause of Lisa's death. This determination can not be made until we have answers to the questions that I have posed to you. Based on the way he has been treated by the police and your office he has concerns that these questions will go unanswered without affirmative action on his part. If he is required to fund a private investigation of his daughter's death he will do so without regard to any embarrassment that it may cause. Your prompt attention to our request is greatly appreciated. If I have not heard from you by January 22, 1996 I will assume that these answers don't exist and advise Mr. Piel accordingly.

Sincerely Yours,

Ross Hickman"

Diane Smith never answered this letter.

This literary ploy of working backward from aftermath to incident has its benefits as will be demonstrated as events unfold. The police reports and testimonies to follow both eludidate and obscure the perspicacious questions brought up by the previous letter of question. It will be seen that a very inadequate investigation was made and any follow-ups were rendered near-useless since all material evidence was either tampered with or removed. No more than a cursory glance at the surroundings was made and witnesses were neither questioned at length nor searched nor investigated further. No fingerprints were taken, a seemingly blatant oversight in view of a gunshot wound. Police procedure seems to have been limited to a Marshall Dillon type preconception of an inevitability, accepted and even expected by the authorities.

319

Backtracking, the Emmet County Sheriff's Department report provides the most comprehensive examination in overview of that poignant evening in terms of official perceptions and procedural conclusions. The factual matter contained in the following will be both augmented and amended by that which follows this official version.

"EMMET COUNTY SHERIFF'S DEPARTMENT
124-8506-94

"NATURE OF
COMPLAINTS: Suicide

"DATE AND TIME: Reported
                     October 8, 1994
                     at 11:26 p.m.

"LOCATION: 218 Arlington Avenue
                     City of Petoskey, MI

"VICTIM: Lisa Michele Piel W/F

DOB: 7/24/57

"NARRATIVE: Det/Sgt. Timothy Roth received a telephone call on 10/9/94 at 00:21 hours (12:21 a.m.) from Lt. Tony Rice, Petoskey Department of Public Safety.   Lt. Rice was requesting Det. Roth's assistance at 218 Arlington, where Lisa resides and was found dead in her bed from an apparent gunshot wound.   Det. Roth contacted Sgt. Betts and requested his assistance as an Evidence Technician. Det. Roth responded to the scene, arriving at 00:46 hours.

"PRESENT AT SCENE: Upon arrival, the following subjects were present in the residence:
– Lt. Tony Rice
– Officer Jim Kushner, P.P. D.
– Reserve Officer Randy Fosmore, P.P. D.
– Art Piel, Harbor Springs, Father of victim

320

- Ronni & Dan Allor, Harbor Springs, sister & brother-in-law of victim
- Dave Reed, friend of victim
- Greg Justis, Petoskey, attorney

"CONTACT LT. RICE: Det. Roth met with Lt. Rice upon arrival. Lt. Rice advised Det Roth that Piel had a gunshot wound to the chest and had been checked for life signs by Life+Link personnel. Lt. Rice further advised the emotions of family and friend present in the house was anti-police, and very antagonistic which is why Lt. Rice was requesting Det. Roth handle the investigation.

"INITIAL WALK-THRU: The house faces Arlington Avenue, a street which runs east-west. Lt. Rice took Det. Roth into the master bedroom at the extreme s/e corner. Officer Jim Kushner was standing guard. Det. Roth recognized the victim as Lisa Piel, former police officer with the City of Petoskey. Piel resigned her position several years ago under allegations of misconduct and Grand Jury investigation into drug trafficking. Lisa was laying on her right side facing south, head on pillows, covered with bed comforter up to the shoulder area. Dried blood was noted on the face and bedding.

"By lifting slightly on the bedding, a small pistol was observed laying on the bed near the left hand and right breast. An entry wound was noted on the left breast. An apparent bullet hole was noted in the upper wall, across the room facing Lisa's back. Friday's (10/7/94) Petoskey News-Review newspaper was observed on the bed. A telephone answering machine was on the glass night stand next to the bed. Lt. Rice indicated to Det. Roth that he had removed the tape cassette and turned this over to Det. Roth. Det. Roth also observed by the phone, a grocery receipt from Oleson's Food Store, dated

321

10/7/94. Det. Roth noted that a quantity of alcoholic beverage had been purchased at that time. Also on the head of the bed near the phone was a Valentine's type card to Jennifer signed L.

"Lt. Rice then took Roth into the living room and showed where glass had been broken on the door at the south end of this room. Lt. Rice then showed Det. Roth where glass had been broken on the side entrance door on the east end of the house. Broken glass was noted to be on the floor in both locations. A smeared footprint was noted on the exterior of the south side entrance door. The house was very neat and in place. The second bedroom appeared to have been emptied of personal effects.

"CONTACT: James David Reed DOB 1/29/40
1185 Lears Road
Petoskey, MI 49770
TX: 348-7560

"Det. Roth met with Reed after the initial walk through. Reed agreed to talk with Det. Roth with his attorney present. Reed stated to Det. Roth that he was close friends with Lisa. Reed stated he met with Lisa at her house 4:30 p.m. on Friday (10/7/94) and she was very depressed over the fight she had had on Wednesday (10/5/94) with her roommate, Jennifer Novenske. Reed advised he had heard from Lisa and Jennifer that it had been a very physical altercation with Jennifer packing her belongings and moving out.

"At approximately 8:00 p.m. on Friday (10/7/94), Lisa left a note on Reed's answering machine stating she just got back from the store and would get back with him later. Reed advised that on Saturday morning he drove by Lisa's house on the way to the laundromat and saw no activity there. Reed stated

322

he called and left a message for Lisa around 10:00 a.m. and approximately 12:00 noon. Reed felt something was wrong because they always get together on Saturday to do something. At approximately 2:30 p.m. Reed stopped by the house and saw her car keys, sunglasses and driving vest in the house. Reed stated Lisa never went anywhere without the sunglasses and vest.

"Reed then went to St. Ignace where Jennifer was staying and spoke by TX to Jennifer's sister, Noel, who advised Jennifer left for Texas that a.m.

"Reed heads back to Petoskey, sees there has been no activity at Lisa's, that there were no lights on. At approximately 7:30 p.m. Reed calls Ronni Allor, Lisa's sister, about his suspicions. When no family gained access to the house by 11:30 p.m., Reed broke out the glass on the door off the living room but was unable to work the lock. Reed then tried unsuccessfully to kick in the side door (east end), then used a sledge hammer wrapped with a towel. Once in, Reed went into the bedroom where he found Piel in her bed. Reed shook Piel by the shoulder, saw the blood, isn't sure if he saw the gun and called Lisa's father, sister and the police.

"Reed stated that when his wife had visited (lives out of state) this summer, Lisa, Jennifer, Reed and his wife had dinner together. Reed's wife advised him that Lisa and Jennifer admitted they were taking Xanax (prescription drug for anxiety) like candy.

"EVIDENCE COLLECTED:
ITEM: A.   Brass casing, .380 cal. located
under Lisa's upper right arm.

B.	Bullet, jacket hollow point, seized from inside bedroom wall north, approximately 21-1/2" from the ceiling.

C.	1 box "Master" 50 ctn. .380 ACP rounds with 8 missing. 1 .22 round also in this box.

D.	AMT .380 auto 9 mm Kurz "back up" model, serial #B05758 registered to Lisa Piel.

E.	Bedspread, electric blanket, sheet w/bullet exit holes near victim's back.

F.	Mattress sheet.

G.	Tape recording from answering machine, TOT Det. Roth by Lt. Rice.

H.	Toxicology kit seized at autopsy and TOT Det. Roth.

"PHOTOS: Taken of bedroom and damaged doors by Det. Roth. Pictures at autopsy by Sgt. Betts. It should be noted that attorney Greg Justis was present in the master bedroom during the evidence collection at the vehement insistence of Lisa's father.

"ANSWERING MACHINE TAPE: Det. Roth listened to the tape on 10/10/94. The first call was from Reed indicating the day to be Saturday and the time before 10:00 a.m. Piel did not respond to this call or the others.

"CONTACT: Art Piel, Lisa's father.

Initial contact took place on 10/8/94. Follow up took place 10/12/94 at Art Piel's residence of 6322 Trillium Trail, Harbor Springs. Present was Sgt. Betts.

"Mr. Piel stated Lisa called on Friday (10/7) to see how her mother was doing as she just had surgery. On Saturday (10/8), he tried calling about a job referral in reference to their wallpaper business they had together, but got Lisa's answering machine.

"At about 7:30 p.m. he receives a TX from his daughter, Ronni, who advised she received a TX from Dave Reed who thought something was wrong. Mr. Piel went to Lisa's house, tried a key that didn't work, thought about breaking in, then decided to look around town for her. Mr. Piel went back around 10:30 p.m., looked around, saw the rumpled bed sheets and thought Lisa might be sleeping. Mr. Piel leaves to get a locksmith and later received a TX from Reed advising to get to Lisa's house. Upon arrival, he's met by the police and Reed.

"CONTACT: Jennifer Lynn Novenske
DOB: 11/10/73

Det. Roth made contact with Jennifer at the Piel residence on 10/12/94. Present was Sgt. Betts.

"Jennifer stated Lisa was drunk on Wednesday night (10/5) and beat her up. Jennifer stated she packed her belongings and told Lisa she needed a few days away. Jennifer went to a friend's place in Conway, then to her sister's in St. Ignace. On Saturday morning at 2:00 a.m. she drove to Detroit Metro and flew to Texas. Jennifer stated she had no contact with Lisa after 10/5/94. Jennifer did state she had a prescription for Xanax but didn't believe Lisa was using them. Jennifer stated there was an incident last February where Lisa was drunk and shot her reflection in the bedroom mirror with a .22 handgun while sitting on the bed.

"Det. Roth was TX'd by Jennifer on 10/17/94. Det. Roth heard from Reed that one of the items Jennifer had taken when moving out was Lisa's small handgun and that Lisa broke into Jennifer's car in Oden and took it back. Jennifer confirmed this to be true.

"FINDINGS: Emmet County Medical Examiner R. Krzymowski has ruled the death of Lisa Piel as a self inflicted gunshot wound. Lisa shot herself in the chest while laying in bed covered with bedding. The bullet exited the lower back, goes through bedding at an upward angle, passes thru the north bedroom wall.

"STATUS: Open, pending toxicology lab results.
"RESPECTFULLY SUBMITTED,
Det/Sgt. Timothy E. Roth #3
Emmet County Sheriff's Department

"Sgt. Everett G. Betts #4
Emmet County Sheriff's Department"

Working backward in this manner chronologically has its advantages in that it is seen how reporting of an incident of this magnitude becomes shaped and compacted, streamlined to shed rough edges, and made to fit neatly into an established format easily dealt with in legal terms. Though the subtleties involved in this next testimony, which events took place just prior to the foregoing, are minute they fill out the scenario of chaos that surrounded and permeated the situation. This report also allows some insight into the emotional status of the moment.

"NARRATIVE: On 10-8-94 at 11:31 p.m., Lt. Rice received a call at home from the Emmet County Dispatch, Deputy Spanuolo, advising Lt. Rice that his assistance was needed at the Lisa Piel residence, located at 218 Arlington Avenue in Petoskey in reference to a possible suicide.

"Lt. Rice arrived on the scene at 11:36 p.m. and made contact with Officer Randy Weston and Officer Jim Kushner from the Petoskey Public Safety department. Lt. Rice was led to the back bedroom area of 218 Arlington Street at which time Lt. Rice observed a white female, known to Lt. Rice as Lisa Michele Piel, white female, DOB: 7-24-57, who was lying on her right side facing south in her bed partially covered with blankets. Lt. Rice observed that Piel was cradling a small handgun near her chest area and that she had a bullet wound in her chest which protruded out her back and appeared that the bullet travelled into the north wall of the bedroom. Lt. Rice also noted that there was blood around Piel's chest, nose and mouth. Lt. Rice was advised by Officer Weston that Life Link Ambulance, which was clearing the scene as Lt. Rice arrived, checked Piel for life signs and determined that she was cold to the touch and that it appears that she had been deceased for some time. After being briefed by Officer Weston, Lt. Rice took over the scene and released Officer Weston to return to the Sheriff's Department to continue with the complaint he was working on prior to this complaint coming in.

"At 11:47 p.m. Lt. Rice placed a telephone call to Officer Rautio at his residence, requesting his assistance at the scene.

"Lt. Rice returned to the bedroom area, looking for a note or any type of foul play around the room. Lt. Rice observed the answering machine setting on the table which was flashing with numerous messages. Lt. Rice, at 11:48 p.m., removed the tape from the answering machine and initialed it, dated it, and put the time of 11:48 p.m. on the tape and secured it with Lt. Rice. Lt. Rice seized the tape right away to prevent someone from accidently erasing the tape by pushing the buttons on the machine.

"Lt. Rice briefly walked through the house and did not observe anything out of the ordinary with the exception of a window in a patio door located on the north side of the residence in the living room area which had been broken out. Lt. Rice also noticed an entrance door off of the kitchen on the east side of the house which also had a window broken out of the door. Lt. Rice made contact with Officer Kushner and a second subject who was identified as James David Reed, white male, DOB: 1-29-40, with an address of 1185 Lears Rd., Petoskey, TX#348-7560, who was identified to Lt. Rice as the subject who called in the original complaint. Reed was with Officer Kushner in the kitchen area and Lt. Rice questioned Reed as to what had happened. Reed advised Lt. Rice that Lisa Piel had been upset over the fact that her roommate, Jennifer Novenske, had moved out of the house last Wednesday and was not going to live at Piel's residence any longer. Reed stated that the last time he had spoke with Lisa Piel was on Friday afternoon, 10-7-94, at approximately 4:30 p.m. Reed stated that Lisa had also called and left a message on his machine and that on Saturday, 10-8-94, around 10:00 a.m., he attempted to call Lisa Piel at her residence but got no response. Reed stated that after not being able to get ahold of Lisa Piel, he became concerned and came to the Arlington address. Reed stated that after observing that both of Lisa's vehicles, a van and a two-door car, were still in the garage and the house was dark, he became concerned for Lisa Piel's safety and attempted to get into the house. Reed stated that he first went to the back of the house where the patio door is and break the window out attempting to get in the door. He stated, however, he was unable to get the door open or enter the residence from that location because of a problem with the lock. Reed stated he then went around to the other service door that led into the kitchen area and did break the window out of that door as well. Reed stated that he was able to get the door open at that location, did enter the house looking for Lisa. Reed stated that as he walked into Lisa Piel's bedroom he observed her lying in the bed and also saw the blood. Reed stated he knew there was a problem and that he did push on her shoulder in an effort to see if she would respond and then he picked up the phone in the bedroom and called the police. Reed then stated that after calling the police he also called Lisa's sister and her father and advised them of the situation. Lt. Rice observed that while questioning Reed, Reed was quite distraught, crying from time to time and also very upset.

"Lt. Rice assigned Officer Kushner as well as Reserve Officer Fosmore to stand by the door and keep track of people arriving at the scene. Lt. Rice returned to the bedroom area and began observing the scene in preparation for Officer Rautio's arrival at the scene. At approximately 11:55 p.m., Officer Kushner yelled for Lt. Rice to come up front at which time Lt. Rice could hear a male subject yelling loudly. Lt. Rice walked down the hallway and was met at the end of the hallway near the living room by a subject identified later as Lisa Piel's father, Art Piel, address of 6322 Trillium Trail in Harbor Springs, TX#526-6855. Art Piel was quite distraught and yelling that he wanted all of the police officers out of the house and also yelling that it was Diane Smith's Prosecutor's office and Scott Croton from the State Police and the Petoskey Police Department's fault for what had happened. Art Piel was very distraught and had to be physically restrained in the hallway and pinned to the wall to avoid Art Piel from striking Lt. Rice. Lt. Rice talked with Art Piel, calming the subject down and advising him that we had to treat it as a crime scene and that he could not disturb anything. Lt. Rice was concerned about Art Piel knowing that he had had heart problems in the past and was quite agitated at the time. Art Piel stated to Lt. Rice that he simply wanted to see her and that he did not believe any of us. Lt. Rice for Art Piel's safety, decided to take Mr. Piel back to the bedroom area. Lt. Rice advised Art Piel that he could not touch anything and that he would have to leave the bedroom shortly after seeing his daughter. Lt. Rice also tried to talk Art Piel out of going into the bedroom and seeing her in the condition she was in, however, Art Piel was quite headstrong and would not listen to reason. Lt. Rice did lead Art Piel back to the bedroom at which time both Lt. Rice and Art Piel walked into the bedroom and walked around to the south side of the bed at which time Art Piel stopped and began crying and then left the room with Lt. Rice without disturbing anything. By the time Lt. Rice went back to the kitchen area with Art Piel, three other subjects had arrived at the scene and were now assisting Art Piel in the kitchen. Two of the subjects were identified as Ronni Allor, who is Lisa Piel's sister and her husband, Daniel Allor. The Allors and Art Piel did sit down at the kitchen table and began to discuss what they were going to do. Lt. Rice was also advised and made contact with another subject who had arrived at the scene who was identified as Gregory Justis who is an attorney in Petoskey. Lt. Rice was advised that Mr. Justis had been called by James Reed to stand by and assist the family.

"Officer Rautio arrived at the scene and Lt. Rice briefed Rautio as to what was going on with the case. Prior to Officer Rautio's arrival, Art Piel had been making comments that the people who didn't care for Lisa were the ones who were investigating the case and that Art Piel made the accusation that he did not trust the Prosecutor's Office, the State Police or Petoskey Police Department and could not trust them to not cover up what was really going on. Lt. Rice also learned that the Piels had a problem with Officer Rautio due to the fact that Officer Rautio's brother, John Rautio, had been involved with the Grand Jury back when Lisa Piel had gotten in trouble. Lt. Rice learned that the situation became quite hostile between Officer Rautio and the Piels at which point Lt. Rice relieved Officer Rautio from the scene at which time he cleared and went home.

"Due to the possible conflict which the Piels believed existed, Lt. Rice placed a telephone call from the cellular phone in 445 to Sgt. Tim Roth of the Emmet County Sheriff's Department. At 12:21 a.m. on 10-9-94, Lt. Rice did make contact with Sgt. Roth and requested his assistance at the scene. Detective Roth arrived at the scene at 12:46 a.m. on 10-9-94 at which time Lt. Rice turned the crime scene over to him and briefed him on what had taken place up to that point. Lt. Rice also turned over the cassette taken from the answering machine to Detective Roth as well as showing him the house and the bedroom where Lisa Piel was located. Detective Roth advised Lt. Rice that he had placed a call to Sgt. Everett Betts, Emmet County Sheriff's Department, to come in as the evidence technician to the scene. Lt. Rice and Sgt. Roth agreed that Detective Roth would be in control of the scene and Lt. Rice would remain on the scene to assist Detective Roth. Lt. Rice took Detective Roth to the kitchen area and introduced him to Reed and the others who were in the room. At that time Detective Sgt. Roth attempted to do interviews while Lt. Rice stood by in the hallway protecting the bedroom where Lisa Piel was located. Lt. Rice also at that time released Officer Kushner and Reserve Officer Fosmore to go on routine patrol.

"After Sgt. Betts' arrival Lt. Rice basically stood by and observed and did assist in holding packages for Sgt. Betts as well as running errands to the Petoskey Police Department to obtain containers to place evidence in.

"At approximately 2:50 a.m., Detective Sgt. Roth requested that Lt. Rice escort the Stone Funeral Home vehicle which had arrived to pick up Lisa Piel and escort them to the Northern Michigan Hospital's morgue and to make sure that Lisa Piel was secured at that facility. At 3:01 a.m. on 10-9-94 the Stone Funeral Home vehicle left the 218 Arlington Avenue address and drove to Northern Michigan Hospital, arriving at the Hospital at 3:04 a.m. Lt. Rice assisted Stone Funeral Home in taking Lisa Piel's body to the basement section where at 3:13 a.m. Lisa Piel was placed into a secured area where the doors were locked. Present at the hospital were two employees from Stone Funeral Home, Lt. Rice, the nurse supervisor and Art Piel who had ridden over with the Stone Funeral Home vehicle. At 3:25 a.m. Lt. Rice cleared the hospital and gave Art Piel a ride back to 218 Arlington Avenue. Lt. Rice made contact with Detective Sgt. Roth and Sgt. Betts who were in the process of picking up their equipment and clearing the scene. Lt. Rice cleared the scene at 3:44 a.m. and went to the Emmet County Sheriff's Department and had a brief meeting with Sgt. Roth and Sgt. Betts. Lt. Rice went out of service at approximately 4:30 a.m. on 10-9-94.

"On 10-9-94 at approximately 9:30 p.m., Lt. Rice came in to the Petoskey Department of Public Safety to do paper work for this incident. At that time Lt.

Rice had a message to contact James Reed at his residence. Lt. Rice did contact Reed at his residence at approximately 9:40 p.m. at which time Reed advised Lt. Rice that he had made contact with Jennifer Novenske who was currently in Austin, Texas. Reed stated that she will be returning back to Petoskey tomorrow evening and will be probably staying with Reed at his residence. Lt. Rice advised Reed that Detective Roth would be advised of her returning.

"STATUS: Closed, case turned over to Detective Roth, Emmet County Sheriff's Department.

Respectfully submitted,

Lt. Anthony Rice

Petoskey Public Safety"

Through all this redundancy of "advised" persons and events is discerned the obvious between-the-lines observations. J. David Reed was the first to discover Lisa; then came Officer Weston of the Police Department; then followed Officers Kushner and Fosmore. Lt. Rice arrived at the house at 11:36 that evening. Officer Weston was contacted at 11:26, ten minutes previous to Rice's arrival. The various officers reacted quickly to the report called in by Dave Reed—too quickly to organize a proper research and detection procedure. As it is said, the correct response is to consider any death a homicide until otherwise proven. Yet no such procedure was followed. It is easily noted that no fingerprints were obtained, Lt. Rice presumably may have obliterated any fingerprints on the cassette tape extracted from the answering machine, little or no attempt to secure the immediate manner in which things were found, and slip-shod techniques of evaluation were used by all concerned. Dave Reed himself was but cursorily questioned as to events and chronology. Continuing to backtrack, these two brief "Narratives" of the first three officers on the scene complete the official findings of that initial investigation.

"NARRATIVE: Officer Kushner was dispatched to 218 Arlington Street by the Emmet County Sheriff's department 10-8-94 and advised to meet patrol unit 448, as Officer Weston and Reserve Officer Fosmore were already on scene. Upon arrival at the scene, Officer Kushner met with Officer Fosmore in front of the residence. Fosmore advised Officer Kushner that this was an apparent suicide, that he had no other information at that time. Officer Kushner then entered through the front door of the house where Officer Weston was standing with a white male subject in the kitchen of the house. Subject later identified himself as James David Reed, DOB: 1-29-40. He gave his address of 1185 Lears Rd., Petoskey. Mr. Reed was very upset. officer Kushner also noted at this time there was a small amount of blood on the sleeve in front of Mr. Reed's jacket. Officer Weston advised Officer Kushner that the victim was in the northeast bedroom of the home and appeared to be deceased. Officer Kushner stayed in the front door kitchen area with Mr. Reed while Officer Weston escorted a paramedic from Life Link to the bedroom. Life Link left the scene shortly after.

"A few minutes later Lt. Rice from the Petoskey Department of Public Safety arrived on the scene and he and Officer Weston entered the bedroom where the victim was. Shortly after that Officer Weston left the scene and Lt. Rice asked Officer Kushner to get a statement from Mr. Reed. Mr. Reed declined to answer any questions until he had contacted his attorney. He, however, did make several statements saying that he last spoke with the victim of Friday, 10-7-94 in the afternoon. He stated she was very upset and he had told her not to do anything stupid. He stated that he had tried several times on Saturday, 10-8-94, to contact the victim but was unable to reach her. Feeling that there was a problem, he broke into the house through a north door and discovered the victim's body laying in the bedroom. Lt. Rice allowed Mr. Reed to use a phone in the hallway where he called his attorney and several other people. Officer Kushner remained in the kitchen front door area of the house and kept a log of the time and names of every one who entered the house.

Officer James Kushner, Petoskey Public Safety"

"NARRATIVE: On Saturday, 10-8-94, at approximately 11:26 p.m., Officer Weston was at the Emmet County Sheriff's Department conducting a breathalyzer exam when Officer Weston was notified by dispatch that they had a possible suicide, 218 Arlington Street in the city of Petoskey.

"Officer Weston responded to that location. While in route Officer requested that an ambulance be dispatched. Also that a supervisor be contacted.

"Officer Weston arrived at 218 Arlington Street and met with a James Reed. Officer noted as he approached the residence, all the lights were on inside. Mr. Reed was standing in the kitchen area, the front door was wide open. Mr. Reed stated to the officer that his friend Lisa Piel had shot herself. Mr. Reed directed Officer Weston to a bedroom in the rear of the house. The officer noted a female, approximate age of 35, lying on her right hand side. The officer could see what appeared to be a bullet exit wound just to the left of the spine. The officer went around to the other side of the bed, checked the carotid pulse and there was no pulse on the victim. Officer noted that victim was cold to the touch and

335

rigor mortis had set in. Officer also noted that dependent lividity was present.

"The officer requested that Mr. Reed exit the room and went back into the kitchen area. The officer advised dispatch by portable radio that the ambulance would not be needed. Approximately that time, Officer Kushner arrived at the scene to assist Officer Weston.

"Several minutes later Life Link Ambulance arrived on the scene. Paramedic Larry Hansen was escorted into the back bedroom and he observed the victim's body, came to the same conclusions that the officer did that no resuscitation would be required at that point in time. Larry Hansen was going to advise the Emergency Room doctor and Officer Weston escorted him out of the residence.

"Officer Weston spoke briefly with James Reed. Mr. Reed stated to the officer that the last time he had heard from Lisa Piel was approximately 8:00 p.m. on Friday night. He stated he had contacted several family members and nobody was able to get ahold of her. he also stated to the officer he broke into the residence in an attempt to check the welfare of Lisa Piel, when he found her in the above described condition.

"Several minutes later Lt. Rice arrived on the scene. Officer Weston turned over control of the crime scene to the Lt.

Officer Randall Weston

Petoskey Public Safety"

As seen, Mr. Reed was allowed to use a telephone after the arrival of an officer, thereby precluding any finger printing of said phone. It obviously was presupposed that a suicide had transpired

336

and indeed no other real assumption was made regardless of the postulated reference to the presupposed potential of homicide.

Mr. Reed, with visible blood on his jacket, was never questioned about this anomaly, nor was he questioned as to the account of his being there for an undetermined amount of time prior to his calling the police. He was apparently not searched for any articles belonging to the deceased that might possibly have found their way into his pockets. His evident manner of distress seemed to have been sufficient to dissuade any further interrogation of his premise for having been there and for how long.

The Autopsy Report in full is interjected here:

"AUTOPSY REPORT

NAME: Piel, Lisa M.   Autopsy #A94-53

AGE: 37   SEX: F   M.E. # 94-25

PATHOLOGIST: George A. Krzymowski

ASSISTANT: William E. Larsen, P.A.

DATE/HOUR OF DEATH: October 8, 1994 approximately 10:00 a.m.

DATE/HOUR AUTOPSY: October 9, 1994 9:45 a.m.

ATTENDING AUTOPSY: Sgt. Betts, Emmet County Sheriff's Department

FINAL AUTOPSY DIAGNOSES

CAUSE OF DEATH: Gunshot wound to heart

MANNER OF DEATH: Suicide

George A. Krzymowski, M.D.

Pathologist"

To bring local procedure into focus, Dr. Krzymowski is a pathologist, not a coroner. This has been somewhat criticized of

337

late for its intrinsic lack of full potential of forensic determinations. As indicated earlier, no account was taken as to the exact trajectory of the causative bullet which entered Lisa's body. Nor was any account studied as to the fact that she was right-handed, lying on her right side, with the reported gun resting near her left hand. Lisa Piel was a very experienced gun handler; would it seem likely that she would pull the trigger right-handedly while lying on her right side? Would it seem logical that she pulled the trigger with her left hand? These questions were never asked.

There was a natural inclination for some local persons to suppose that Lisa died of drug complications. This State Police report by the Forensic Science Division of East Lansing dispels all these rumors quite conclusively.

"Subject: LISA PIEL (D)
Evidence Received:
1 - Sealed Michigan State Police Specimen Kit
(TriTech) containing:
1 - Tube with approx. 9ml. blood
1 - Tube with approx. 8ml. blood
1 - 35ml. capacity bottle with 35ml. urine
1 - 35ml. capacity bottle with 35ml. urine
Results of Analysis:
0.20% Blood Alcohol
Analysis of the urine failed to show the
presence of cocaine metabolite, barbituates,
benzodiazepines, cannabinoids or opiates.
Laureen J. Marinetti-Sheff
Laboratory Scientist"

A post mortem examination concluded that Lisa's position at death was consistent with peripheral findings. A "pooling of blood under the right arm in addition to an impression of a cartridge shell within the pooled blood on the ventral (abdominal or front) surface of the upper right arm" seems to verify that this is indeed the arrangement of her body when she died. There were discovered "blue-black to green ecchymoses (bruises) of the left inner thigh and right anterior thigh," unexplained and unquestioned. The cartridge shell was not examined. This post mortem merely certifies the position in which she was found, the wrong hand near the gun.

Backtracking further, these statements by Nancy Simon, a friend of Lisa's who lives in Bloomfield Hills, Michigan, are printed in full:

"FRIDAY OCTOBER 7TH:

"I called Lisa at approximately 11:00 a.m. We talked for almost an hour, discussing many things. We basically caught up on our lives, she told me that Jennifer had moved out a few days ago. I asked her if anything in specific had happened and she replied 'we have been fighting a lot lately.' At this point I didn't ask her anything else regarding that situation, and Lisa did not sound as if she wanted to discuss it further. I do remember, however, asking her if she and Jennifer were partners in her wallpapering business because I was concerned for her financial status with her company. Lisa informed me that Paperchasers was strictly her own and that Jennifer only worked for her a few times. She said Jennifer worked part time at Birchwood for security. We discussed real estate continuing education, my husband and myself and had just taken our 6 hours, and Lisa told me she was scheduled to take hers at the Holiday Inn the following Monday. Our conversation began to get quite upbeat and I put Jake on the phone. He and Lisa talked and I could hear her laughing (loud enough because Jake had the phone and I was standing next to him). During our conversation I asked her if Jonathon and I could come up and stay with her the next week as Jon had to make a prison visit to a client in Kincheloe and I was looking forward to seeing the fall colors. She seemed glad I'd asked and said 'yes.' She might have said 'sure' but

339

anyway it was a set thing. Lisa then asked what we were doing 'tonight.' I told Lisa that we didn't have any plans and she asked if she could come down to our house. At that point I said sure and was very happy thinking she was going to come down. I gave her directions from I-75 since she was only at our new house last fall (before we had moved in) and we came from Beverly Hills, where we used to live so she wanted more direct directions.

"FRIDAY OCTOBER 7TH AT APPROXIMATELY 12:30 PM

"I called Lisa and got her answering machine. I assumed that maybe she was getting ready to come down. I left a short message for her to call as soon as she got my message so I could plan dinner for us.

"Friday night at approximately 8:30 Lisa left a message on our machine. To the best of my knowledge she just said 'it's Lisa, give me a call.' We did not listen to the message until Sat. a.m. sometime, as we assumed she was not coming down by 5:00 p.m. and made other plans.

"Saturday a.m. I had a friend over which was planned much in advance and had to leave to go see a friend's new house, etc.

"Sat. p.m. Art called and asked Jon if Lisa had come down to our house.

"Sunday at 9:00 a.m. Art called and told me about Lisa. He mentioned a man named David Reed, whom he said had found Lisa at her house.

"SUNDAY OCTOBER 9TH AT APPROXIMATELY 11:00 PM

"I had been thinking about this David Reed and who he was since Lisa had never mentioned his name to me. I called information and got his telephone number. I called him and told him who I was and asked him to tell me what had happened.

340

At first he was uneasy about how I got his number but then was cooperative in his responses to me. I recall him telling me that Lisa mentioned to him she was thinking of coming down to my house (he asked if I was the one with the baby), that he had been at her house with her and left her at approximately 7:30 p.m. and that Lisa said she would not do anything 'funny.' I asked him how he knew Lisa and he said he lived just down the street from her and met her and Jennifer because they were neighbors. He told me he watched Art walk around Lisa's house and waited until he left to go up to her house himself. He told me he saw her keys on her kitchen table and decided to break in because her car was in the garage. Then he said he found Lisa in her bed and telephoned Art and told him to come over right away. He told me that Lisa had shot herself and told me what type of gun, but I do not recall what exactly the type of gun he said it was now, but I know he told me specifics about the gun.

"I'm not sure of all the things I asked him but he seemed to suggest that he and the girls were very close."

This following note, brief and undated, apparently was found in Lisa's house since it is stamped by the Sheriff's Department as evidence.

"Dave—I'm not in the right state of mind to do this today—not to mention I bought a 16" not 12". They must of been in the wrong slot.

Sorry—
I'll have to start over.
(signed) Lisa"

This foregoing note remains unexplained. This completes the recognized and verified evidential compilation of sequence of events immediately culminating in Lisa's death. Other evidences exist but are again not readily verifiable, if ever, the shroud of silence being cast shortly thereafter, upheld and emboldened by fear and time. There are allegations, theories, hear-say and similar hints of other mitigating points and versions attenuating the chronicle of events.

Retrospectively, nothing further can be ascertained. The only other "document" available from this time frame is at once—in Warholian terms—a "glorification of the mundane," and a testament to the living. This is a grocery receipt from Oleson's Food Store nearby to Lisa's house. This receipt is dated 10/7/94, 7:45 p.m., the night before her death. The $10.97 amount marked "liquor" accounts for the .20 blood alcohol level indicated on her death certificate. The rest of the purchases totaling $44.60 are assuredly not indicative of someone planning on ending her life that very next morning. One does not buy three packages of meat for a "last supper." Neither does one concern herself with fourteen coupons of refund for one's last night on Earth, such as are found listed on this receipt.

In this next double chapter Art Piel himself takes the stand, so to speak, with retrospective thoughts and findings on Lisa's death as well as Lisa's life. Having been met with conflicts ranging from the blase to the vindictive, much of these allegations are unprovable since any and almost all attempts at verification are met with hostility and silence. Some documentation exists but mostly toward the vindictive attitude pointed at Art. The reader is left to his/her own perceptions and opinions.

The sage of Lisa Michele Piel, dead at thirty-seven years of age, does not end there.

16

Criminal Business,
Ordinary People
Part A

This two-part chapter portends to pull many loose and conflicting ends together. In this format will be dissected the scattered remains of Lisa's Story, hopefully to accomplish a reestablishing of the premise of her life and purpose, for what is a person without a purpose? Lisa had purpose. That purpose unfortuitously interfered with other lives already in progress. This interference was dealt with scurrilously and in a borderline illegal manner under the auspices of legalities. This borderline was stretched thin, so thin that the telling of Lisa's tale may well prompt a re-telling of the legal premise that heralded her resignation. Death has a way of living far beyond the grave. Martyrs are not expected around northern Michigan, and are assuredly not welcomed. Martyrs, however, appear where they are most unwanted.

Lisa's name and honor will no doubt be cleared one day. She was a nice girl caught in a web of intrigue that existed before her advent. She interfered with the status quo, not only locally but countrywide, as any undeniably chauvinistic male will freely admit to. She was not wanted—nothing personal—in a long-term man's role. Much of the country, and perhaps the world, still feels that way. Many feel that equality of many types is superimposed forcefully upon an unwilling populace by a minority of powermongers. This editor, as do all editors, has friends who are of this potentially archaic viewpoint. After all, changes happen rather quickly now, as in, horse and buggy to jet planes and moon rockets in one hundred years time. Many people just can't keep up with the velocity. Many don't want to. Many who even want to can't bring conscious values into acquiescence with ethical and moral decisions.

The small town is feudalistic and provincial in outlook. Without the big conglomerates of megalopolis, urban centers the world wide would still be in the throws of this feudalism, warring neighbor to neighbor, such as is seen in second and third world cultures even now. In rural areas such as this, intimidation is allowed more sway due to the lack of monitor capacity by powers of equalization. In trying to preserve the pristine countryside and capacious freedom of movement many freedoms are curtailed by dint of supposed omnilateral predisposition.

The Yuppie crowd, when they migrated north in search of a cleaner, better lifestyle in contrast to the dirty cities, brought their values of homogeneity of purpose with them. Many of these types were and are of the legal professions, such as lawyers, judges, business persons of influential means, and in general persons who saw fit to mold their desires for a congenial lifestyle into a culture that didn't quite live up to their expected visions. Hence come incongruities of cultural premise. Moral and ethical premises are bent to fit a new mode of lifestyle: that of a new breed of ethicist imposing values upon an older and more basics-oriented social order. Northern Michigan, lower peninsula, is made up of emigrants from the older world: Scandinavia and Western Eurasia primarily, Northerners who sought a northern but freer style of living and working. They found it here in Northwestern Michigan.

With the world changes rapidly encroaching, the bucolic small-town areas were caught without precedent of how to deal with these changes. They had not the big-city means nor groups of revitalization nor ways of compromise at their disposal. The conflicts were allowed to implode. They still wave Old Glory down by the courthouse, as Merle Haggard has sung. The muddle of legalistic balance gropes with anachronistic blinders, a testament to superimposed changes upon a culture not prepared.

Art Piel sought not sympathy but empathy for Lisa's tragedy; he found fear and hostility. In frustration he lashed out. Every avenue was blocked, if not by prevaricative bureaucracy, by sedation and staidly of societal mores. His every move was countered by misrepresented charges, blockades, and threats of legal recourse.

Many instances of letter and police record bolster the attitude of authority in these various undertakings of Art Piel. Even searching for answers to seemingly commonplace requests, such as photographs and documents pertaining to Lisa's death and previous records, were met with stonewall negativity. Why? Qui bono?–in legal terms–who benefits?

345

Many things happened subsequent to Lisa's death, most promulgated by Art Piel, and most all of these happenings resulted in little or no progressive good nor insights into underlying truths. Art, self-admittedly distraught, sad and angry, attempted many contacts with police personnel who had been involved with Lisa, as said, to no avail, but simply provided the authorities with fodder for further convolution of art's questionings into allegations of his potential mental instability, his actions into potential investigatory vindictiveness by official decree of law and order. The authorities seem to have silenced every attempt by Art to bring Lisa's story to the surface for analysis. True, he went slightly overboard in a few instances due to his anxieties and the automated preclusion of acceptance as a rational questioner; he was maligned at every instance with legal maneuverings to silence and repel his every move.

These excerpts to follow point out succinctly this manner of silencing in all of its ramifications. It is a thorough and inauspicious process in its entirety of scope to successfully bar anyone's entrance into the inner sanctums of jurisprudence, anyone who is not wanted.

On January 6, 1995, Lisa's mother wrote to the City Manager of Petoskey, thus:

"Dear Mr. Korthauer:

As Independent Personal Representative and mother of Lisa M. Piel, I am requesting copies of any and all files related to Lisa during her tenure as an employee of the City of Petoskey as a police officer."

The reply: Jan. 20, 1995

"Dear Ms. Piel:

"I am writing in response to your January 6 letter that requested copies of employee files related to Lisa M. Piel. I have been advised by legal counsel that the City cannot release such files. Therefore, I am unable to grant your request.

Sincerely,

George Korthauer
City Manager"

From Diane Smith, Prosecuting Attorney for Emmet County:

"MEMORANDUM

"TO: Tim Roth
FROM: Diane M. Smith
RE: Lisa Michele Piel
DATE: March 30, 1995

"This is to inform you that I have reviewed the reports submitted to me in this matter and am satisfied that your conclusion that Ms. Piel's death was a suicide is well documented and substantiated. I therefore recommend that this matter be closed"

Again from Diane Smith on June 27, 1995, concerning a meeting with Art Piel who was requesting the return of negatives of pictures taken at Lisa's death. She says: "In your particular case they feel it is vital to retain the negatives in the event that it turns out that your daughter was murdered. If someone were to come forward a few years from now and confess to murdering Lisa, we would have to have the pictures for evidence." In this same letter, Ms. Smith adds: "With regard to your second request, I have talked to several people and have not been able to find anyone who would be willing to consider having a picture of Lisa hung at City Hall . . . to recognize her as the first woman police officer."

And further from Ms. Smith:

"Dear Mr. Piel:

"I am sorry it has taken me so long to get back to you in response to your request to have the police report of the investigation of your daughter's death amended to delete any reference to drug trafficking.

"I have reviewed the report and discussed it with Tim Roth and find no need to make any deletions."

On September 13th of 1995, Art wrote Sheriff Jeff Bodzick requesting the closing of Lisa's files and further information concerning a statement by Tim Roth that "he knew something about Lisa that I did not know:"

September 13, 1995

Sheriff Jeff Bodzick
450 Bay Street
Petoskey, MI 49770

I am putting my request in letter form, per our conversation on September 8th of last week.

I would like to sit down with you, Roth and Smith to talk over the following:

(1) Closing of Lisa's file and release of pictures and the negatives.

(2) Tim Roth's allegation, when he stated "He knew something about Lisa" that I did not know. This was said in the presence of Diane Smith.

(3) Roth's report relating to Lisa's "drug trafficking."

I do not want any hear-say, this is why I want the four of us to meet in person (not by letter) that I may state my case and ask questions, so this matter can be settled once and for all.

Art Piel

Here follows more of the curious workings of judicial suppression of "evidence" held against Lisa Piel, seemingly in a sort of "abeyance" state, potentially to be used should any more relevant information be forthcoming. Attorney Michael Buckingham raises some interesting arguments, all to no avail.

Michael B. Buckingham P.C.

ATTORNEY & COUNSELOR AT LAW
321 E. LAKE STREET
PETOSKEY, MICHIGAN 49770

MICHAEL B. BUCKINGHAM

SCOTT R. ECKHOLD
OF COUNSEL

TELEPHONE
616-348-9595
FACSIMILE
616-348-9599

February 17, 1997
FAXED on Even Date

Mark Blumer
Assistant Attorney General
6520 Mercantile Way #1
Lansing, MI 48913-0001

Re: **People v Lisa Piel, File No. 92-118-FY**

Dear Mr. Blumer:

Please find enclosed a Motion for Suppression of File and a Notice of Hearing regarding the same.

Merely as a refresher, your office took over the file from the Emmet County Prosecutor's Office due to a conflict of interest with Diane Smith. Ms. Smith is no longer the prosecutor. Robert Engel is now the Emmet County Prosecutor. I have spoken with Mr. Engel and he has no objections to our motion but he still believes the conflict with the office exists. Consequently, I am writing to you.

If you have no objections to closing the file, would you please sign the enclosed order so that I may present it to the court.

This is being prompted simply because the parents have not been able to bring closure to their daughter's death. Every time they reach a point where they think they have overcome her death, a reporter or some curiosity seeker reviews the court file and then calls them up.

Hopefully, you will have no objections. If you have any questions or comments regarding the same, please feel free to contact me.

Respectfully Yours,

Michael B. Buckingham

MBB/ceb
Enclosures
xc: Arthur and Gloria Piel

(letters\piel)

350

STATE OF MICHIGAN
DISTRICT COURT FOR THE 90TH JUDICIAL DISTRICT
EMMET COUNTY

PEOPLE OF THE STATE OF MICHIGAN,

Plaintiffs,

File No. 92-118-FY

v

Hon. Richard W. May

LISA PIEL,

Defendant.

_____/

Mark E. Blumer (P24029)
Assistant Attorney General
On Behalf of the People
Office of the Attorney General
Criminal Division
6520 Mercantile Way, Suite 1
Lansing, Michigan 48910
517-334-6010

_____

Michael B. Buckingham (P32801)
Attorney for Defendant
321 E. Lake Street
Petoskey, MI 49770
616-348-9595

_____/

ANSWER TO MOTION FOR SUPPRESSION OF COURT FILE

NOW COME the People of the State of Michigan by Attorney General
FRANK J. KELLEY and Assistant Attorney General Mark E. Blumer and in answer
to the Motion for Suppression of Court File state:

The People sympathize with the problem expressed in the motion for
suppression of this Court's file concerning Lisa Piel. However, there are two issues
which prevent this Court from granting the relief prayed for by Mr. and Mrs. Piel.

351

First, Mr. and Mrs. Piel lack standing to propose the motion before this Court and, second, the relief sought is contrary to both the rules of this Court and the public interest.

The rules of procedure for all courts of this state, as adopted by the Michigan Supreme Court, are superior to all other laws of this state with the exception of the state constitution. *People v McDonald,* 201 Mich App 270; 505 NW2d 903, app den 444 Mich 946 (1993). The only constitutional entry regarding this issue will be found at Const 1963, art 6, § 19, which declares that this and other courts of the state are courts of record. The People have found no law specifically on this topic except that a reasonable and rationale interpretation of the phrase "court of record" means that it is a court of "public record." This interpretation is supported by the rule discussed below which starts with the premise that records will not be sealed absent some very narrowly applied exception.

MCR 8.105(D) details the conditions by which a court may order a record of the court to be sealed. Absent some constitutional interference with this rule, it stands as the controlling authority on this issue. The premise of this rule (paragraph 1) is that the court may not seal any records unless certain procedural criteria are satisfied. First of the requirements is that a party must file the motion for suppression. With all due respect, Mr. and Mrs. Piel, the parents of Lisa Piel, are not parties to the action entitled *People of the State of Michigan v Lisa Piel,* File No. 92-118-FY, of this Court. Therefore, the People's first objection to this motion is that the movants lack standing.

Even if this Court finds the Piels are appropriate parties for this motion the remainder of MCR 8.105(D) prohibits the requested action. This Court must find, on the record, that there is good cause to seal the documents. The People respectfully refresh this Court's memory that Lisa Piel was a law enforcement officer in Petoskey, Michigan, who was charged and convicted of carrying out certain illegal acts while in uniform. A plea was reached with Ms. Piel and the matter was settled with the state. The People respectfully suggest that corruption in law enforcement and a subsequent plea reached with the Defendant are matters of vital public interest which persists even after the death of the Defendant. Therefore, it is against the public interest for this Court to approve suppression of such a file. MCR 8.105(D)(2)

Further, MCR 8.105(D)(5) says that a court may not seal an order or opinion. This Court's acceptance of the plea agreement between the parties, as well as the subsequent order dismissing the charge against Lisa Piel, (after completion of her one-year probation) are orders contained within the prohibition of this paragraph and may not be suppressed as requested by the parties. Finally, as described in the motion for suppression, this apparently is a matter of continuing interest in the local community served by this Court. Pursuant to MCR 8.105(D)(6) any party can subsequently move this Court to reopen the file if this Court grants the relief requested and may appeal a decision of this Court if such reopening of the file is denied. Thus, granting of the relief requested by the movants here will subject this Court to continuous litigation on this file. It is not difficult to imagine who such other legitimately interested parties would be including, for example: local news media, police unions, similarly situated defendants, and future police administration officials.

353

In conclusion, the People respectfully suggest to this Court that the action proposed by Mr. and Mrs. Piel is not allowed. While understandably important to their peace of mind, is clearly contrary to the public interest, the proper administration of justice and the rules which guide the record keeping activities of this Court.

Wherefore, the People respectfully request that this Court deny the relief prayed for. Further, the People waive oral argument with respect to this motion.

Respectfully submitted,

FRANK J. KELLEY,
Attorney General

Mark E. Blumer (P24029)
Assistant Attorney General
Criminal Division
PO Box 30218
Lansing, MI 48909
(517) 334-6010

Dated: February 26, 1997
cases/blumer/piel/answer

354

PEOPLE OF THE STATE OF MICHIGAN,
Plaintiff,

vs.   File No. 92-118-FY

LISA PIEL,
Defendant.
_____/

MARK BLUMER (P24029)   MICHAEL B. BUCKINGHAM (P32801)
Assistant Attorney General   Attorney for Defendant
State of Michigan   321 E. Lake St.
6520 Mercantile Way #1   Petoskey, Michigan 49770
Lansing, MI 48913-0001   (616) 348-9595
(517) 334-6010
_____/

NOTICE OF HEARING

        PLEASE TAKE NOTICE that the attached Motion will be
brought on for hearing before the Honorable Richard W. May,
District Court Judge, and held in the 90th District Court, County
Building, Petoskey, Michigan, on the 28th day of February, 1997, at
1:30 p.m., or as soon thereafter as counsel may be heard.

                        Respectfully submitted,

Dated: _2-17-0?_

                        MICHAEL B. BUCKINGHAM (P32801)
                        Attorney for Defendant

(notices\piel)

355

PEOPLE OF THE STATE OF MICHIGAN,
Plaintiff,

vs.   File No. 92-118-FY

LISA PIEL,
Defendant.
_____/

MARK BLUMER (P24029)   MICHAEL B. BUCKINGHAM (P32801)
Assistant Attorney General   Attorney for Defendant's Parents
State of Michigan   321 E. Lake St.
6520 Mercantile Way #1   Petoskey, Michigan   49770
Lansing, MI   48913-0001   (616) 348-9595
(517) 334-6010
_____/

MOTION FOR SUPPRESSION OF COURT FILE

NOW COME the parents of Lisa Piel, Arthur and Gloria Piel, by and through their attorney, Michael B. Buckingham, and state:

1. Arthur and Gloria Piel are the parents of Lisa Piel.

2. Lisa Piel is deceased.

3. Prior to her death, Lisa Piel entered a plea under a deferred sentence and the matter was ultimately dismissed on October 28, 1992.

4. Because of the circumstances surrounding their daughter's death, certain people have been curious regarding her death and have periodically have sought to review the court file in this matter.

5. The parents are seeking to bring closure to their daughter's death, but unfortunately, the curiosity seekers who review the court file and then contact Ms. Piel's parents regarding the same serve only to rekindle the parents' sorrow.

6. There is no constitutional right for the public to have access to court files.

7. The parents of Ms. Piel are seeking to have this Honorable Court suppress the file in this matter from public disclosure.

8. The undersigned attorney spoke with the Emmet County Prosecutor, Rober Engle, who stated he did not object to the request.

Respectfully submitted,

Date: 2-14-97

MICHAEL B. BUCKINGHAM (P32801)
Attorney for Defendant

(motions\piel)

357

2   90TH JUDICIAL DISTRICT COURT (EMMET COUNTY)

3

4 THE PEOPLE OF THE STATE OF MICHIGAN,

5 v   File No. 92-118-FY

6 LISA PIEL,

7

8 Defendant.

9   _____/

10

11   MOTION

12   BEFORE THE HONORABLE RICHARD W. MAY, DISTRICT JUDGE

13   Petoskey, Michigan - Wednesday, March 12, 1997

14

15 APPEARANCES:

16 FOR THE PEOPLE: MR. MARK BLUMMER (P 24029)
17   ASST. ATTORNEY GENERAL
                 6520 Merchantile Way, Ste. 1
                 Lansing, MI. 48913-0001
18   (517) 334-6010

19

20 FOR THE DEFENDANT: MR. MICHAEL BUCKINGHAM (P 32891)
                 ATTORNEY AT LAW
                 616 Petoskey St., P.O. Box 426
21   Petoskey, MI. 497700-0426
                 (616) 347-6580
22

23 RECORDED BY: Candace L. Godley   CER 3330
                 Certified Electronic Recorder

24

25

TABLE OF CONTENTS

PAGE

1   Petoskey, Michigan

2   Wednesday, March 12, 1997 - 11:45 A.M.

3   THE COURT: This is file number 92-118-FY. And this

4 is the time scheduled for a motion filed by Mr. Buckingham to

5 suppress the Court file.

6   Mr. Buckingham?

7   MR. BUCKINGHAM: Thank you, your Honor. If the

8 record could also reflect that part of Assistant Attorney

9 General Mark Blumer's response was his waiver of oral argument

10 and that he is not present.

11   Your Honor, Mr. Blumer raises an issue that I had dis-

12 cussed at the very onset with my clients, Gloria and Art Piel,

13 who are the parents of Lisa Piel, who is deceased. There is a

14 court rule, Michigan Court Rule 5.709 J. that allows the

15 Probate Register to open up a previously closed probate estate

16 case for good cause. I believe that we can have Gloria Piel

17 re-appointed, under the Probate code, to reopen a file which

18 was file 94-010013-IE. It was an independent Probate file

19 where Gloria Piel, the mother of Lisa Piel, was appointed to be

20 the personal representative of the independent state of her

21 deceased daughter. It was subsequently closed on September 19,

22 of 1995. That, I would submit to the Court, puts Gloria Piel

23 in the shoes of Lisa Piel. I concur, and am standing here

24 before the Court being as honest as I can. the Assistant

25 Prose---excuse me, the Assistant Attorney General, when he

3

360

1 states that he researched and there are not any cases to give
2 him guidance, I've done the same thing. I've run it through
3 West Law. There isn't anything that is providing me with
4 guidance of whether or not a personal representative can ac-
5 tually be a party as the term is defined under Michigan Court
6 Rule 6.105 D. I agree that that's the applicable Court Rule to
7 suppress a file. I have a different interpretation of what
8 that Court rule means but I agree that's the applicable rule
9 for the Court to follow. I would point, just by way of anal-
10 ogy, Priscilla Presley, the ex-wife of Elvis Presley, has been
11 able to keep the estate of Elvis Presley open for two decades
12 because there's value in Elvis Presley's name; and the endorsem-
13 ent that his name and attachment that his name can give to
14 products. That isn't what the parents of Lisa Piel are seeking
15 to do but nevertheless, there's still a value to their
16 daughter's name. And what they're seeking to do is put closure
17 on their daughter's death. I would ask, ---I concede to the
18 Court that we do not have the Probate estate re-opened at this
19 point. I gave that some thought and concluded that, yes, I
20 could probable run to the Probate Court and do that but that
21 would be like blind-siding the Attorney General's office at the
22 last minute and not giving them the opportunity to respond as
23 to whether or not the personal representative actually was a
24 party. What I would ask the Court, if I could, is for some
25 guidance. I have discussed it with Art and Gloria and we know

4

361

1 that you don't have to give us guidance. You don't have to
2 give us your best guess as to how,---what the outcome of our
3 motion would be if we could get through the party issue. But
4 they don't want to spend unnecessary funds. I don't want to do
5 futile work and open up a Probate estate if the Court's of the
6 opinion that the personal representative couldn't be a party.
7 I would make the analog in Michigan and the only cases, line of
8 cases I can find, is that there's a statute that certainly al-
9 lows the personal representative to bring a wrongful death
10 case, in the name of the decedent. That's the same sort of
11 thing that the personal representative is a party, if you will,
12 if the plaintiff in an action. I cannot find any precedent,
13 one way or the other, for the proposition that we are propos-
14 ing. Just as the Attorney General can't find any contrary to
15 it. There are---
16   THE COURT: I guess I'm not, Mr. Buckingham, listen-
17 ing to you and reviewing the motion, you know. I understand the
18 difficulty that Mr. and Mrs. Piel have had with this or with
19 the file being opened. I guess I agree with the Attorney
20 General that, uh, in the Court Rule, this is the only Court
21 Rule that allows for suppressing files and basically it's the
22 Supreme Court's position that all Court files should be open to
23 the public unless there's good cause. To suppress them re-
24 quires the party to---requires a party to file a motion to sup-
25 press it. I guess as to guidance, I guess my off-the cuff

5

362

1 opinion would be that even the personal representative would
2 not be considered a party for the purpose of this motion. And
3 I can't say that definitively at this time because I haven't
4 done any research myself on that particular issue but I guess I
5 think the analogy would be whether ---can an personal represen-
6 tative file a motion on behalf of a decedent to set aside a con-
7 viction. You know, that person has no prior record ---
8   MR. BUCKINGHAM: Sure, for an expungement.
9   THE COURT: -----for five years then the person can
10 file a motion to have the conviction set aside, basically to
11 clear up their name so that they don't have,---you know, if
12 it's a child wants to clear up their record of their parents or
13 the line of cases, there are a line of cases that are---where
14 people are on appeal and during the appeal process, you know,
15 can the personal representative continue that appeal to have
16 the Defendant's name cleared and have the conviction set aside
17 or is the--- and I guess my off-the-cuff recollection, and I
18 haven't done any thorough research either, is that, you know,
19 once the individual Defendant is deceased while a case is pend-
20 ing appeal, that the appeal is automatically dismissed.
21   MR. BUCKINGHAM: That's correct. It is.
22   THE COURT: Being moot. I'm not---I'm not aware
23 where there ----
24   MR. BUCKINGHAM: I used to do appellant work in a
25 prosecutor's office and I'm certain that's the case, your

4

1 Honor.

2 THE COURT: As you're aware, Mr. Buckingham, as Judge
3 I have only limited discretion in certain types of issues and
4 sometimes I have no discretion, even though, I guess, people
5 would like me to have discretion. I guess by analogy, and it
6 doesn't apply to this, but you know, I had a small claims court
7 yesterday where a seventeen year old bought a car and, you
8 know, paid a couple of payments and when he was 19, two years
9 later, he hadn't been making any payments but, you know---
10 equity would say, you know, this 19 year old owed this seller
11 $700 for this car he received but the law says that he was 17
12 when he entered into this agreement and I couldn't enforce it
13 whether I felt equity required me to enforce it or not.

14 MR. BUCKINGHAM: Sure, I understand.

15 Your Honor, there are a just a couple of matters, if
16 I could state on the record. There are some inaccuracies in
17 the recount of history by Mr. Blumer that my clients would like
18 to simply have put on the record.

19 First, their daughter was never convicted of any
20 crime. The plea was held under abeyance and subsequently dis-
21 missed. So to allege, as he has, that she was a convicted felon
22 or misdemeanor, regardless of what the conviction--there was no
23 conviction.

24 Secondly, your Honor, it makes reference to her
25 having been placed on probation for a year. The Court file

364

1 would reflect, and I have a transcript that supports it, that
2 she was not placed on probation for a year. It was for six
3 months and this matter was held in abeyance.

4 They would also strenuously object to the word
5 "corruption of law enforcement" and make that applicable to her
6 daughter. The offense to which Miss Piel did not fight, that
7 was the basis of the plea that was taken under advisement, was
8 an accusation that while she was off duty she may have seen
9 somebody use controlled substance and she didn't arrest them
10 while she was off duty and didn't report it to the police. Not
11 that she, during the time that she was actively working as a
12 police officer, she failed to carry out her charge. It's some-
13 what of an anomaly that attorneys get to have time off when
14 they're off duty, judges get to have time off but evidently the
15 police department, or the City Police Department feels that you
16 are on duty 24 hours a day, seven days a week, 52 weeks out of
17 the year. That was the basis of the complaint to which she did
18 not fight. Not admitting any corruption or ----

19 THE COURT: I would agree with you, Mr. Buckingham.
20 From my review of the Court file it indicates that Judge Varnum
21 took a plea under advisement for 6 months to an amended charge
22 or an added charge of Neglect of Duty and all the other
23 original charges were dismissed.

24 MR. BUCKINGHAM: Yeah, thank you.

25 THE COURT: I'm sorry. I guess, you and Mr. and Mrs.

8

365

1 Piel, that I am not able to, I'm just not able to grant that

2 motion.

3   MR. BUCKINGHAM: Thank you for your help.

4   THE COURT: Thank you, Mr. Buckingham.

5   (Hearing concluded 11:56 A.M.)

6   * * * * * * * * * * * *

7

8 STATE OF MICHIGAN)

9   )

10 COUNTY OF EMMET   )

11

12   I certify that this transcript, consisting of 9 pages, is

13 a complete, true, and correct transcript of the proceedings

14 and testimony taken in this case on March 12, 1997.

15

16 April 10, 1997 _____

17   Candace L. Godley   CER 3330

18   90th District Court

19   City-County Bldg.

20   Petoskey, MI. 49970

21

22

23

24

25

                           9

366

Not long after this decision by the court, Lisa's mother wrote to Mr. Blumer, dissecting yet again the obvious aspects of this matter, that Lisa was indeed off-duty and was, in fact, never convicted of any other charge than off-duty observation of criminal intent. As a mother's words are most poignant when dealing with her daughter's rights, this brief letter is printed in full:

"Mark Blumer
Office of Attorney General
Criminal Division
6520 Mercantile Way, Ste. 1
Lansing, MI 48913-0001

Dear Mr. Blumer:

"I am writing this letter in response to the Answer you filed in my daughter's case where my husband and I sought to suppress the court file. In your answer, you attempted to refresh the court's memory. Unfortunately, several of the 'facts' that you cited were incorrect. First, my daughter was not convicted. She pled under a plea agreement, and ultimately all charges against her were dismissed. Second, I am greatly offended by your assertion that my daughter was a corrupt law enforcement official. I believe the charges of the Grand Jury were that my daughter, while off duty, did not report alleged criminal activity in her presence, not that she was 'on the take' or did anything inappropriately herself. It is an anomaly that virtually every profession, including probably yours, is 'off duty' at some time. But apparently that is not true for police officers.

"I would respectfully request that in the future when you seek to refresh the court's memory, that you refresh yours first.

"Since you state in your Answer you sympathize with our family's feelings, I trust you will understand why these errors in your answer were disconcerting us us.

Sincerely,

(signed) Gloria Piel

To which Art Piel adds a quote: "I guess if you want justice, you go to a whorehouse; if you want to get fucked, you go to court."

17

Criminal Business, Ordinary People
Part B

This final analysis adds a further dimension to LISA'S STORY that actually almost leads into another story: ART'S STORY. While investigating Lisa's demise and the attempts at clearing her name of charges on file against her, Art himself was met with the same obstructions that Lisa experienced. All of these reports to follow are directed toward Art Piel, not Lisa. In the aftermath of her death the Piels were obviously suppressed in their attempts to vindicate the inferences of guilt against Lisa, as seen in the frustrating legal hyperbole of the preceding chapter. These prior letters, reports, and documents seem now, in editing, but rhetorical avoidance and going through the motions of jurisprudence without bipartisan equanimity. The court, the judge, the police forces, the prosecutor, and even a jury have the *law-to-uphold* predominance, all paid for by the public, and hence, surely have the upper hand. These previous documents read like grandiloquent but scanty and predetermined acquiescence to the letter of the law with no intent to listen to the logical argument and request of the bereaved.

Once again, so much for "justice."

Be that as it may, that portion of legalities is explained away by the remote potential that *new evidence* should appear one day to suggest further intrigue in the life and death of Lisa Piel. The word "homicide" was even used by Diane Smith, the prosecutor. So, Lisa was and is denied, first: honorable status of being the first police woman of Petoskey, Michigan, second: withdrawal of all charges held against her, on record but unproven as well as unfounded. What is one to do?

Indeed, what is one to do when all legal avenues are blockaded? When seemingly an entire community is unwilling to respond to any other determinant than "guilty as charged," and the more heinous, "good riddance."

The human psyche reacts to such discrimination with a bitterness. Repression, suppression, and police *force* do not create acceptance, only acrimony. With no avenues of approach left to either clear Lisa's name or investigate further into the events leading to her death, Art understandably became frustrated. His deeds thereafter, self-admittedly, were acted out from this thwarted point of view. He couldn't let go of it; nor could he accomplish anything by available routes. He saw the evolution of Lisa's life and career end in dissolution, aided and abetted by all legal forces, and sanctioned by the public. The local press had no kind words for Lisa. The police wanted to obliterate all trace of her. Judges and prosecutors involved whitewashed and shelved the whole affair. As suggested earlier, the *political* aspirations of some in power may have had something to do with decisions–or *non-decisions*–of appeasing the public. The voting public.

Art Piel did some strange things following these barred indifference rulings and bias. Non-violent, but strange. Such things as mailing and presenting bloody reminders of his daughter's death to two persons. Stalking, a charge much in the news as of the 90's, was immediately brought to bear against him. Other incidents, such as threatening comments, surfaced and were investigated. A hint of harassment was forthcoming in the midst of these, being perpetuated from the initial *around the courthouse* pursuits by him in search of parking–for both business dealings and his stated confrontation with police personnel. The major manifestation of notice by police in this sequence was Art's attempt at contacting Scott Croton, a former officer and at that time a security worker for a local business. Following this, a letter received by Mr. Croton's wife, mistakingly perceived as a Christmas card but containing a bloody sample, led to a PERSONAL PROTECTION ORDER (P.P.O.) against Art Piel.

Compounding this, the aforementioned "verbal threat" directed toward one of Lisa's former roommates led to a concerted effort by conjoined police forces to investigate Art, himself, with ramifications of *mental instability,* potential violence, and even criminal intent. These investigations, actually having taken place in earlier chronology (1995), promulgated a psychiatric evaluation and much discourse via intra-office police agencies both local and state-wide. The legal eyes were upon Art Piel. Frustration acted upon begets retaliation by the forces of opposition. Now *Harassment, Stalking, and Threat* were being insinuated against him.

These pages to follow picture the actual documents accumulated against him, and working in retrospect to the events following Lisa's death, culminate in a letter by Art outlining his actions and reasons thereof. Other comments by him are interspersed, for he has much on his mind concerning the mis-workings of government procedure. Though documents are not placed in date chronology, they appear as such because of the buildup process of their inceptions. That is, culminations tend to evoke a retrospective rethinking of all sequences leading up to the prognosis of *instability* on Art's part and the intensifying investigation on the part of authorities.

This book being the story of Lisa Piel, and not necessarily a unilateral representation of all directives (as stated, the only legal response being written documents), Art Piel insisted upon the inclusion of these latter events that they be not brought back against him at the publication of this writing with the culpability of omission. The strategy of official *Intelligence,* if offended by these revelations herein, will undoubtedly vilify any person and action that they may attach legal connotation to. As will be seen once again, all legal matters are automatically geared toward *defendant* status of the accused. Guilty by charge and not by verdict.

The P.P. O. follows, with the previous, bolstering actions added to convey the stalwart intensity of the official stance versus Art Piel's vexation. To preface this, a short introduction by Art purports to negate credibility of these reports.

"The next few pages will show a little how the police worked when they were after Lisa. Anytime she disagreed with the police department they would lie in their report about her to discredit her and she could not do anything about it. When you disagreed with the area's police or said anything about them, they would come after you. What you are about to read is just about what type of things that were done and said about Lisa in her years on the department.

"Again, the police can say and write anything about you in their reports and you can not do a thing about it. The next pages are about what they said about me for trying to ask questions

372

about Lisa. The only thing true in the following reports is I did send Croton a card with Lisa's picture and bloody bedding and I did say he deserves it. It does not have anything to do with the following reports. But I also hand-delivered the same type of card to Diane Smith on her last day in Petoskey, saying you and your inSANE group destroyed Lisa mentally and physically. It was not given as a threat but as something to remind Smith of what she did on her part to Lisa. It is something I believe she will keep."

–Art Piel, 1-98

STATE OF MICHIGAN		CASE NO.
57th JUDICIAL DISTRICT / JUDICIAL CIRCUIT	SUMMONS AND COMPLAINT	96 - 4048 - PH

Court address: 200 DIVISION ST., PETOSKEY, MI 49770   Court telephone no. 348-1748

Plaintiff name(s), address(es), and telephone no(s).		Defendant name(s), address(es), and telephone no(s).
SCOTT CROTON 145 HARDWOOD LANE HARBOR SPRINGS M I 49740	v	HENRY ARTHUR PIEL 6322 TRILLIUM TRAIL HARBOR SPRINGS MI 49740

Plaintiff attorney, bar no., address, and telephone no.

(PRO PER)

NOTICE TO THE DEFENDANT: In the name of the people of the State of Michigan you are notified:

1. You are being sued.

2. YOU HAVE 21 DAYS after receiving this summons to file an answer with the court and serve a copy on the other party or to take other lawful action (28 days if you were served by mail or you were served outside this state).

3. If you do not answer or take other action within the time allowed, judgment may be entered against you for the relief demanded in the complaint.

Issued 12-26-96	This summons expires 3-27-97	Court clerk Carol M. Godfrey

*This summons is invalid unless served on or before its expiration date.

☒ There is no other pending or resolved civil action arising out of the same transaction or occurrence as alleged in the complaint.

☐ A civil action between these parties or other parties arising out of the transaction or occurrence alleged in the complaint has

been previously filed in _____ . The docket number and assigned judge are:
                            Name of court

Docket no.	Judge	Bar no.

The action ☐ remains ☐ is no longer   pending.

VENUE	
Plaintiff(s) residence (include city, township, or village) SAME AS ABOVE	Defendant(s) residence (include city, township, or village) SAME AS ABOVE

Place where action arose or business conducted

EMMET COUNTY

I declare that the complaint information above and attached is true to the best of my information, knowledge, and belief.

12-26-96
Date

Signature of attorney/plaintiff

COMPLAINT IS STATED ON ATTACHED PAGES. EXHIBITS ARE ATTACHED IF REQUIRED BY COURT RULE.

MC 01 (6/95) SUMMONS AND COMPLAINT   DEFENDANT   MCR 2.102(B)(11), MCR 2.104, MCR 2.107, MCR 2.113(C)(2)(a), (t

374

ORIGINAL DATE	INCIDENT NO.
Mon, Dec 23, 1996	078-0003339-96
TIME RECEIVED	FILE CLASS
1730	13003

| WORK UNIT | COUNTY |
| PETOSKEY | Emmet |

| COMPLAINANT | | TELEPHONE NO. |
| TERI CROTON | | ( ) - |

| ADDRESS: STREET AND NO. | CITY | STATE | ZIP CODE |
| 145 HARDWOOD LANE | HARBOR SPRINGS | MI | 49740- |

| INCIDENT STATUS | | |
| Open | | Computer #01 |

Intimidation/Stalking

INFORMATION:

On this date at approx 5:00 p.m., the complainant, Teri Croton , was home going through the day's mail when she opened a letter addressed to her husband, Scott Croton, with no return address. Inside the envelope, which she believed contained a Christmas card, was a remnant of a bloody bed sheet with a picture of the suspect's daughter, Lisa, stapled to it. Also attached, was a note to Scott from the suspect, Art Piel, which stated:

"This is a cut from Lisa's bloody beding(sp). I thought you would want to from it (sic) for your office as a trophy, for your part in the big kill. Lisa will not be home for X-mas again this year."

After opening the letter, the complainant became very upset and felt threatened by the note. The complainant's husband, Scott, had received unannounced visits from the suspect, Art Piel, at his place of employment, Boyne Highlands, on previous occasions. These visits were reported in complaint #78-2213-95/9800-7. The suspect, Piel, blames Scott Croton for causing his daughter's suicide, due to his part in an Emmet County Grand Jury several years prior. Lisa Piel was a Petoskey City Police officer who lost her job as a result of this grand jury investigation. Piel had been showing up at other public buildings as well as having contacts with public officials (also chronicled in the aforementioned complaint). As a result of Piel's actions, I requested a profile be done on Mr. Piel by the Michigan State Police Investigative Resources Section. On 01-26-96, a typewritten assessment was forwarded to me by D/Sgt David Minzey of the Investigative Resources Section/Violent Crimes Unit. As part of the assessment, Minzey stated it was his opinion that the risk potential of Mr. Piel is moderate to high. A copy of the assessment is kept with this report.

VENUE:

EMMET COUNTY , LITTLE TRAVERSE TWP
145 HARDWOOD LN

DATE & TIME:

MON, DEC 23, 1996 AT 1730

| PAGE | INVESTIGATED BY | REPORTED BY | REVIEWED BY |
| 1 of 3 | D/SGT BRUCE DYKEHOUSE | | |

ORIGINAL DATE	INCIDENT NO.
Mon, Dec 23, 1996	078-0003339-96
TIME RECEIVED	FILE CLASS
1730	13003

COMPLAINANT:

NAM: TERI CROTON

		RAC: W	ETH:
NBR: 145	DIR:	SEX: F	OPS:
STR: HARDWOOD		DOB:	SSN:
SFX: LANE		HGT:	SID:
CTY: HARBOR SPRINGS	ST: MI	WGT:	FBI:
TXH:	ZIP: 49740	HAI:	MNU:
TXW:		EYE:	PRN:

VICTIM:

NAM: SCOTT CROTON

		RAC: W	ETH:
NBR: 145	DIR:	SEX: M	OPS:
STR: HARDWOOD		DOB:	SSN:
SFX: LANE		HGT:	SID:
CTY: HARBOR SPRINGS	ST: MI	WGT:	FBI:
TXH:	ZIP: 49740	HAI:	MNU:
TXW:		EYE:	PRN:

INTERVIEW VICTIM: Scott Croton

Shortly after arriving at the Croton residence, I was contacted by Scott Croton. He stated he was very upset that this letter was mailed to his home. He stated his address is not listed in the phone book and the suspect would have had to do some above average research to obtain his address. Croton stated following Mr. Piel's visits to him at his place of employment (Boyne Highlands) the previous year, he called and left a message for Piel on his answering machine telling him not to have any further contact with him or be showing up at his place of employment. Croton was very adamant that this was a stalking type complaint and he wants the suspect prosecuted on criminal charges.

EVIDENCE:

1. A white envelope addressed to Scott Croton, 145 Hardwood, Harbor Springs, MI 49740 with a Gaylord postmark dated 12-21-96. The envelope contains a.cardboard backing with a piece of bloody bedding and a picture of Lisa Piel in a Petoskey Police uniform. It also contains a letter from Art Piel to Scott Croton. Value nil. UD-14 signed and submitted.

UD-30:

I supplied Scott Croton with a UD-30 this date.

PAGE	INVESTIGATED BY	REPORTED BY	REVIEWED BY
2 of 3	D/SGT BRUCE DYKEHOUSE		

ORIGINAL INCIDENT REPORT PAGE 1	TIME RECEIVED 09:00A	FILE CLASS 98007

	WORK UNIT PETOSKEY POST	COUNTY EMMET	
COMPLAINANT SCOTT CROTON		**TELEPHONE NO.** 526-3004	
ADDRESS: STREET AND NO. 600 HIGHLAND DRIVE	**CITY** HARBOR SPRINGS	**STATE** MI	**ZIP.** 49740

INCIDENT STATUS

[[5]]   CLOSED

NATURE OF INCIDENT

SUSPICIOUS SITUATION

VENUE:

Boyne Highlands Resort, 600 Highland Dr., Pleasantview Township, Emmet County.

INFORMATION:

Complainant is a retired MSP Detective and is presently employed as Security Director at Boyne Highlands Resort in Harbor Springs. He reported that during the week of 10/16/95 through 10/20/95 a subject had come to his office and asked to speak to him. As the Complainant was not in his office at the time, the person was asked his name by another employee and told the subject he would radio Croton to come to the office to see him. The subject refused to give his name and merely sat in a chair in the office with a blank look and said nothing. A short time later, the subject left the office. This happened on two occassions during the aforementioned week. On friday, 10/20/95 the subject again showed up at the front desk of the resort and again asked for Croton. The employee advised him that she would contact Croton by radio and asked the subject his name. The subject again did not give any further information and just stood there for a few minutes at which time he left. Another employee recognized the subject as ART PIEL and later asked Croton what PIEL wanted with him. Croton stated he does not know ART PIEL and would not recognize him if he saw him. Croton was however involved in a Grand Jury investigation in the course of his employment with the Petoskey Post during which ART PIEL's daughter, LISA, was convicted of Possession or Use of Cocaine and subsequently lost her job as a police officer with the City of Petoskey. Approximately one year ago this month, LISA PIEL committed suicide and ART PIEL has been having a difficult time accepting the death as a suicide. CROTON expressed his concern that ART PIEL somehow holds CROTON at least partially responsible for his daughter's death and feels that PIEL may be targeting him for some sort of retribution. Contacts with other

PAGE	INVESTIGATED BY	REPORTED BY	REVIEWED BY
1	D/SGT. BRUCE DYKEHOUSE		

public officials and a threat against a witness by ART PIEL have also come to the attention of this officer. All available police reports and documents from other agencies are attached to this report.

SUBJECT:

ART PIEL, w/m, approximately 50 years of 6322 Trillium Trail, Harbor Springs, Michigan.

CONTACT WITH BEHAVIORAL SCIENCE SECTION:

I contacted Dr. Gary Kaufmann at the MSP Behavioral Science Section and discussed this complaint with him. Dr. Kaufmann suggested the report be forwarded to D/Sgt. David Minzey for profiling. I also discussed the possibility that personal protection orders be sought for the individuals involved. Dr. Kaufmann advised me that if they were, I confront ART PIEL with the orders and question him regarding his intentions with the contacts.

ACTION TAKEN:

As of this date, no further contacts of suspicious nature have been reported on PIEL. No personal protections orders have been obtained as of this date. It is possible with the passing of the anniversary of LISA PIEL's death, the subject has ceased his contacts. It is also a concern with the approaching holidays the contacts will resume. This report has been forwarded to D/Sgt. Minzey for profiling. At this time the complaint will be closed, to be re-opened at the suggestion of D/Sgt. Minzey or the resumption of contacts by ART PIEL.

FINAL DISPOSITION:

Closed.

| AGE | INVESTIGATED BY | REPORTED BY | REVIEWED BY |
| 2 | D/SGT. BRUCE DYKEHOUSE | | |

ORIG Mon .., 1996	INCIDENT NO. 078-0003339-96
TIME RECEIVED 1730	FILE CLASS 13003

SUSPECT:

NAM: HENRY ARTHUR PIEL

		RAC: W	ETH:
NBR: 6322	DIR:	SEX: M	OPS:
STR: TRILLIUM		DOB: 02/08/1930	SSN: 375-28-0823
SFX: TRAIL		HGT: 6'01"	SID:
CTY: HARBOR SPRINGS	ST: MI	WGT: 195	FBI:
TXH: (616)526-6855	ZIP: 49740	HAI:	MNU:
TXW:		EYE: BLU	PRN:

CONTACT SUSPECT: Henry Arthur Piel

On 12-26-96 at approx 9:00 a.m., I contacted Henry "Art" Piel by TX at his residence. I informed Mr. Piel who I was and who I worked for. At that time, Mr. Piel asked me to spell my name for him which I did. I told Mr. Piel I was requesting him to come in and see me at the State Police Post so I could talk to him about a matter that had come up. Mr. Piel asked me what that matter was and I advised him it was a letter that had arrived at the Croton residence, to which he replied, "Yah, he deserved it." I told Mr. Piel that I would like to talk to him about his motive for the letter and he stated, "I don't want to talk to any Petoskey people."

Mr. Piel went on to state that he had had it with the Petoskey Police and stated, "All of Petoskey - hell's coming there." I informed Mr. Piel I would still like to speak to him about the matter and he went on to state, "I have transcripts, something's coming up." Mr. Piel stated he would not come in to see me; however, I left him my phone number in the event he changed his mind.

STATUS:

Open. Pending review by Emmet County Prosecutor.

PAGE 3 of 3	INVESTIGATED BY D/SGT BRUCE DYKEHOUSE	REPORTED BY	REVIEWED BY

As has been seen, Art's actions were obviously disconcerting to the forces of *public safety*, or at least those that were personally involved with the life and death of Lisa Piel. Add to this some political considerations on the parts of officialdom, couple this with a dogged determination to silence all reference to clearing Lisa's name, an impropriety arises as to the concerted effort to further frustrate all attempts by the Piels to garner any understanding or even an unbiased ear, and what remains is a record of seemingly futile attempts at making a point.

Seemingly, that is because the more the authorities declaimed Art's displays of frustration with hints of instability or even illegality the more Art persevered. As a protagonist, he was initially ineffective due to efforts that were emotionally driven. The offensive taken by these authorities, however, does bolster the insinuation of malfeasance on their parts.

Malfeasance means using power of authority in a personal and an unlawful way. It being still unknown just what benefit was and is derived from the slandering of one's name by these local authorities, one may only presume that it instigated from within an organization which wants and accepts no outside influence but desires its clandestine activities unscrutinized and unquestioned. Detractors are naturally silenced as soon as possible by threat of legal recourse, whether it be psychological or corporal.

This P.P.O. previous brought the psychological aspect into the spotlight. This, added to the next reference to threats on Art's part against a former roommate of Lisa's, occasioned officials to prepare a file on Art of some significance. They were watching him closely now, but not necessarily letting him know about it. A large file exists in the Petoskey City Hall about all of Art Piel's activities outlined here. This was much to his surprise when he eventually inquired into this possibility and discovered the bulk of written reference to himself. He was walking in Lisa's footsteps, it seemed.

We continue with more retrospective reports leading to the accumulation of this "dossier."

Another preface by Art to more reports about his activities:

"The following reports and letters were lies that were being said about me when I was going around trying to ask questions. All these reports were given to me along with the P.P.O. (Personal Protection Order)."

DEPARTMENT OF STATE POLICE

DATE: 10/20/95

"TO: D/Lt. Carl Goeman, Seventh District
        Headquarters

FROM: D/Sgt. R. Sexton, St. Ignace

SUBJECT: Mr. Art Piehl

Per your request reference Mr. Art Piehl

On Monday or Tuesday (10-9, 10-1995) I was contacted by Mr. Novenske of St. Ignace. He is the father of Jennifer Novenske. Jennifer is currently living in Austin Texas. Mr. Novenske reported that Mr. Art Piehl called her over the weekend and told her that within 5 years she was going to be a quadriplegic. The call was tape recorded and reported to Austin Texas PD. Mr. Novenske is concerned because his daughter, Jennifer used to live with Mr. Piehl's daughter in Petoskey at the time of his daughter's suicide. Mr. Novenske is extremely concerned for his daughter. After speaking with Mr. Novenske I spoke with Petoskey

PD for some more background information to see if there is a substantial concern. I recontacted Mr. Novenske and advised him. I also contacted Austin Texas PD. I spoke with their intelligence unit and gave them the same information that the threat should be taken seriously.

My notes on this incident have been destroyed and no complaint was taken. If you need more detailed information contact me and I can recontact involved parties."

"TO: File Memo

FROM: Captain G. Michael Vargo,
        Petoskey Public Safety

DATE: October 20, 1995

RE: MR. ART PIEL

Captain Vargo was contacted by Detective Carl Goeman from the Traverse City Post of the Michigan State Police. He indicated he had been contacted by ex Post 78 Detective Scott Croton. Croton told him that Mr. Art Piel had shown on two different occasions at Croton's work place acting strange, asking for Croton and then disappearing when Croton showed up. Detective Goeman will be conducting an investigation and is requesting copies of any information that our Department may have in reference to the Grand Jury case and the death investigation of Lisa Piel.

This information was compiled by Captain Vargo and sent to Detective Goeman at 218 West 14th Street, Traverse City, Michigan, 49684."

"TO: File Memo

FROM: Captain G. Michael Vargo,
        Petoskey Public Safety

DATE: October 9, 1995

RE: MR. ART PIEL

Captain Vargo was contacted by Detective Sexton from St. Ignace. His phone is 906-648-8383. He indicated he had been contacted by the parents of Jennifer Novenski, who had been Lisa Piel's friend and room mate.

Apparently sometime over the weekend preceding 10-9-95, Jennifer had received a threatening phone call from Art Piel while she was in Texas where she has been living since the incident here in Petoskey with Lisa Piel committing suicide.

Apparently Mr. Piel threatened her with the fact that she would be a paraplegic or quadraplegic within four or five years and he would make sure of it. Detective Sexton was given all the information that Captain Vargo had from previous contacts with Mr. Piel and was given a partial run down of the Piel case as to her death investigation."

"Synopsis Contact Art Piel.

10-9-94: Detective Roth responded at the request of P.P.D.to handle a shooting death with the victim being Lisa Piel. Upon arrival, Detective Roth was approached by Art Piel, father of Lisa, who was extremely upset (understandable), loud and demanding to have his lawyer, Greg Justis, present with officers when the investigation took place. Piel made insinuations about cops being responsible for Lisa's death, not trusting police.

10-12-94: Det. Roth and Sgt. Betts went to the Art Piel residence, Harbor Springs at Piel's request. Present was Mrs. Piel, Jennifer Novenske, Nancy Simon and Geraldine Zarenmski. Art Piel was clam, composed, and thanked Det. Roth and Sgt. Betts for the job we did on the investigation. Art Piel stated he knows his daughter killed herself but was having a problem understanding why. Art Piel requested Det. Roth look into Dave Reed, who discovered Lisa's death. Art Piel had specific questions about Reed he wanted answered. Piel would become enraged when talking about P.P.D., specifically Ken Burke and Mike Vargo and would refer to Lisa's "Black Book," that she kept while working for Petoskey P.P.D.

10-14-94: After talking with Reed, Det Roth advised Art Piel of the interview. Piel seemed satisfied with the answers and again expressed his gratitude.

11-31-94: Det. Roth received information from M.S.P. Lt. McCord that Art Piel was at his department complaining about Det. Roth's investigation and requesting M.S.P. take over the complaint.

Nov. 94 thru March 95: Piel came into the department numerous times demanding all the physical evidence and alleging his daughter was murdered, that is was a police conspiracy and cover-up. Piel would be very upset and demanding. Piel would talk about Lisa's "Black Book" that had all the cop's names in it that ever did her wrong and how he was going to get even. Eventually, as Piel's visits progressed into accusatory yelling and threats of getting even, Det. Roth ordered Piel from the department and barred his return.

March 95 to present: Det. Roth has seen Piel on several occasions at the county building where he would stare at Det. Roth with a hollow blank look. On one occasion, Pros. Smith requested Det. Roth's protection as Piel was in the lobby of her office. When Det. Roth entered with Ms. Smith, Piel jabbed at Det. Roth with his finger and stated, "Get the hell out of here." When Det. Roth advised it was a public building, Piel apologized. Piel then stared at Det. Roth with a blank stare and accused Det. Roth of letting Office Rautio (Petoskey P.P.D.) Into the bedroom with his dead daughter so that Rautio could see her naked because Rautio always wanted to have sex with Lisa. Piel referred to Lisa's "Black Book" and accused Rautio of drug trafficking. Piel stated his daughter was murdered, then admitted she killed herself, then stated it was a conspiracy amongst the police.

3-30-94: all evidence in the matter TOT Atty Mike Buckingham acting on behalf of Art Piel. All pictures were requested. Det. Roth had copies made at the Photo Depot, Petoskey. Det. Roth heard that when Piel picked up the pictures, he demanded the negatives and became quite upset when advised by The Photo Depot that Det. Roth has them.

11-7-95: Undersheriff Wallin stated he observed Piel circling the county building in his vehicle.

Closing: It is Det. Roth's feeling that Lisa's suicide has substantially changed her father, more so than any other suicide Det. Roth has handled. After several contacts with Piel, Det. Roth was left with an uneasy feeling that Piel may attempt retaliation for hurts real or imagined. Det. Roth learned from the county clerk's office that Piel had the section for occupation on his daughter's death certificate changed to reflect Police Officer. A bronze plaque was also placed on the garage of her house stating, "Lisa's Place. In memory of Lisa Piel. The only female police officer for Petoskey."

Respectfully submitted,

D/Sgt. Timothy E. Roth"

EMMET COUNTY SHERIFF
PETOSKEY, MICHIGAN

"TO: File Memo

FROM: Captain G. Michael Vargo,
             Petoskey Public Safety

DATE: October 10, 1995

RE: CONTACTS WITH MR. ART PIEL

Due to recent police contacts with Mr. Art Piel, Captain Vargo finds it necessary to include file memos in the Piel file.

On 3-21-95, at approximately 11:00 AM, Captain Vargo working in his office, was notified that a gentleman by the name of Art Piel was in the front lobby area and wished to talk to Vargo. Vargo approached Mr. Piel and asked what he could do for him. Mr. Piel exhibited a very tense and upset stature about his person in that his arms were behind him, he was standing almost at attention, staring straight forward with non-blinking eyes at Captain Vargo. His jaw was set in a determined manner and he appeared to be very angry.

This caused me to keep my distance and to expect possibly the worst from Mr. Piel as far as a physical confrontation or an armed assault.

When I asked Mr. Piel what I could do for him, he stared straight at me, appearing to look straight through me with stone cold non-blinking eyes and did not say a thing, only taking a step closer to myself. I stepped back, keeping my distance and asked him once again what I could do for him. He took another step forward toward me finally stating in a very low monotone voice, "I just wanted to see a crooked cop." I asked him what he meant by that and he restated it exactly in the same low monotone voice and using the same body language that he displayed earlier.

Fearing for the worst and not knowing what Mr. Piel might do next, I asked him who he was as I had never met him before. To this he stated, "You know very well who I am. You worked with my daughter," once again displaying the same low monotone voice and physical demeanor.

I am unsure how many times he repeated as we stood looking at each other, the statement, "I've always wanted to see a crooked cop." He also stated "I just came down here to get a look at a crooked cop," over and over again. After listening to this for a short period of time it appeared as though he was starting to raise his voice. I feared he would create a disturbance in the lobby area as there were other people doing business at the other city offices.

I advised him if he continued to be loud and intimidating, disturbing the business routine of the building, that he could be placed under arrest for being a disorderly person. To this he indicated, "That's what I would expect from a crooked cop."

I advised Mr. Piel that his business here in the building appeared to be concluded and that I no longer cared to talk with him as long as he continued to be threatening. I advised him he had better leave the building.

As he left the building, I followed behind him and followed him out into the street to his vehicle which was a two tone Ford pickup, believed to be Burgundy and silver in color with a sign on the driver's door indicating something about Piel Construction.

Having never met Mr. Piel before it appeared to me as though he was in some type of a trance in that he walked very slow and deliberate, staring straight ahead. His eyes were glassy and did not blink. He did not move other than to take two steps in my direction, causing me to back up and had his hands behind his back standing as though he were at attention. All of this seemed very peculiar to me and it caused me to realize that he could be a very dangerous person. I feared for my well being. Since this happened, I feel afraid for myself and my family.

I contacted Mr. Piel's attorney, Mike Buckingham, to find out what the problem was. Buckingham indicated Mr. Piel was not dangerous and did not mean to be threatening police officers. I advised Mr. Buckingham that Mr. Piel was no longer wanted in our city offices if he continued to act threatening. (Apparently Mr. Piel had been in to see the city manager and our public safety director at least 2 or 3 times). They both have no further business with him.

Mr. Buckingham said he would advise Mr. Piel to stay away from the city offices. He also said he would alert the proper authorities if he heard his client threaten any police personnel.

Mr. Buckingham indicated he would only be Mr. Piel's attorney during the process of Mr. Piel trying to obtain Lisa Piel's personnel file.

At this point Art would like to interject his strong viewpoint about these concatenations of events, directed in particular toward Mike Vargo:

"As God is my witness, what really happened when I, Art Piel, went to see Mike Vargo, not just my opinion or how I saw it, the total truth and exactly what was said and done.

"Mike Vargo walked out of the office area to me; just as he was stopping to talk, he said:

'Am I supposed to know you?'

"I replied, 'No, I am Lisa Piel's father.'

"Vargo said, 'I have nothing to say to you.'

"I replied, 'Oh, I did not come here to talk, I came to see what a real dirty cop looks like.'

"I stood there for a couple of seconds and then walked out of the building. Vargo walked right behind me so close I could feel him.

"Mike Vargo is a liar of the worst kind. This is how he works, as told to me from an ex-cop. He is a pathological liar.

"I think it is the people's right and need to know that Mike Vargo is a dirty lying cop. He should be fired from his job as a police officer. A liar is the lowest kind of human being, and anyone who protects him is as guilty as he is. Of course, where there is one liar, there is another liar."

Then this by Art to address the St. Ignace report by the State Police there. This note is printed in its unexpurgated form and precedes a somewhat longer letter pertaining to several aspects of Art's thwarted attempts at information gathering as well as the allegations accumulating against him.

I always thought of the State Police as the West
Point of police work; not true. Sergeant R. Sexton of
St. Ignace wrote a report about me (Art Piel) to Carl
Goeman, Seventh District Headquarters, that Mr.
Novenske told him I threatened his daughter,
Jennifer–which is a lie. Mr. Novenske and his
daughter are liars, and Sexton talked to Petoskey's
Mike Vargo, the biggest liar of all. Now, tome, that
makes Sexton a liar. I would think he would check a
report like this out before slandering someone, and
then destroying his notes. Good State Police work.
Sexton, you get your police friends and the
Novenske's and show me and the world where I
threatened or said anything to Jennifer Novenske as
your report said.

Art Piel"

The allegation pertaining to the Novenskes evidently stemmed
from some casual remark made out of context and not directed at
all toward Jennifer Novenske–a snowballing effect that in police
hands escalated to this as yet unresolved accusation, perhaps still
considered by authorities to be cause for "dossier" material on Art
Piel. Though Art admits readily to some ineffective and emotional
displays due to the loss of his daughter's career–and his daughter–
his outspoken frustration at "legal" proceedings lead him to speak
the truth as he knows it. Unresolved allegations, in fact and as
has been seen, provided the basis for almost all charges having to
do with this story in its entire evolution.

A bloody remnant of bedding is certainly a disconcerting article
to receive in the mail, especially at Christmas time, as mr. Croton's
wife did, and as Prosecutor Diane Smith did as well at her
departure from city work, delivered in person by Art Piel.

Art does not deny these actions. Nor does he hesitate to
explain descrying his banishment from the "halls of justice" that

would not and will not listen to requests for any other terminologies of said "justice."

Though Art's actions were undoubtedly blatant, he was left with no alternative but silence due to the unremitting pressures brought to bear against any research of facts or attempts at release of Lisa's files or charges. No alternatives, that is, until this book.

Everyone in the legal professions involved with the Piels either "clammed up" or initiated allegations stemming from any and all overt actions on art's part. He was clearly being ostracized by dint of inference and invidious threat. All avenues were, and remain, blocked.

Art's letter of late 1997 to the State Police Post of Petoskey, next, will serve to preface his somewhat longer Statement to come.

September 17, 1997

"Bruce Dykehouse
State Police Post
1200 M-119
Petoskey, MI 49770

"Mr. Croton said I did above average research to obtain his address, I did not. All I did was ask someone where Mr. Croton lived,they told me the name of the subdivision and street, his name was on the mail box. Obtaining this information did not take any above average research. If Mr. Croton said I was stalking him, Mr. Croton had better get his dictionary out.

"I went to visit Mr. Croton at his office and asked if he was around. There were about 3 or 4 men in the office area, one person said Mr. Croton was not in, and said he would try to reach him on his car phone. He asked for my name and I said, "if I give you my name he may not want to talk to me" and we all laughed a little. The young man contacted Mr. Croton and said Mr. Croton will be in the office in about 15 to 20 minutes. I did not set in a chair with a blank look, I was standing in the doorway in front of some steps. I did not have time to wait and said I would see him later and left the building. I did not refuse to give my name, almost every one in Mr. Croton's office at that time knew who I was. I came in the office again when I was in the area. There was one man in the office doing paper work and I asked him if he was Mr. Croton, he said no and that Mr. Croton was on the road. I left the building.

"One other time I went to Mr. Croton's office and asked the woman at the desk if Mr. Croton was in, and she said no. I sat on a bench for a minute, and left the building. I was not stalking him and did not go out of my way to see him. I just wanted to talk to him whenever I was in the area.

"Mr. Croton called me and left a message on my answering machine indicating he knew who I was, and "I know you want to ask questions." He did ask that I not come around his place of work but I thought if we met, we could talk. I was not jumping out from behind trees to talk to him.

"I sent the picture and bedding of Lisa's to let him know how I felt. I am sorry Mrs. Croton opened the card and that they felt threatened. It was not meant to be a threat.

"Dykehouse reports I am 50 years old, I am 67. Lisa Piel was not convicted of possession or use of cocaine. She lost her job because she knew people who were using drugs. One of them being her superior officer, who was also selling drugs. Her superior officer said he would kill her if she reported him, his name will come out in the future.

"The anniversary of Lisa's death or holidays, has nothing to do with what is going on. I am doing an investigation of Lisa's death and the loss of her job. This will go on if need be, to my death and then my family will take over.

Re: Roth Report

"After Roth got to Lisa's house and he spoke to the officer's that were there, I asked Roth if he knew Lisa, and he said he knew Lisa was a police officer. I was not loud and demanding lawyer Greg Justis to be in with the investigation. Greg Justis is not my lawyer and never was. I never saw him until that night. He was the lawyer for David Reed. David Reed said that Justis should go with Roth to investigate so there are not any dirty trick's going on and I agreed.

"When Roth and Betts were at my house I asked questions about Reed that I wanted answered. I did not become enraged when talking about the Petoskey Police Department, although I did not have anything good to say. Roth need's a dictionary. There were 4 other people in the room, Roth is a liar. Roth said he advised me of an interview he had with Reed, he did not.

"My wife and I, with an investigator went, to the Michigan State Police and spoke to Lt. McCord to ask him to take over the investigation of Lisa's death. We told him we felt it was incomplete. We did not know this was something he could not do. I think all the Michigan State Police could do for us is call Roth and tell him 1/2 truths about us and about Lisa. I said that there was a conspiracy among the police to get her out of police work. It is a fact that there was a conspiracy to do just that. My 2-1/2 year investigation has got me a little closer to the truth of Lisa's death and loss of her job. It takes money and time and I will keep going little by little until my death to get the truth. I have people telling me they are afraid they will get there head shot off.

"When I picked up pictures at the Photo Depot in Petoskey Roth said I demanded the negatives. I did not demand the negatives, I asked where they were. The man at Photo Depot said the negatives went back to Roth, that they belong to the public and anyone can see them. He also said he can go up and get the pictures anytime he wants. Yes, after that I was upset to think that the pictures were made up in a place like that and not in a crime lab. Up to this time I saw Roth 2 times, at Lisa's death and at my house.

"My first visit to the Sheriff's Office the sheriff took me back to his office. We talked and I asked him if Lisa's case was closed and if I could get her belongings back, such as her gun, bedding, death pictures, etc. He was very pleasant and told me the case was not completed. D. Smith still had to complete her end and sign it. As I was leaving I said, "I think you're the only one I can trust, thank you."

"My second visit to the Sheriff's Office was approximately 2 to 3 weeks later. I asked for the Sheriff and he came out to the entrance area of the department. We talked and he said he had not heard anything from D. Smith. He talked about going to another Prosecutors office to have the case closed and that maybe D. Smith was too close to the case. He said he would look in to it and let me know. I thanked him and left.

"My third visit I made an appointment to see the Sheriff. The woman at the front desk said the sheriff could not make it. She said she was supposed to call me but time got away from her. I asked when was a good time to drop in.

"My fourth visit sometime later, the Sheriff was not in and I saw Roth in the area so I asked to see Roth. He came to the window and I asked Roth if he knew if D. Smith signed off on the case and when did he think I could get her belongings. I never got upset and demanding. He said, something like case not going to be closed and that I am not getting back the things. He told me to get out. I felt bad that he talked to me the way he did. I told my wife when I got home, "all I want to do is talk to him." In Roth's report "Piels visits progressed into accusatory yelling and threat of getting even" all lies.

"My fifth time to the building to see D. Smith, she came out and I told her I came to talk about Lisa's death and closing the case, she said, wait just a minute, left and came back with Roth. This is only the fourth time I've seen Roth. I did say get the hell out of here and I did apologize. D. Smith told me at another meeting after this one, she got Roth because she did not know anything about the case. He said I then stared at him with a blank stare. Another lie, we were talking too fast to each other. I did not accuse Roth of letting officer Rautio of the Petoskey Police Department into the bedroom. Rautio was in the house and bedroom, and I told Rautio to get out of the house. He left about 45 minutes to an hour before Roth got to the house. Lisa has no black Book she left a diary of some sort of day to day working on job. I may have said she was murdered one time to Roth, but I have always said she killed herself, but I also said I felt there was something wrong. There was no real investigation of her death. And the day I met D. smith when she had Roth come with her Roth told me he knew something about Lisa that I did not know and when we were talking fast at each other, I did say hell is coming to Petoskey.

"On 11-7-97 Undersheriff Wallin stated he observed Piel circling the County Building in his truck. I am a general contractor in Emmet county and in the late summer 1995 and through to spring

1996 I was in and out of the Emmet County Building Department, sometimes 2 to 3 times a week and Nick White was the architect on the job I was working on and I had to see him sometimes 2 times a day. So I sometimes had to drive around 2 or 3 times to get a parking place. Take Wallin's parking place away at the Sheriff's Office in the afternoon and he may have to do some circling around. I met with D. Smith at the County Building after 5:00 P.M. one time and I also met with Smith and Engle at each meeting I was told I have to see the Sheriff to talk about what I would like to have. After that I called to talk to the Sheriff and he told me to make a list of what I want to talk about, send it to him and he would get back to me in 24 hours. I wrote the letter September 13, 1995, and have not heard from him to this date. I called the Sheriffs office many times after that and he would not talk to me. I feel being a tax payer in Emmet County, I should be able to talk to Roth or the Sheriff about Lisa's death. If Roth is not man enough to meet with me he can have me cuffed and have 2 or 3 officers in the room. Or is he just like I hear in the area. He is not any older then his son.

"D./Sgt. Minzey of the Investigative Resources Section Violent Crimes Unit. There is two sides to every case, or are you part of this conspiracy among the police in this area. With their lies and half truths too? You have destroyed my reputation. This whole report has gotten in to the hands of a newspaper. The reporter Richard Bachus told me he could not tell me a name but he said it was a law officer in the City of Petoskey or the Emmet County sheriff's Department who told him the report is in the Clerk's office freedom of information.

"D./Sgt. Minzey stated it was his opinion that the risk potential of Piel is moderate to high. I never saw or met Minzey, he has never talked to me, but makes a judgement on lies and hear say, just like a grand jury.

"Mike Vargo Petoskey Police Captain wrote a report on his first and only meeting with me. Every page and word told lies, I came in to talk to him about Lisa and this is what really happened:

"I came in to the City Building and asked for Mike Vargo, after about 2 minutes he came out. He walked out to me, just as he was stopping to talk he said, "Am I supposed to know you?" and I replied "No, I am Lisa Piel's father." Vargo said, "I have nothing to say to you." and I replied, "Oh, I did not come here to talk, I came to see what a real dirty cop looks like." I stood there for a couple of seconds and then walked out of the building. Vargo walked right behind me so close I could feel him and he stood on the City building porch in the rain and watched me get in my truck. I am no angel but I do not lie, and I face up to my wrong doings. Vargo's report and the ones before are out and out lies. A lying cop is the dirtiest thing there is.

"Yes, I came to see the City Manager after Lisa's death 3 or 4 times to get her file. My wife was head of Lisa's estate and had a right for me to come in to see the City Manager and give him a letter about the estate. We have a right to see her file. That took about 2 months to get, I believe Dick Smith, City Attorney had most of her file destroyed. Our attorney thought that was very possible. The attorney also told us at 2 different meetings that Dick Smith hated Lisa, also said there was no doubt

400

in his mind and some other attorneys in town thought that there was a conspiracy to get Lisa off the Police job.

"My wife and I had one meeting with the City of Police Postelnick, and City Manager together. I do not believe they felt threatened in any way. The report to Carl Goeman, District Headquarters, from R. Sexton, St. Ignace said that I threatened Jennifer Novenske. That is not true. I did not threaten or say anything that the report said I did. I would not say those things to Jennifer. After Lisa's death my wife and I have talked to her 2 or 3 times a month. She calls us or we call her. She is one of the key persons to know what happened to Lisa. She sent me 3 tapes about a month or so ago of her talking to a very key person. Which were very hard to understand, I paid $1,000.00 to an ex-FBI agent to have him clean up the tape, which he did. I would never shut the door on Jennifer by threatening her. Vargo when reporting the Jennifer matter, put his own words in his report when he sent it out.

"I could go on and on but it is very hard for me to write things down on a letter. There is so much to talk about, but no one will talk to me so I will go it alone. A one man grand jury, like a grand jury I will be the judge and jury all in one. My investigation on the loss of Lisa's job and her life is very warm. It is opening up a can of worms. I always thought the law was to get the truth of any matter or death. Jennifer Novenske tried to talk to Tim Roth after Lisa's death and he would not talk to her.

"Lisa Piel was young, beautiful and a very caring person. She loved and was loved my many. She died a lonely gruesome death.

"Through this whole ordeal my wife and I have gotten nothing but resistance and empty promises from local law enforcement agencies. This can only lead us to believe that they have something to hide. We will keep searching for the truth. We are not alone.

Art Piel

xc: Carol M. Godfrey
        Robert Engle
        D. Sgt. Minzey
        D. Lt. Goeman
        George Korthauer
        Chief Postelnick
        Tim Roth"

18

A
Tentative Conclusion

etting back to Dave Reed, that most enigmatic of figures involved, the Emmet County Sheriff's Department has a letter from him addressed to a Pete Castillo, who is involved somehow with investigation. Mr. Castillo had obviously said or written some allusion to Mr. Reed's being responsible for Lisa's death. Dave Reed articulates well that perhaps Castillo himself had some part in it, him knowing ". . . how to set the scene to simulate a suicide . . ." He also in this letter suggested, ". . . urge Jennifer into some therapy . . ." Evidently this Pete Castillo had been responsible for taping phone calls between Reed and Novenske, as Reed warns him in this letter as well. He adds that all his documents are secured with the Piel family in "the event of any harm" to himself.

Art Piel, in turn, relates that Mr. Reed possibly went home to obtain a sledge hammer and a towel with which to break into Lisa's house on that tragic night. That seems an extravagant motion and relegates some planning to the continuity of that evening. Both Mr. and Mrs. Piel said Lisa had told them of Dave Reed's advances toward her in an amorous way about a month prior to her death. She had reportedly told him she did not see him in this way, but only as a friend, at which Mr. Reed got mad and was said to have "cried." Mr. Piel also states that no one looked into neither Reed's nor Jennifer Novenske's potential involvements in Lisa's demise, whether for good or for ill. Jennifer left the state suddenly after this occurrence, her trail never being followed up for time schedules.

Lisa had been seeing a therapist sometime recently prior to her death. Somehow Mr. Reed got this person's phone number and called shortly after the night in question, saying to this therapist that Lisa was fully dressed rather than clad only in the panties she was found wearing. This therapist told Art thereafter that "her business is to listen to people, and that's exactly what he told her." Art adds, "she loved life, her bed was messed up bad, she was caught off guard, never went to bed undressed."

Art also alleges that Dave Reed "told somebody how many bullets were left in her gun clip." As to the blood on Reed's coat, "he said he had to shake her to see if she was alive; well, when I saw her you didn't have to shake her. When I saw Lisa in her death bed, her eyes were open. She had been crying; her eyelashes were stuck together." He further postulated that when someone takes their own life, they don't hold their eyes wide open, they would naturally close them tightly–for the big sleep.

Lisa's bottle of liquor and glass, of course, were not fingerprinted. Not one fingerprint exists from that entire investigation, which in itself would seem to preclude any finalization of summary. By the testing thereafter she had evidently drunk half of the bottle existent–which bottle, half-full, her mother still has. All in all, the prognosis seemed to fit in indicating self-taken life. Art said later, "95% chance she killed herself; yet . . . question."

It actually was a dark, rainy night when Lisa Piel died. Art Piel had come looking for her that evening, tried to get in and couldn't without breaking something. He went around to her bedroom window, saw her disordered bedclothes, and since the window was open about four inches, called out, "Lisa, it's Dad." No answer. He then left and went out looking for her. It was later reported that Dave Reed had seen this visit by Art Piel. Reed said he watched Art walk around the house, then leave. Then Reed is said to have gotten a sledge hammer, waited for a neighbor's nearby lights to go out for the night, and broke into Lisa's house. The time schedule remains open to conjecture. As much as an hour, or perhaps even more, are unaccounted for since the only verifiable times are those recorded by the police personnel. Art speculates that Reed stole Lisa's address book, which would account for his having called several friends and relations soon after that. It is of course possible that Mr. Reed did any number of things having been presumably the only other person in that house besides Lisa for that undisclosed amount of time. The answering machine tape, for instance, might have been listened to or tampered with, as Art Piel suggests. And then, Art says that Dave Reed told him "they'd find Jennifer's finger prints on Lisa's gun." None of this appears in police reports. A private investigator affiliated with Art Piel stated it "looked like there was a struggle," presumably when viewing the photos of the scene.

When Dave Reed called Art Piel at his home to tell him he'd better get over there, Art said, "It was the worst drive of my life." As one might imagine.

All these recent statements are unofficial, of course. Truth spoken is different from truth considered and polished, as in legal procedure. These latter comments were given freer rein to widen the spectrum of emotions involved. After all, "hear-say" was fully allowed in the Grand Jury trials. The no "blacks and whites" of this story are most closely perceived when collecting the variegated asides and addenda's to the official version, but as the official version has as many holes and lacunae as any other rendition, these casual remarks certainly allow raw material for conjecture.

Alvin Toffler, author of "Future Shock," followed up that sociological classic with "The Third Wave," which alludes to the post-technological revolution in this and other countries, and ultimately with the entire world. He says:

"We can either resist the thrust toward diversity, in a futile last-ditch effort to save our Second Wave political institutions, or we can acknowledge diversity and change those institutions accordingly.

The former strategy can only be implemented by totalitarian means and must result in economic and cultural stagnation; the latter leads toward social evolution and a minority-based 21st century democracy."

Setting one's viewpoint above the horizon of these past chronicled events it may be seen that a clash is in progress. It is not immiscible like oil and water but an acculturation process, or "melting-pot" of acceptance, one toward another. If indeed the Big Brother tactics of "double-think" and totalitarianism are allowed full sway, the world would surely be lacking in diversity and assuredly freedom.

Dr. M. Scott Peck, author of "The Road Less Traveled," and an eminent psychiatrist, wrote "People Of The Lie" as a follow-up to the former title, which still appears on local bookseller's shelves. In "People Of The Lie" Dr. Peck discusses the potential of a confluence of psychiatry with religion, and dares to probe into the labelling of "evil" as a treatable term of disease. Psychic disease. He offers a paradym in its simplest form as equasion: ". . . wherever there is evil, there's a lie around." This train of thought is broached because in the next four-fold personality disorder described by him lies a strong hint as to the sickness of fear and vindictiveness inherent in the foregoing biographical sketch of personalities and area mores. "The time is right," he says, "I believe, for psychiatry to recognize a distinct new type of personality disorder to encompass those that I have named evil. In addition to the abrogation of responsibility that characterizes all personality disorders, this one would be specifically distinguished by:

- (a) consistent destructive, scapegoating behavior, which may often be quite subtle.
- (b) excessive, albeit usually covert, intolerance to criticism and other forms of narcissistic injury.
- (c) pronounced concern with a public image and self-image of respectability, contributing to a stability of life-style but also to pretentiousness and denial of hateful feelings or vengeful motives.
- (d) intellectual deviousness, with an increased likelihood of a mild schizophrenic disturbance of thinking at times of stress."

That four-point analysis, it would seem, defines with exceeding accuracy many persons who wear the black robe. It also filters down into the realm of all keepers of the peace and anyone who wields authority over others. Many of those who wield the law place themselves above the law. Interpretation of law is a basically one-sided proposition. The rhetoric of bureaucracy is so all-inclusively on the side of prosecution that the ordinary person does not stand a chance of getting a fair trial unless he or she is rich, as in the well-known case of O.J. Simpson, once this person is accused. O.J., whether actually guilty or not, was exonerated but did spend one full year behind bars nonetheless. The entire

407

accusatory body, defense lawyers, jurors, reporters, and all concerned got paid for their time; O.J. got one year and paid all their salaries, in essence.

Scaling these grandiose theories and examples down to accommodate small-town, America, the same basic premise holds true, but lacks the diversity of the big city with all its necessary compromises and acceptances of this diversity. In the small town the grip is often iron-like since, as one local man says, "they'll either kill you or paint a picture of something you're not, and run you out." This same person dared to file a grievance against Prosecutor Diane Smith in 1993 or 1994 which resulted in her being investigated for misconduct. Four months later this person was charged with two felonies. Please see Dr. Peck's four-fold theory above, clause (b) in particular.

And then, as Frederick Douglass said more than a century ago, "power concedes nothing without demand; it never did and it never will."

Art Piel had a plaque made for the front of Lisa's house, which he maintains now, keeping it for relatives and friends of the family. a photo of this appears in the center section of this book. Lisa Michele Piel died at thirty-seven with more than half of her life expectancy unfulfilled. Her mother and father want nothing less than total abrogation of all charges and innuendos held against her.

Art has, of course, talked to many persons concerning all the facts and fictions of this case. One friend told him flatly, "Art, I'm afraid to get my head shot off." Art even concedes he can't name names. And this is the man, Lisa's father, carrying on this crusade. He can't name names because these names are friends who fear for their very lives. And this is in the beautiful small town of Petoskey Michigan and surrounding area, Ernest Hemingway country, home of the Shining Big Sea Water, where people come seeking purity of life and lifestyle, simplicity of society.

There is a symbol used in philosophical circles that is known as "Occam's Razor." It refers to the "most likely truth" of a given argument or situation. Looking back over all the facts and theories

408

contained herein, the reader will no doubt appraise himself of all said and arrive at an opinion either of most likely truth or predisposed judgement, depending on his/her wont and disposition. The law of the land often reflects only opinions, not realities. Much of "evidence" is not allowed in many trials, being ruled inadmissible, by virtue of the "opinion" of the prosecutorial / judgmental team. The small-town court system is an anachronism in times such as these, most issues now being out of their league, they being but equipped for the old-style, good ol' boy, lasso the bad guys-type, cops and robbers, judge 'em and hang 'em justice that held sway not all that long ago all across America. And this despite the new input of legalists whose agendas tend more toward personal opportunities than equilateral justice. The people of Petoskey were no more ready for Lisa than the people of Nazareth were ready for the man Jesus.

Times and mores are changing. "Women-folk" are not relegated to the kitchen and the bedroom exclusively anymore. Diane Smith, as prosecutor and a woman herself, might well have given Lisa Piel her due as the first and only female on the force, but instead used her as a political stepping stone toward the black robe she so desired. The opportunist got the better of the altruist; it is plain which is which.

As to some of the other players in this drama, Chief Ernest Kraus is said to be working as a guide of some sort in Arizona; Ken Burke is living and working in Florida but his occupation is not known; Matt Breed is still a Petoskey officer; Croton, as mentioned, works in security; Earl Doernenberg is retired and may have cancer; and Diane Smith is an editor for a lawyer's news periodical in Lansing, Michigan.

For whatever reason or reasons the majority of these persons moved on, there exist still some segments of this old guard tactic and philosophy of guardianship. "To serve and protect" is not the main credo under which they operate. The younger officers are said to be mostly unaffected by the old corruptions. some of the now older ones may still harbor some atavistic feelings of malfeasance. Joe Rautio is no longer on the force; his brother John, after his stint in jail, is back in the drywall business and advertises locally. One-time Officer Schaefer quit the force and is in the insurance business. His reasons for quitting are open to conjecture. Many were said to have left when City Manager Korthauer hired on. Dave Reed, who started Citizens Against Legal Misconduct (C.A.L.M.) in 1996, to monitor police activities in Emmet county, is reported to be "jerky and jittery about Lisa" whenever the topic is broached in conversation. Alice Waybrant, one of Lisa's former roommates and Grand Jury testifiers, stopped outside Lisa's house one day, grieving for her, at which Officer Matt Breed came by in a cruiser and ordered her to "leave the premises." Earl Doernenberg told Cheryl Sieradski's father that Lisa was a lesbian and that she, a long-time friend of Lisa's, should "stay away from her."

There are other mysterious figures in this scenario, some benign, some malignant, of which no trace can be found. Vague allegations of set-ups and plea bargainings abound throughout, but of proof, nothing else exists. Lisa's friend, Gerri Zaremski, was arrested on a bogus charge not long ago and exonerated ultimately with a sizable monetary settlement, the inference being that she was a friend of Lisa's and open to harassment by deputies and police officers. she was overwhelmingly acquitted, however, which attests either to her and her family's good standing in town or a possible change in the winds of prejudice, maybe a little of both, or a majority of one inference and a minority of the other. The societal climate changes but slowly. Yet change, short of totalitarianism as suggested, cannot be stopped. The greatest deterrent to freedom of diversity is fear. The ubiquitous "I have to live here," like an old broken l.p. record, resounds in the well-kept thoroughfares, side streets, front lawns, marinas and nightclubs of Northern Michigan. The fear of having a picture painted falsely outweighs any ethical indignation a local citizen might harbor.

Lisa's story is perhaps unique in that she experienced a dramatic chain of events, and certainly Dickensian arch-enemies in her thirteen-year tenure, concluding in the most poignant of all endings: death. Premature death. That is why "interrupted" is used in the title, to accentuate the very real thought that the interruption had to do with the rest of her life. She was not a martyr by choice, but by chance.

Lisa Piel's birth sign was LEO. A helpful astrologer in New Jersey, VINCENT STARCASTS, offered these insights into Lisa's general tendencies of her birth date of July 24, 1957. "Noble character; people pleaser; artistic nature; high standards that she expected others to live up to; she couldn't always live up to these standards herself; good person; law enforcement was below her; a feminist but didn't quite believe it; potential of being ostentatious; a showman; theatrical; likes pleasure and amusement; tends to dramatize spontaneously for possible stimulation; enjoys basking in the sun; into herself–main attraction; risk of becoming effete through overindulgence, possibly complete discharge of emotional batteries resulting in jaded insensitivity; sincere and sympathetic; can benefit through superiors." Thank you, Vincent.

A thinking, caring, compassionate person might say, as Gerri Zaremski has said, that a "need to clean house" is immanent; others will say and have said that nothing will change. Realistically, something will change but not everything. Art Piel and family want the charges against Lisa exculpated and her honor and name vindicated. This is not far-fetched. Lisa has no actual "record." When seen in total retrospect, as this book purports, no wrongs were ever done by her, only the most minor of peccadillos. In contrast, many wrongs were perpetrated against her, most by authoritarian figures. It's not that hard to see. It is only fearful to acknowledge it publicly. As to her death, the bumbling, incompetent manner of investigation might easily be utilized as a tool to upgrade techniques and means of such archaic methodologies of detective work, negating all stated premises and potentially be used as future teaching guides as to the importance of improving outmoded and erroneous reactions to crime scene evaluations. But, with the cry for more law and order seems to have come more law and disorder. More laws hamper police work rather than create more harmonious neighborhood, more laws allow for more vindictiveness on the parts of disgruntled neighbors. Where once neighbors settled differences by argument, fights, compromises, promises, apologies or whatever, now the court and the officers of the law must intercede for the individual, not always with equanimity in mind. Indeed, many officers "have to arrest" someone now, making "Robocops" out of potentially mitigating influences.

Updating on the remainder of the Grand Jury participants—and this is strictly hear-say"—Julie Woodruff (Woody) and Alice Waybrant are said to have been "addictive personalities who straightened themselves out" prior to the Grand Jury. Lora Hinkley, whose brother was recently (1997) arrested, seems to have been at variance with the law on numerous occasions. Kathy Boyer, whose father was a State Trooper, is alleged to have falsely testified—again, hear-say—Lisa having arrested a member of the family once on drunk driving charges. Linda Postle, Lisa's friend and one-time roommate, was said to have "fed Lisa to the lions," quote anonymous.

The only other member of said jury, John Rautio, is a convicted drug dealer. A shadowy figure, un-named and unknown, reportedly said, "Lisa died because of a drug sting." His particular case was thrown out of an in-process court plea-bargain under "mysterious circumstances." Another loose end to a concatenation of myraid loose ends.

Other persons un-nameable, were contacted by Art Piel for input. All but one "clammed up" after initially speaking freely about Lisa. Some even claimed "wrong number" when re-contact was attempted. There would seem to be some pervasive threat in the atmosphere surrounding Lisa and her experiences yet. Even, or perhaps especially, former police personnel refuse to speak up or have their names mentioned. There is no insight or integrity in the aftermath tactics of war. And war it was, with many victims. The main actress, whose story this is, will not be sidelined much longer under the shroud of culpability. As she slowly rises to martyr status, some of the persons involved will belatedly rise to the occasion; the detractors will either disappear into the theatre wings or utilize the law to discredit and scapegoat.

The shroud of secrecy is perforated now. It took Lisa's father to initiate a small monument to her. If Lisa had died in the line of duty perhaps the City would feel compelled to attest to her positive accomplishments. As it stands, the threat to the City of revealing dubious practices past and present, precludes any recognition on their parts of Lisa's worth or position in the cultural skein of change. It will perhaps take a new regime to "clean house" of the accumulated detritus of deals and coverups, scapegoating and vengeance-ridden hypocrisy innate to the bureaucracy of this and other towns. Frank Serpico is back in the forefront of this quest once again. He says he envisions a day when the corrupt cops are afraid of the honest ones.

Lisa's Story tips the scales. Unfortunately, as always, someone has to get shot, locked away, crucified or exiled as catalyst for change. It is not known if more than one sacrifice to this process of evolvement will surface. This is possible. A sequel to this book is also possible.

LISA'S STORY

"Through this whole ordeal
my wife and I
have gotten nothing but resistance and
empty promises from local law
enforcement agencies.
This can only lead us to believe that
they have something to hide.
We will keep searching for the truth.
We are not alone."

–Art Piel

A STATEMENT

BY

ART PIEL

T his concluding statement by Art Piel, though reiterative, lends a compacted, thumbnail sketch of events in retrospect as perceived and lived through by him, his family and friends. This brief treatise was transcribed from both letter and tape recorded versions of his feelings of catharsis at the compiling and editing of this story: LISA'S STORY.

STATEMENT BY ART PIEL

"Our daughter, Lisa Michele Piel, joined the Petoskey Police Department September, 1978 under a C.E.T.A. program. In September, 1983 she received a private investigator's license for the State of Michigan. Lisa was with the Petoskey Police Department for thirteen and one-half years.

"Her chief, Ernie Kraus, and several other officers who were not certified officers (Lisa was Michigan certified, training at Grand Valley State College) did not like women police officers. She was harassed starting from the beginning with sexual and verbal comments. She was constantly being written up with minor infractions.

"Within three years of being on the force there was talk because of her age to have her work undercover as a narcotics agent, which she felt, as we did, was an entrapment to catch her with some drugs. That did not go through because she had talked with us (parents) about it!

After years of making her life miserable, Diane Smith, Prosecutor, and the police department, with the Grand Jury, charged her with cocaine possession and misconduct in public office. Lisa was forced to resign February 14, 1992.

For about two years after resigning her job she started drinking quite a bit, was depressed and put herself into a rehabilitation center. After coming out of rehab she tried getting work with her private investigator license, which did not work out well in a small town.

"She started a wallpaper business which was going very well but, as the construction business goes, up and down. Still grieving over the loss of her job, with bills piling up (owning her own home, car and work van) and the death, 1989, of her brother at forty years of age, plus losing her kidney in 1991, her father having by-pass surgery after a heart attack in 1992–on October 8, 1994, she was found in her home in bed, dead from a gunshot to the heart.

"After her death I, Art Piel, started to look into why she lost her job and what was behind it, looking through her papers and notes she had left behind and talking to people and attorneys. One attorney we talked to, Mike Buckingham, told us he talked with some other attorneys and all agreed there was no doubt that there was a conspiracy by the police department to get Lisa off the force. Even the Prosecuting Attorney, Diane Smith, told us that it was not her but the police department that wanted her out of the department. I believe that is true because she knew too much of what was going on in the force, the way things were being handled, and that they thought she was a lesbian.

"Buckingham told us the City of Petoskey, city attorney, Richard Smith, and all, hated Lisa, so I feel that when my wife tried to get Lisa's papers from the police records and was turned down twice–two months later when they gave us some papers to see, there was nothing there to see–I told Mike Buckingham that I think City Attorney, Richard Smith, destroyed them, Buckingham said that is possible.

"Ernie Kraus, the Chief of Police, said he did not like women police officers. This he said at a dinner party we were at. There's no doubt there was a conspiracy because she was the only one that they were after in the police force. She did not do any drugs; she did not sell drugs; they couldn't find any drugs; all they had were scared witnesses that testified what Croton and Breed wanted them to say.

"She pleaded guilty to knowing somebody that had done a controlled substance. Well yes, she did. She knew Burke had done controlled substance. He sold it. She knew his wife was doing it. She knew a lot of people–in fact, she told Burke one time that John Rautio was doing drugs or selling them. He told her to mind her own business. So she said, 'well then, screw it.' They were just after her because she knew what was going on in that department, the things that were going wrong, the dirty cops. Not all of them,

417

but mostly her superior officers, and a few under the superiors that were over her. She just got to be too smart and wouldn't go along with the flow. They did everything they could to get her out, wrote her up on any little thing. After a while she just toughened up to the point where she didn't take it anymore. She started getting grievances against them. She knew she was in a man's world but she worked hard to get there. She had gone through the police academy which only less than half of her fellow officers had done including Chief Kraus!

"She was a good cop. Diane Smith wanted to get somebody big, you know, what they call the Big Cheese, so that Diane would look good and could get her judgeship–she wanted to run for judge. But if they talk about dirty cops, Chief Kraus drank and had a bottle of vodka in his desk, and this was not only reported from Lisa but from other cops that have resigned since then. He came in drunk or with booze on his breath every morning and never stuck around for the whole day, Ken Burke, another superior, was the department drunk, crashed police cars, Lisa and Jennifer saw him at Carley's in Petoskey, a restaurant/bar. She saw him there with a police car parked in back, eleven o'clock at night, lots of times. Lisa and Jennifer saw him in Boyne City at a bar and he was in there smashed, drunk. He had a city car parked outside. The City Manager and Chief of Police kept a blind eye; he was their good old buddy. Everything Lisa did, she did wrong, but Burke could take off a week at a time and never even call in. She just missed calling in to take a break, they'd write her up. What people call it there is the Gestapo. No doubt in my mind, her superior officers were the Gestapo. Ken Burke beat people up. He was even fired from a job in Gaylord. Who knows where he came from before there, how many people he's beat up? That's over and above being an officer. Burke was a rotten cop and yet nobody ever did anything about him. He could do anything he wanted. Matt Breed, another cop, was drunk driving in Petoskey, crashing into a light pole. There was a small article in the paper–I heard he got two days off; I don't know if he even got that. Breed had been driving a city car in this offense. He was one of the officers investigating Lisa's alleged drug thing, alleged drug use–which is a lie. Matt Breed, he was right on it, him and Croton. But nobody would see Ken Burke, nobody knew about the Chief, Kraus, that is.

"On the night of Lisa's memorial, as a friend of her's, Alice Waybrant, stopped at Lisa's house at 218 Arlington and sat in the driveway grieving (she had lived there once), Matt Breed came along in a police car and told her that she couldn't stand there, that the Piels didn't want her there, that she should leave the premises. What kind of a cop is this? Gestapo.

"Another reason why they want her out of there, they thought she was gay; they thought she was a lesbian. Couldn't have a lesbian cop in Petoskey. Earl Doernenberg told Ken Sieradski, who used to own Sunrise Electronics, to keep his daughter away from Lisa because she was a lesbian. This was her Sergeant, Earl Doernenberg. He wasn't even a certified cop. Bob Engel of the Prosecutor's office called her a lesbian to the Grand Jury. He got the people on the Grand Jury to ask the witnesses questions of: does she have a boyfriend?; does she go out?; and things like this just to discredit her.

"Bob Engel told Lisa once he likes to pile on charges. Engel asked one of the witnesses on the Grand Jury, with Lisa's being an officer, she must have known John Rautio was doing drugs. A police officer should know that. Yeah, she knew he was doing drugs. But if a police officer's supposed to know that then they all should have known John Rautio—including his brother, Joe Rautio, a police officer, couldn't help knowing his brother—was in drugs. Joe Rautio went home for lunch most of the time to his mother's house where his brother and Alice had been doing drugs during the day or the morning. Alice said that she and John were high when Joe came home. Why didn't they question Joe? Well, the reason is Diane Smith told me that the police didn't tell her about anybody else. The just told her about Lisa. Then when I talked to the City Manager and the new Chief of Police they said, 'no, it was the State that was after her, they had nothing to do with it.' But when she had her court date they were sitting in the court getting their enjoys of watching her go down.

"Lisa should never have signed the agreement, but her attorney, who was the wrong attorney, a friend of Diane Smith's, was told not to bargain with Diane, that we want to fight the case because she had done nothing wrong. Nothing! I don't think they had one thing on anybody except circumstantial evidence. Even John Rautio, why didn't they trace back where he got his stuff? If they really wanted to stop drug trafficking why didn't they go back and find the big guy instead of running around finding all the little people who were victims? No, they thought they'd just stick around this area and get at the little guys, hurt a lot of people that were just victims of the drugs because it was way out of their league to go after the big dealers. They wouldn't dare go into the big city looking for any big guys, following a trail from John Rautio all the way back to probably the Detroit area. No, that was way out of their league; they just like to hit on the little people. Then the sad part of it is these little people they hit on hadn't done any drugs in a couple of years. They were getting on with their lives; they were past that kid stuff, had kids and getting jobs and getting on with their lives. But they had to go back six years because Diane Smith said that you can't let a criminal go just because he hasn't done anything in a couple of years. Well, they didn't rob a bank they didn't kill anybody, they didn't do anything to anybody, except themselves.

"You hear a lot of stories when you're going around talking to people but I was told a story from a friend of mine who was invited to a party in Petoskey. He was invited, he said, by an attorney from Harbor Springs. The attorney told him to come to this party because there were going to be a lot of people out for business—doctors and lawyers and cops and big people around town—you can come and meet these people. Well, when he got to this party which was on Howard Street, approximately 1989, eight to ten years ago, he said that when he got in there there were two people he knew for sure. I can't name names because everybody's afraid, but he did say that one was an attorney and one was a real estate agent, and there were other attorneys, doctors, and he said there were four—and I asked him a couple of times—there were four Petoskey Police Officers. One of them brought in some cocaine and set it on a table. When he saw this he took his wife and he got out of there. He knew there was something going on. I can't mention his name, but, he doesn't want to talk about it anymore to me. He thinks he's said too much already. Everybody I talk to doesn't want to talk. One person told me, 'Art, I'm afraid to get my head shot off.' That's exactly what he said. That was the man that told me that he heard that Burke threatened to kill Lisa. Ken Burke threatened to kill Lisa, her superior officer threatened to kill her if she told about his drug dealings. Blumer down in Lansing, Assistant Attorney General, called her a dirty cop, said she was corrupt. He doesn't even know what corrupt means. He was the prosecutor on her case because Diane Smith said it was a conflict of interest. She liked to get the dirt but she didn't want to look dirty doing it.

"Burke, as Lisa said in her notes, had a rape charge against him, or an assault on a woman. The woman was a friend of Kit Lieberman's who was a former Emmet County Deputy. I talked with Kit but she didn't want to talk anymore to me about it. She gave me the girl's name which I'm going to leave out because the girl said she was going to call me but she never did. Everybody's afraid. A few attorneys, not a lot, a few, say, 'we have to live here.' They don't want to buck the police.

"It was Burke who told Lisa that he had a drug charge against him and he had a rape charge against him. The police department made Lisa out to be the bad cop; Lisa never came to work drunk, or drugged, or having had a drink. They always tried to catch her doing something but there was nothing to catch her on. She liked her job. She came from a police family. She wanted to be a good officer. She was inexperienced when she first started. She made mistakes like new cops do; she had the training but she didn't have the experience. She gained that quick–how to watch your back! They're not all bad there, but you don't know which ones are which; you have to watch your back. After losing her job, an officer by name of Rick Mitrick, a young officer in Petoskey, was just on the department for a short time when he resigned because of the things that were going on there; he didn't like the way things were operating and what they were telling him to do and how to run his life. Rick Mitrick liked Jennifer and came over to Lisa's house to see her. Lisa and Jennifer both told me that Vargo and the chief told him to stay away from Lisa's house. You know, being a cop, you don't get very many friends. And then both Vargo and the chief tell somebody to keep away from her house. Vargo is an officer that told a lot of lies about me in a paper that's on public record about when I tried to meet with him; and I can't do anything about it; he just lied up and down about me, what I did, what he thought I did, he just made lies up. I can't do anything about it. The only thing I can do is just call him a liar. LIAR! And I'll take Vargo on anytime, or anybody, at a lie detector test about any part of this situation. Of course, I know they say in Michigan the lie detector isn't admissible, but yet they used to want Lisa to take a lie detector all the time so she could make herself clean from police hear-says and things they wanted to try to get against her.

"If you're a person somebody's trying to get something on, whatever it is, when you're new on the job, you sure as heck aren't going to keep doing it for thirteen years. But they just kept on because it was her they wanted. She lived in misery sometimes. And that apparently, maybe, brought her around to shooting herself, we don't know. There's about a ninety-five percent chance that she did shoot herself, maybe a little more. But then there's always that question that keeps popping up in my mind because there wasn't an investigation properly done. Tim Roth told me he knows something about my daughter I didn't know, when I was talking to him and Diane—of course, we weren't talking, we were arguing. But he said, 'I know something about your daughter you don't know.' But yet he won't talk to me about it. I called Sheriff Bodzyk's office and wanted to talk to him about this; he said to put it all on paper and he'd get back to me in twenty-four hours. That's been well over two years ago.

"There was no investigation; they didn't care. I think they just figured it's good riddance. She just knew too much. And when you know too much and don't play along, you're out; they'll get you out. Diane Smith once asked me why Lisa didn't leave town after losing her job. Why should she leave town? She was not guilty. That's why Diane Smith left town, I think: she was guilty. I heard she couldn't stand Petoskey. This was told to me by an attorney. About the investigation of her death—I didn't know all deaths are considered homicide until proven otherwise–they didn't even try to prove anything. There were people walking all over the house–police, Reed, even myself, everybody was walking in and out of the bedroom. I didn't know that that should have been blocked off. The glass she was drinking out of wasn't fingerprinted; nothing, in fact, was. David Reed, supposed to have been her friend, told me that night that 'I'll betcha they'll find Jennifer's fingerprints on the trigger.'

"But they didn't take any fingerprints as far as I know. They just took some pictures and measurements, and said it's suicide. Doctor Kryzmowski, the area pathologist, presumed it to be suicide without having seen the death photos because that's what the police report said. Northern Michigan doesn't even have any forensic people to go out to the scene of death. It was a farce. And Roth didn't care. The way he talked to my wife a couple times was, I think, very rude. And he told lies about me. I guess the question is, why David Reed, who didn't know my other daughter, Denise, Ronnie Denise Allor, called her the night, that Saturday night, and said he was worried about Lisa, that she'd been depressed. Then he said, 'well, what are you going to do about it?' She said, 'well, I'll call my dad,' so she called me and I went over to Lisa's house, and I didn't have the right key to get in. So I walked around the house–it was raining, October the 8th. I looked around, looked through the window screen. Lisa's window was open four inches, I could see the bedcovers. I put my flashlight in there and I knocked on the window and I said, 'Lisa, it's Dad.' And then I went around to the back door and I pulled the screen hook off, thought maybe the key I had might work in the door. I was tempted to go in, break in myself, and I didn't, so I drove around town, thought maybe I'd find her car sitting someplace. I didn't see her anywhere so I came back to her house and looked around again. I called my daughter, Denise, again from the car and told her what was going on and she said, 'well, maybe she went down to Nancy's down in Bloomfield'–her friend, Nancy Simon, who she had talked to the day before for about an hour. So I went home and called Nancy and she said no, they talked but Lisa didn't come down. She talked about coming down; she didn't come down. Just then, after

I hung up, I got a call from David Reed. He was in Lisa's house, told me I better get over there. So I got in the car and drove over—it was the worst drive of my life. I got there, it was full of people. It's a little house, doesn't take much to fill it up—seven, eight people. In and out of her bedroom—all to look-see.

"The next day, Monday, Reed came by Lisa's house. Nancy Simon had come up from Bloomfield. Gerri Zaremski was there and my wife and I when Reed came by and told me that he had been standing outside watching me walk around the house. Why did he want to get in there by himself? Then after I had gone Reed watched for the neighbor next door to go to bed after watching TV. When the lights went off, then Reed got his sledgehammer and a towel and smashed two doors in. Why was Reed apparently so anxious to get in—without me?

"I don't know how long Reed was in Lisa's house but I do know he listened to her phone recorder tape, picked up her sunglasses and what else I don't know. What else did he do in there? He had blood on his jacket sleeve. He said he had to shake her to see if she was alive. Well, when I saw her, you didn't have to shake her. Why was he so interested in getting in her house? Why are Jennifer and Reed so close? On a Wednesday, October 5th it was, before her death, Lisa and Jennifer had a bad argument. They had been drinking. Lisa had gone to rehab in Traverse City but it's hard to stay sober when you have people who don't care about you enough not to drink around you.

"Jennifer told me she had some tapes of her and Dave Reed in a phone conversation but she was scared to death to give them to me because if he found out she'd be in trouble. She finally sent them to me. But yet every time she came here from Texas where she lived, to visit her mother, she'd make a beeline right over to Reed's house. Jennifer said she had to drive to Detroit to get an airplane on the night of Lisa's death. Nobody checked her; maybe she took the Cherry Capital Airport to Detroit. That way she could have had about an hour at Lisa's. Who knows all this? Nobody ever questioned it; nobody ever looked into it. These are things that just haunt me. These are possibilities that just haunt me. But Roth says, 'well, if you think she was murdered, I'll never close the case.' Roth acted like a little boy, said he'd never close–he can't never close–the case. That's what I heard, but what do I know? All I know is I'm puzzled. A lot of questions are unanswered. And nobody wants to talk to me. Roth avoids me completely. I was in the county building one day as Roth was coming upstairs and as soon as he saw me he turned around and went back down again. The Sheriff doesn't want to talk to me. They say when I come around I make threats. Well, when you make threats you don't get very far. How could you ever want to threaten somebody and then ask a favor of them, or a question? That doesn't make sense. Well, I'm through trying to talk to these people; I'm just telling my story like I see it. I'll continue on with my investigation. I've talked to at least four people about her death. My trips have taken me to Cheboygan County where 'they' all say she was murdered. That's all they can tell me; they don't want to tell me anything else.

"Getting back to Dave Reed, he had called and talked to Lisa's therapist–who he did not know nor that Lisa was seeing her. Reed told her that Lisa was fully dressed when he saw her. The therapist told me that that's her business–to listen to people–and she knew that's exactly what he told her. Again, why did he want to get in that house by himself? That's the big question. Lisa told her mother and I that Reed wanted an affair. When he was at her house one time she said she did not feel that way for him but that he was a good friend and all that, he got kind of belligerent and she had to ask him to leave. This was a short time before her death; I don't know the exact date but it was within a month or so.

"People think because you plea bargain, that you're guilty, but that's not true. It takes money to go to court. I wanted to go through with it but Lisa was tired. She was just not herself, and then we stopped to think: what are we going to do, buy her job back for a hundred fifty thousand dollars? Our attorney told us it would cost two hundred thousand though, I learned better, but nevertheless it's just like buying Lisa's job back. Why buy a job back when nobody wants you there? So it's just better to get it over with. That way the prosecutors win. That's why they have plea bargains; they pile the charges and then this way they never lose. It's a business, big business, the court business. That's what

425

is going on in Petoskey courts. They're not trying to get people healed. If you find a person that's using drugs, you don't give him or her jail time, you take them for help; you find a drunk, you don't just lock him up, you get him sober and get him some professional help. That's the way Lisa always felt when she found somebody drunk driving; she took them home, told them to cut this stuff out and get themselves straightened around. She had one or two people she helped and they sent her letters thanking her for helping them get straight and not ruining their lives by arresting them.

"She always liked kids and old folks. Lisa talked to her friend Nancy down-state for about an hour, Friday, October 7, that evening. She called me about seven o'clock Friday night, asking how her mother was doing. Lisa had gone shopping Friday evening; she had her grocery receipt with her in bed when she died; she had her newspaper, News-Review, open to the real estate page. It was Friday, that's a big real estate time and because she was going to put her license in with a local realtor the following Monday. She was going to start working at the real estate plus her wallpaper business. Lisa loved life; why would she sit in bed with her shopping list? Because she was a coupon clipper she had about seven dollars worth of coupons when she went shopping Friday night. She always was very thrifty, checking, making sure the numbers were correct on her shopping list. And she was looking at the real estate page. She had had quite a bit to drink. Her bed was messed up badly. Clothes were all over. She was all undressed except her panties. She never went to bed undressed. She was caught off guard. We had a private investigator, a former F.B.I. man, who told us that it looked to him like there had been a struggle. But he said since there were so many people, and David Reed in there, you're really not going to get anything from the pictures because everything had been disturbed.

"When I saw Lisa in her deathbed her eyes were open, her eyelashes seemed to be stuck together. She'd apparently been crying. Her eyes were open. I think a lot of times your eyes would be open when you get shot by somebody but if you're going to shoot yourself you're usually going to close your eyes. She had been

426

crying. Her eyes were wide open. She looked like she had shot herself with her left hand, or she would have had to, the way the gun was laying. She was right handed. When you've had quite a bit to drink it's pretty hard to shoot yourself right through the heart. A lot of people don't even know exactly where their heart is.

"Also about Dave Reed, he told me and somebody else how many bullets were left in the gun clip. Very strange. Lisa did have a drinking problem. She didn't drink every day but when she did drink she didn't know when to quit. When she lost the job was when she really started drinking. She was very depressed. Her therapist told us that one of the things was the loss of the job. She had her own home; she had a lot of bills to pay. She owned a couple cars. She had money in the bank. She had stocks. She was just depressed over the thirteen years of hell and people wondered why did she stay there? Well, just because she wanted that job. Just think, you're coming to this nice little town of Petoskey and you're lucky enough, being a woman, to get a job on the police force there, but not knowing what kind of a police force it is and what kind of law enforcement is going on there.

"Courts and police, I believe, are interconnected. They all stick together. They've got the attorneys baffled because otherwise the attorneys wouldn't be able to get all the lucrative work in court if they didn't play along. We went to court and tried to have her files expunged. Being as she's dead, Blumer, the Assistant Attorney General, said that the public needs to know about this. Of course, the judge agreed with him. I believe these prosecutors and judges, they'd just as soon kick a dead dog than a live one. My dad always said to me, 'nobody likes you when you're down and out.'

"Lisa, most of the time, had a girl living with her. I think they all, the police department, etc., thought she was a lesbian because she had a partner living with her. Well, when you've got a house and things she had, there's a lot of upkeep and you need a partner to help keep the payments up. Simple as that. Sure, she knew girls that were gay and there's no crime if you're a police officer to know somebody that's gay. It probably wouldn't be a bad thing if the Petoskey Police Department had a couple gay officers–might bring a little humanity to the department. So I think when they figured she had a girl living with her that she was gay. But if she had some fellows living with her she would be a whore. She had some friends that would stay at her house from out of state for two, three weeks, but I guess if you've got a girl living with you, that makes you gay, whereas if she had guys living with her she'd be a whore. So no matter which way she went that's what they would think of her.

"The night of her death Officer Weston spoke briefly with James Reed. Reed stated he had contacted several family members and nobody was able to get in touch with Lisa. Reed also stated that he broke in the residence to check the welfare of Lisa Piel. David Reed said he contacted several members of the family—there aren't several, there are only me and my daughter, Lisa's sister. And he only contacted Lisa's sister which he had never met before. Why didn't he call me first? It's either that or the police don't hear right. I just don't understand where he contacted several people. But he watched me walk around the building. Interesting.

"Officer James Kushner noticed Reed had some blood on the sleeve of his jacket; well, if he just shook her on the shoulder, it's almost impossible to get blood if he only shook her on the shoulder. You'd have had to get into her face or part of her body to get blood. Or reach for the gun to see how many bullets were in the clip.

"Police walked through the house looking for a note but Reed had already been in there, and if there was a note he might have taken it. Then Rice let Reed use the telephone. That seems kind of funny. This is a crime scene; before you can say that it's suicide there should have been a crime investigation, shouldn't have been letting just anybody pick up a telephone because there could have been fingerprints on a telephone, or, it just seems that everybody's trying to cover something up to make it look like suicide because they all think that she was gay, that it was a gay lovers' quarrel, but it wasn't. Lisa told me, her dad, at two different times she was going to ask Jennifer to leave because Lisa tried to get herself off of alcohol but she had somebody like Jennifer who didn't want to give up her lifestyle to please Lisa. But she was living in Lisa's house, and she even told the hairdresser that my wife and Lisa went to,

Jennifer went to, that after Lisa got out of the rehab, she says, she wasn't going to change her lifestyle just because Lisa's got a problem. Well, Lisa had to ask her to leave, was going to but apparently they got in an argument. I guess she was having a hard time telling her to leave. So naturally when you have a couple of drinks you get in an argument and that's what happens. Lisa had her own life to live, and Jennifer too, so they found it better to part ways. I believe that Lisa was upset because she started drinking again, mostly due to the loss of her job. Her business was going good but it was slow.

"Rice says they removed the tape out of Lisa's cassette on the answering machine. Reed had already listened to it. He could have erased any part of it because we believe he had access, according to Jennifer, to Lisa's answering machine and could get her messages so he knew what she was doing all the time. So he wanted to check the tape, which he did. And also, her phone book has been missing, the personal phone book. It's never been found. Reed said he didn't have it but yet he calls all kinds of people that he didn't even know, never even heard of. Rice secured the tape, marked it and secured it. Well, it was already too late. Did Rice drop it in a plastic bag to check maybe for fingerprints, see who was fooling with it, or who touched it last? Reed told Rice that Lisa was upset because her roommate was going to move out. But Lisa threw her out. She cared about her but she wasn't going to cry over her. Everybody thinks they know Lisa so well. They don't know her as well as her mother and I do. Especially her mother. Reed said that he checked to see if Lisa was home and he said that both vehicles were in the garage. Well, that's pretty hard to see on a dark, rainy night. There's only one little window and it's in a window well and you'd have to get on your knees and use a flashlight and I think the glare would not let you see in there. I think he must have known something because he'd been watching Lisa's house all day Saturday. According to Rice, Reed said he was unable to get the door open or enter the residence from the location because he had a problem with the lock. You mean his key didn't fit? There was no problem with the lock. It had a deadbolt and he just couldn't get in unless he had a key and it didn't work for him.

"The police say that I was distraught. Yeah, I probably was, and had to be physically restrained in the hallway and pinned against the wall. There were four big people in the hallway and it's only not even three feet wide. We were all pinned against the wall. I was just trying to get through because I wanted to see her and they didn't want me to because they thought I was going to mess the place up. And Rice told me it might be a criminal case. Well, hell, they had all been walking all over the place and Reed had been in there for possibly a half hour before he called anybody. He did whatever he had wanted to. And then how are you going to secure a place that's already been ransacked? They don't know what they're talking about or what they were doing. Two former officers have since told me that they're all incompetent.

"Then Rice says, yeah, we had to calm him down and we've got to treat this as a crime. Yeah, Rice said he advised me that he had to treat it as a crime scene and that he could not disturb anything. Then why was he letting everybody and his brother walk through the bedroom? Joe Rautio was no detective. In fact, there isn't a detective in the whole damn town that's worth his salt. There was nothing done. Everybody was walking through the house, using the phone, and she'd already been disturbed. Who knows who might have touched the gun? Maybe the one with the blood on his sleeve. Rice said he couldn't talk any sense to me, I wouldn't listen to reason. Well, there was no reason. The reason was that they shouldn't have been there. They were too close to it. They were too involved in her losing her job. Then Rice told me there's a new detective in town. Well, 'new' was an old detective, a deputy that became what they call a detective. That's Tim Roth. Obviously, if I'd known that, nobody would have gotten in there. I'd have had to call the State Police from another county because they were all too close to Lisa. But they were there to 'look-see.' And Rice kept referring in his report that the Piels did this and the Piels did that and the Piels this . . . there was only one Piel that was doing anything. My wife wasn't even there. And my daughter who is a Piel, Lisa's sister, her name is Allor now, she had nothing to say. So what are they trying to do, are they trying to get more people

430

involved so they get a better case? Same old stacking the evidence. Attorney Gregory Justis was called by James Reed. I'd never seen the man before. I never knew him. And Tim Roth said that I insisted that Mr. Justis, the attorney, go in Lisa's bedroom with him for the death investigation. One other thing that comes to mind, Lisa and I talked about was when she was involved in a murder case that took place in the area. A young man murdered two people and put their bodies in a septic tank. The police had a lead that the killer might go after a young lady in Petoskey. So Lisa was picked to sit in the young lady's house one night with a shotgun, and waited to see if the killer would come after the young lady. Lisa said she was a little nervous and would check over the radio to her partners, 'are you guys still out there?' But Lisa was more afraid that her partners would not back her up when and if something would happen or if there was any shooting, she would have got shot from the so-called friendly fire, the police would say, sorry, that's part of the job. On some other cases Lisa called for back-up of the Petoskey Police and no one came. She said she was lucky at the time because the State Police picked up the call and came by. There are some real good State Troopers.

"Also, one reason I believe Scott Croton worked extra hard on Lisa's case, because he and his wife were real pissed off about Lisa not asking Mrs. Croton to handle the real estate deal when Lisa bought her house, Lisa knew she had her license. Lisa knew a lot of people with real estate licenses, she just went to the listing sales person. The Croton's held that against Lisa for all these years. That is the kind of people they are, and in my talks in the past years I heard they were not very well liked in the area.

"I believe City Manager George Korthauer knew they were not planning on having Lisa Piel for very much longer, because the City of Petoskey did not provide locker rooms and shower facilities for women officers as they did for men when they built the new City building and police department. Lisa was always looking forward to the new facilities—which never came about.

"If I have hurt anybody's feelings, or they don't like what I have said, those that don't like what I believe to be the truth, if they are without sin, then start throwing your stones."

Art Piel, 1997"

Epilogue

Officer admits exposing himself," the headline read in the Detroit Free Press of November 20, 1997. "Statement comes in harassment suit," by Kelly Longton of the Ecorse Police Department against Police Chief James Hunt. Kelly Longton, age 24, is a female rookie officer. The article says that "in October, a Wayne County Circuit Court Judge ruled that Ecorse discriminated against its two female officers by failing to provide locker-room facilities similar to males'."

Sound familiar?

This current hearing is based on an apparently self-admitted statement by a male cop that he exposed his genitals to Longton while both were in a squad car parked in an alley. He said Longton told him she "wasn't interested."

A long-term policewoman, now Lieutenant Smith, of nearby Warren, Michigan, said this had happened to her while on duty about 18 years ago. Other female police officers in metro Detroit say Longton's allegations come as no surprise to them. After Longton initially brought charges last December about the lack of locker room facilities, "17 Ecorse police officers signed a petition requesting Chief Hunt step down until the matter was resolved. Hunt and the officer who said he exposed himself remain on duty." Longton said she changed clothes at home rather than use a broom closet, and shared a toilet with female prisoners at the precinct.

Lieutenant Smith said, "there's a handful of people you can't get to change their attitude." Kelly Longton has had several disciplinary complaints filed against her since she herself began these proceedings. One such complaint was for not wearing her hat, another for "using a department camera without permission," for taking a photo of sexually explicit magazines in a police squad room, sending it with a report to higher authorities.

And this is 1997, not 1978.

In a November issue of the Northern Express of Traverse City, concerning women on the job, Dawn Wagoner of the Grand

Traverse Sheriff's Department says, "I think our department, for the most part, is very progressive. People think you have to be a big bruiser, and that's just not true, I think departments are looking more for intelligence."

Intelligence, compassion, methods of deterring incipience of crime, these and more are the wanted wave of future law enforcement as even the middle and upper classes sometimes get snagged in the web of dragnets by increasing numbers of laws and constabulary. In some cities, walking patrols have been initiated with great success in terms of community acceptance. A cop on foot is much more approachable for even casual conversation than one in a patrol car. Passing by a police precinct, such as the Petoskey State Police Post, does not conjure thoughts of stopping in for a neighborly chat. Everything is authoritarian, cold, and rhetorical. The fleet of cars and other vehicles, all painted the same colors and logos, are military in appearance and function. One almost expects to hear emanating from a loudspeaker: "Resistance is futile, you will be assimilated," as in "The Borg," a hornet's nest-oriented race on "Star Trek" TV series and movies. The separation of police from the public has created this mistrust, one to the other, that left to develop as such results in estrangement of values–values which should be fundamentally the same and of one accord.

Entrapment has become a major ploy in police work. Lisa Piel was approached once in her career with the mission of undercover work. Due to her young age, it was thought that she could infiltrate drug-exchange scenarios, feign friendship, and bust the local dealers. On discussing this potential with family and friends, she decided, with due apprehension, that dealing with drugs would not place her in the best of reference frames with the authorities because of the obvious possibility of their using confiscated drugs as probable evidence against her as a potential middleman or user. She wisely refrained from this position.

In preparing this book, a measured amount of secrecy was exercised. It was thought, realistically, that any publicity would not only cause a tightening of information but also some reprisal on the parts of authorities. There are many avenues of reprisal, both legal and monetary, with the added social effects which might well be the more harmful in a small-town setting.

There is a work-out gymnasium in downtown Petoskey that is frequented by many persons. The ownership has ties to the Sheriff's Department through family and friends. A number of people have recently had their memberships cancelled by the club for no apparent reason other than legal publicity contrary to the police departments of Petoskey. Those cancelled are among the business and legal community, even encompassing a lawyer or two who had represented a client adverse to police harassment. The aforementioned J.D. Reed, founder of Citizens Against Legal Misconduct, is among those stricken from the membership role, and this under less-than-polite auspices. This ostracism has many inroads of subtle attack.

Persons known to the police and sheriff's departments as protagonistically opposed to their practices are routinely singled out and pulled over for breathalizer tests and any other legal maneuverings available to hassle and harry an individual driving home or elsewhere. With car phone communications and distant computers it is easily possible to interrupt a person's schedule by several hours if an officer harbors any reason to do so. This happens; this and more, as seen in the experience of Gerri Zaremski mentioned earlier who was actually thrown down in the snow and held there, thence spending more than half a day in jail— and all for nothing, no crime, no disturbance, absolutely no wrongdoing. Unless one reverses the allegations and points a finger toward the ones disseminating the well-armed force known as "To Serve And Protect."

This must stop. And it has ceased to be a common problem in areas where the corruption of police departments has gotten so markedly evil as to become noticeable in areas other than their own. Some police departments have turned themselves entirely around, becoming good neighbors to the communities which they defend. As of 1997, with some discernible minor changes, this has not occurred in Northern Michigan. Dave Reed's C.A.L.M. organization has cut the incidences of malfeasance somewhat as of late. Publicity is what is needed. Publicity is hard to get in an area where the one and only newspaper tends to take the side of law and order on the surface of its stilted, never-admit-wrong, stance of bureaucratic linguistics. The pendulum swings both ways.

The previous cry for more law and order has turned to more law and disorder. It is up to the community, to the police or the courts, to create change. Art Piel has come forward with this well-documented plea for–not bargaining but–truth. But the reign of silence prevails for the most part. Most others are content to go about their lives with no thought to fixing anything that they can easily ignore within the beauteous landscape of Northwest Michigan.

But not all others. A Letter To The Editor, perhaps never printed, dated 11/13/91, and signed by the pseudonym of Mr. Joseph Anthony, decries the Grand Jury findings, John Charles Robbins' reportage thereof, Diane Smith's political platform, and suggests that the public outcry reported was not so much in response to Lisa Piel's alleged conduct as it was to the "cheap sensationalism" surrounding the entire affair.

This letter writer says, "One would think you had ear plugs not to have noticed the overwhelming rebuttal from the public," this directed primarily to Robbins but peripherally to Prosecutor Smith and her Grand Jury as well. Mr. Robbins takes a lot of flack of this sort, but continues to present his one-sided versions of every story assigned to him.

Mr. "Anthony" continues with, ". . . in effect they've done nothing but spend a huge amount of money to capture 49 people in an eight-county region! And most of these were for offenses very small and that happened years ago. . . . that's a hell of a way to get a conviction on her (Lisa's) record without any physical evidence! Doesn't that sound like something out of the McCarthy era?"

If Mr. Anthony is correct, the cost of that Grand Jury was "$76,000. so far," to which he poses the challenge, ". . . I would like to know how much drugs have been seized–let's see a picture!" He adds, as to ". . . Diane Smith's political platforms, there are a great many, many citizens that are sick and tired of you (John Robbins) trying to make her into some single-handed hero trying to make some huge impact on our beautiful northland with the politically popular issue of drugs."

A former friend of Lisa's summed up the inferences to Diane Smith: "Diane Smith made a big name for herself and a few officers looked like real Federal Agents to ignorant community members but nothing really was accomplished. End result, broken lives, that's it, broken lives. Diane Smith ran for judge, did not get voted in."

Perhaps there truly are many persons locally who side with the underlying truths pointed out in this writing, but who need the catalyst of open publicity to come forward. Like the recapitulative hearings of reparation in South Africa currently, it is expected that many tales of guilt and whitewash might be told if conducted without retribution. The South African tribunal, which sounds strangely like Kurt Vonnegut writings, seeks to get at the truth of genocide and apartheid in return for commutation of admitted offenses. In New Orleans, more than fifty cops have been arrested since 1993 for felony offenses, inclusive of rape, murder, and robbery. No wonder no one wants to talk.

Lisa's former friend adds this testament to her memory: "I along with a handful of other people I know can easily be held responsible for my friend's death. How much can one heart break? The thing is, had people not been basically forced to fear so badly for their futures, perhaps a little more truth may have been told and a few less fabricated stories to save one's self. After the Grand Jury unfortunately my friendship with Lisa began to fade. We were angry, bitter people full of pain and blame. I believe she tried hard to go on, however she had been robbed and her world had been raped. Diane Smith and her little clan used the fall of a good officer and a fabulous person for political gain and all that was accomplished was the destruction of Lisa's entire world.

"Lisa passed away and I to this day still question the fate of that loss. No matter who pulled the trigger I blame and will always blame Diane Smith and her crusade for political gain. I can do nothing to change that.

"Diane Smith is so heartless that even after Lisa's death I approached her to inquire about the expungement of my felony, she told me it was out of her hands. I needed to contact the judge. I did just that and was told that she was in fact the only person with the ability to allow such an action. Not only does she limit my abilities to prosper in life (this has), she destroyed one of my dearest friends and proceeds to lie about all of it. I have a great deal to live with. I honestly feel confident in who I am and I believe there will be forgiveness for the wrong I've done. My heart is true. May God help the rest."

This last statement was, of course, by one of the girls forced to testify against Lisa Piel. As chronicled, it's a dirty system, in which no real punishment of crime is consummated. Wheels turn and money is appropriated and spent, but a status quo of acceptable corruption is allowed by the slow and steady agglutination of legal and business back-slapping while practicing forms of usury against other segments of the population. The scapegoats are those who buck the system in either criminal or altruistic terms. Lisa was no criminal. Not by any stretch of the imagination. In point of fact, there is no real hard-core crime in Northern Michigan. The drug lords never venture north on business. Keeping the peace has never been a problem. Drink and drugs remain the basis for investigation—and it might be added: revenue. Why then, the heavy-handed approach toward citizenry and the reported misuse of power accompanying the hypocritical stance of double standards of what's right and wrong and for whom? If a segment of the business/legal crowd use drugs with impunity, where do they get off arresting others for the same things they are reportedly doing? Respectability, as disclosed earlier by Dr. Peck, is the best cover for illegal/immoral motives. Not unlike a Nineteen Eighty-Four scenario, the protectorship of society is sometimes entrusted to the ones with the least empathy towards its wards. The statements of Lisa's friend spell out poignantly just how destructive this can be to the personal psyche, and also how destructive these intentions are to the community. People are scared and embittered here. And not of the robbers; the cops!

Obviously, not everyone is "buying" this hypocrisy; it's the fear factor that wins by intimidation. Through War On Crime and War

On Drugs implementation the legal forces have garnered more power lately, power which, like technology, is the "barrel of wine to an alcoholic" syndrome as given to us by Theodore Kaczynski in his Unabomber Manifesto. Power corrupts. Many are the victims, in many different formats. Lisa's Story is the most glaring example of this in recent times.

J.D. Reed's C.A.L.M. group, from which he recently stepped down as president, is active in this venue, which certainly adds to the enigmatic mystique of the man. The rumored interest from TV shows like Maury Povich and such, if proved actual, might shed some light into these dark corners of culture, or may have only a sensational and short-lived nova effect. The real struggle lies with the populace, those who ought never to have allowed these travesties to take root in the first place. By absent-mindedly trying to nip in the bud drug use and drunk driving, the point is missed and the ideal time has long passed. In point of fact, only the most visible, minor detractors from the social order are being sought out and made examples of. Lisa Piel was made an effigy of for adjacent low-down, self-aggrandizing motives. Her story is not over. If this book succeeds only in clearing the way for more equilateral treatment between societal elements, a success has been achieved. The true intent of this research is, however, to exonerate Lisa from any complicity in the morass of corrupt skullduggery that is hubristically taken for granted by the purveyors thereof as the right-and-proper, good values responsible for maintaining a decent society. This is the real travesty of justice—when "justice" itself is the purveyor of hate and harm.

"May God help the rest," as spoken earnestly and ingenuously by one of the victims, bespeaks of the cathartic effect of facing the truth. Unfortunately, there are some who have no intention of facing the truth—at least not in public. When evil is exposed, it lashes out viciously. It is the task herein to allow enough light to pervade to render backlash unprofitable and dangerous to those who seek to hide anything having to do with this account. As the Bible says, by their deeds will they be known.

"May God help the rest."

Mitchell Jon MacKay

440

LISA'S STORY

It is for LISA, family and friends

that this story is told.

Perhaps she has more friends

than are willing to come forward

and speak on her behalf.

Maybe this story will provide

the impetus for more people

to reveal what still remain

mysteries in this tale.

NOTES

NOTES

NOTES